VIETDAMNED

VIETDAMNED

How the World's Greatest Minds Put America on Trial

Clive Webb

Profile Books

First published in Great Britain in 2025 by
Profile Books Ltd
29 Cloth Fair
London
ECIA 7JQ
www.profilebooks.com

1 3 5 7 9 10 8 6 4 2

Typeset in Garamond by MacGuru Ltd
Printed and bound in Great Britain by
CPI Group (UK) Ltd, Croydon CR0 4YY

A CIP catalogue record for this book is available from the British Library.

ISBN 978 1 80081 233 8
eISBN 978 1 80081 235 2

CONTENTS

INTRODUCTION

Sitting within feet of a No Smoking sign, he took a drag on his cigarette before leaving it to smoulder in the ashtray. Leaning towards the microphones, he momentarily looked up from his typewritten statement at the throng of newspaper reporters and television camera operators that filled the cavernous congress hall. After days of harrowing witness testimony and deliberation, it was time for him to announce the decision.

The date was 10 May 1967. Outside, on the streets of Stockholm, a coolness filled the morning spring air. Inside the Folkets Hus, the soberly modernist building that occupied an entire block of the Swedish capital, the recessed ceiling lights shone a bright warmth on the stage from where the tribunal president addressed the audience.

What followed was no ordinary ruling, but nor was this any ordinary tribunal. The accused was the United States government; the charge, that it had committed war crimes against the Vietnamese people.

Thirteen years earlier, Vietnam had been partitioned into two states. Fearing the threat of invasion by military forces from the northern Democratic Republic of Vietnam, President Dwight Eisenhower sent American military advisers to support the defence of the Republic of Vietnam in the south. The path from there had been less than straight but steadily led successive administrations in Washington to an undeclared war. American policy was determined by the domino theory, the belief that the surrender of South Vietnam to the communist forces of the North could cause all of Southeast Asia to topple. In March 1965 the administration of President Lyndon Johnson launched Operation Rolling Thunder, the sustained aerial bombardment of North Vietnam. Within days the first ground troops landed at the South Vietnamese coastal city of Da Nang. Vietnam was now an American war, and a conflict that US forces were confident of winning. Yet soon they would be mired in a bloody stalemate that in time led to withdrawal and defeat. As the American military sank deeper into the quagmire, so the tribunal intended to determine whether they had resorted to increasingly immoral and illegal actions, indiscriminately injuring and killing civilians on both sides of the border. Vietnam, Washington claimed, was a fight for freedom and democracy against communist tyranny. Yet the saviour seemed to have become the scourge.

Who, though, was brave or foolish enough to bring the most powerful nation on earth to account for the brutal excesses of the war?

The man at the microphone was one of the most eminent philosophers in the world, Jean-Paul Sartre. Sitting with him around the horseshoe table on the congress hall stage was a coterie of distinguished figures from the world of arts and letters, among them his partner Simone de Beauvoir.

Sartre might have been the captain of this strange vessel, but it was not he whose imagination conceived the design and stoked the engine room boiler. That was the inspiration of another of the world's greatest thinkers.

Bertrand Russell was renowned as an advocate of world peace. He had written books, walked on marches, addressed audiences at rallies and over the airwaves, even served time in prison because of his beliefs. By the time the United States became embroiled in Vietnam, the philosopher had established himself as a sort of international ombudsman, publicly intervening in some of the most contentious aspects of world affairs, from the Hungarian Revolution to the Cuban missile crisis. So omnipresent was he that the satirical magazine *Punch* published an article with the gently mocking strapline, 'Everywhere diplomats and negotiators are asking, "Should Bertrand Russell replace the UN?"'[1]

The philosopher was in his nineties, his body failing but his mind still sharp, when the United States entered the Vietnam War, and he was one of the war's earliest public critics. His attacks cut so deep that when President Johnson showed reporters his surgical scar after undergoing a gall bladder operation, *Private Eye* ran a front-cover photograph with the caption 'That's the last time I invite Bertrand Russell to lunch'.[2]

Russell's idea of bringing together prominent cultural and political personalities to bear witness to unrestrained American military action owed its inspiration to the Nuremberg trials following the Second World War, when the Allied forces indicted and tried former Nazi leaders for crimes against humanity. Too frail to leave his rural retreat in North Wales, Russell turned to Sartre to serve as president of the tribunal. No less active in the material world of global politics and war, the pair shared a moral revulsion at American intervention in Vietnam. Between them, what Russell and Sartre did was an act of daring.

Think about opposition to the Vietnam War, and what comes to mind? College students occupying campus buildings and clashing with National Guardsmen? Young men burning their draft cards? Demonstrators bearing placards as they march through the streets?

When Russell first announced his intention to investigate

American war crimes, much of that lay in the future. It was not until after the tribunal had met that opinion polls showed a groundswell of public unrest about the war, and even then only a minority believed military intervention had been a mistake. Nor was there any coordinated global opposition. For all that *Punch* ridiculed Russell's pretensions as an international peace-keeper, the United Nations failed to intervene. The Burmese Secretary General U Thant denounced the war as a reproach to the conscience of humanity, but his words were not met with action. If the United Nations let slip the mantle of leadership, human rights organisations made little effort to catch it. Amnesty International remained neutral on the war, offering only limited support to incarcerated draft resisters. Only the International Red Cross interceded to assist suffering civilians. Today, whistle-blowers and investigative journalists routinely expose the wrongdoings of governments. But at the time of the tribunal, almost no reporters dared to depart from the official line about the war. Russell and Sartre were filling a moral and political vacuum, placing their reputations on the line by attempting to coordinate a global response to the conflict.[3]

This is a story that shows how determined Washington was to silence critics and control the narrative about the war. The scale of the US government's lies not only prolonged but also transformed the nature of the conflict. That Sartre announced the ruling on that spring day in Stockholm was testimony to the strength of his character, given that the Johnson administration had done everything within its power to prevent the tribunal from taking place; the CIA infiltrated the tribunal, securing confidential information about its plans from informants, some unaware who they were speaking to, others consciously betraying their collaborators. That was only one front in the counteroffensive. Washington further conspired to bully other governments

into denying the tribunal a place to convene, conducted surveillance on the participants and threatened their freedom of
movement. Its other tactic was to smear the reputations of the
tribunal members, aided and abetted by a compliant press that
parroted the story Washington wanted to tell about the war.

The smearing of Russell and Sartre was cruel and relentless.
Sartre was a has-been, commentators wrote, a once brilliant
intellectual who had traded philosophy for propaganda. And
those who surrounded him were even worse, a bunch of third-
rate novelists and intellectuals who had swallowed the lies of
an enemy state and were now regurgitating them with gleeful
hatred towards the United States. The potshots fired at the rest
of the tribunal were nothing compared to the abuse directed
towards Russell, the tribunal's founder. Cartoonists dressed him
in the clothes of fantasists from the world of fiction. He was
Lewis Carroll's Mad Hatter, whose view of the world through the
looking glass turned reality upside down. Or he was Cervantes'
deluded Don Quixote, readying his horse for a fight against a
dangerous foe but merely tilting at windmills. One of the towering intellects of the twentieth century had collapsed into the
ruins of senility.

Posterity has not proven much kinder. Russell's biographers
have been more circumspect about his supposed mental decline
but no less caustic in appraising his motivations. One account
attributes the philosopher's anti-war activism to 'a quite colossal
vanity', his concerns about the war motivated less by a sincere
commitment to the welfare of others than the selfish concern
of a feeble and elderly man to reaffirm his faltering influence
in world affairs.[4] The tribunal has also been all but forgotten,
omitted from the contentious public conversation about the
meaning of the Vietnam War.

Histories of the war typically represent it as being fought on two fronts: the military conflict that occurred in Southeast Asia and the battle to sustain public support in the United States. Yet Vietnam should also be seen as a global struggle. In an era when the rest of the world was able to witness the fighting in real time, the war became an international test of the United States' super-power status. The story of the Russell tribunal demonstrates how it stirred the consciences not only of the American public, but also of people around the planet. In focusing on a group of individuals from around the world and the international reception of their work, this book is, in essence, a global history of the anti-war movement.

This is also a quintessential story of the sixties, a decade in which public intellectuals commanded headlines as much as show-business celebrities. In later decades, ambitious international campaigns harnessed the power of celebrity to address problems ignored by governments, yet it was in the revolutionary ferment of the 1960s that a small cluster of intellectuals and artists had the conviction – and the conceit – to call to account the most powerful government in the world and attempt to alter the direction of its foreign policy. Some of those stories are notorious. John Lennon and Yoko Ono promoting peace by lying in bed at the Amsterdam Hilton hotel for a week. Muhammad Ali standing defiant outside an armed forces induction centre, after refusing to be drafted. Jane Fonda perching on a North Vietnamese anti-aircraft gun. All of these incidents were essentially symbolic gestures of protest. What distinguished the tribunal led by Russell and Sartre was that the focus was less on their personalities than the evidence they presented of alleged American wrongdoing.

My purpose, in part, is to rescue the last decade in the long life of Bertrand Russell from the dismissive treatment of other biographers, to reveal him as a flawed but profoundly compassionate man determined to bring peace to a war-torn world. But the book also brings to light the activism of other luminaries of the literary world – Günther Anders, Sara Lidman, Peter Weiss and especially Simone de Beauvoir and Jean-Paul Sartre.

Above all, the tale told here is about what the tribunal uncovered, the ruthlessness with which politicians and the press attempted to discredit their evidence, and the lessons to be learned about our continued need to hold to account those in power.

The writing of history often focuses on decisive turning points – the winning of wars, the rise and fall of politicians, the advances in science that change the way we live. This is a messier story, and drawing a decisive conclusion is difficult. Now, as then, the tribunal will seem to some a futile act of hubris, to others an honourable failure. In the immediate term it did little to influence public opinion or government policy, yet it established a precedent that shapes political activism to the present day.

This, then, is a story that reveals much about attempts to use the power of celebrity to effect global political change, about the fine line between veracity and voyeurism in exposing the ugliness of war, and about the power of the surveillance state. Above all, it is an account of what the world was able or willing to learn about the Vietnam War. Those warnings would come with a clearing of the throat and a voice speaking with slow and deliberate measure into a stage microphone.

1

THE COMING OF WAR

Gathered in faltering spring sunlight, the 20,000 people in London's Trafalgar Square on Easter Monday in 1963 had little reason to suppose the annual demonstration by the Campaign for Nuclear Disarmament would be best remembered for a poem. By the time the author performed it during the International Poetry Incarceration at the Royal Albert Hall in June 1965, his words were seared into the political consciousness of young activists across the country. Conservatively attired in a pale summer suit and tie, his voice at first a little diffident, Adrian Mitchell soon had his audience spellbound. 'To Whom It May Concern' had an incantatory tone, like a nightmarish version of a children's nursery rhyme:

> I was run over by the truth one day.
> Ever since the accident I've walked this way
> So stick my legs in plaster
> Tell me lies about Vietnam[1]

The poem had grown more salient in the months since Mitchell had first performed it at the London peace rally. While he delivered it in the Royal Albert Hall, American bombers were pounding the towns and cities of North Vietnam and combat troops had taken the war to the communist forces that threatened the precarious political regime south of the border. And the lies and deception about the war were getting worse. Falsehoods about what had forced the United States into the fighting, about its financial cost, about the scale and success of military operations and, in time, about the brutal excesses committed not only by cruel enemy forces but also supposedly humane and heroic American soldiers:

> You put your bombers in, you put your conscience out,
> You take the human being and you twist it all about

How had the United States become embroiled in a conflict nearly 9,000 miles away in a 'little pissant country', as President Lyndon Johnson called it?[2] A conflict that would rage for close to a decade and cost the country $168bn, the lives of over 58,000 soldiers and injure 153,000 more, the ruin of a presidency, the division of its people and the deep wounding of national pride? How could 'The Best and the Brightest' of their generation responsible for government policy have been proven so wrong? And what, other than rage in verse, was anyone prepared to do about it?[3]

The Vietnamese fight for national freedom had ancient origins. China had ruled the country for a thousand years from 111 BCE and briefly occupied it again in the fifteenth century. The Vietnamese had otherwise maintained their independence until the French arrived by force in 1858, their soldiers stepping onto dry land to seize control of what is now the coastal city of Da Nang. There was fierce resistance in other areas of the country, but by 1883 Vietnam was completely under colonial control.

What sort of a colony had the French inherited? Like much of Asia, most of its people were peasants who toiled the land just as generations of their families had before them. Industrially underdeveloped, the country afforded little opportunity for individual or collective advancement.

Vietnam might have been poor and oppressed, but some were determined to change its future. A nationalist movement started to take form from the early twentieth century. The leader who would become synonymous with the struggle for independence was Ho Chi Minh. Born Nguyen Sinh Cung in 1890, he led an itinerant life for three decades that took him far from his homeland. His travels through the United States, Britain and France imbued him with an admiration of Western liberalism. That turned to disaffection when he and other Vietnamese exiles petitioned the Great Powers during the Versailles peace negotiations following the First World War to honour their commitment to national self-determination by liberating the country from colonial rule. Alienated, Ho turned away from liberalism and towards the communism of the Soviet Union and China. It was the Second World War that finally brought him home.

By the end of 1941, Japanese forces occupied all the colonial territories in Southeast Asia. Ho led the newly formed Viet Minh in a nationalist insurgency that, following the Japanese surrender to Allied forces, established a provisional government in Hanoi on 2 September 1945. The proclamation of a new Democratic Republic of Vietnam consciously emulated the United States' Declaration of Independence from Britain in 1776. Vietnamese nationalists were encouraged by the rhetoric of the Roosevelt administration in Washington that identified decolonisation as a central aim of the war. Hopes were high that the new republic would receive the moral blessing and material support of the United States, but anticipation soon soured to bitter disappointment.

First there was the fact that France was unwilling to cede

Indochina. By December 1946 talks with Viet Minh representatives had broken down. Eight years of warfare followed. Second there was the decision by the United States to support France, with the Cold War the decisive factor. In January 1950, China and the Soviet Union granted diplomatic recognition to the Democratic Republic of Vietnam. With Washington in a strategic battle with Beijing and Moscow for global dominance, the American civil and military establishment feared that Vietnam would capitulate to the malign influence of their communist foes. There was also a need for the United States to buttress its brittle relationship with the French who were essential to maintaining the security of Western Europe from Soviet influence. And so between 1950 and 1954, Washington essentially underwrote the French war effort, the $2.6bn dollars it expended amounting to 80 per cent of the cost to 'save' Vietnam.[4]

The money was not well spent. American President Dwight Eisenhower despaired that the French army was 'a hopeless, helpless mass of protoplasm'.[5] Its soldiers lacked ability, and back home the French people had lost the will to win. On 7 May 1954, following a long siege, Vietnamese forces captured the French military stronghold at Dien Bien Phu, with more than 2,000 French soldiers killed and 11,000 captured.

The day after the fall of Dien Bien Phu, representatives from nine nations convened in Geneva to determine the future of Indochina. Envoys from Hanoi looked forward to the creation of a unified and independent Vietnamese republic, a hope that was smothered by a negotiated settlement that temporarily divided Vietnam at the 17th parallel pending national elections two years later.

Temporary turned out to be permanent. Nineteen fifty-six came and went without an election; Washington had only reluctantly sent representatives to Geneva, and even then officials pondered the possibility of air strikes to repel the political advance of the Viet Minh.

The Cold War determined American foreign policy towards Vietnam. In the minds of Washington planners, the country was part of a larger geostrategic struggle against China and the Soviet Union. The spread of communism to southern Vietnam would be a win for Beijing and Moscow – and if Vietnam fell, the rest of Southeast Asia could follow. The analogy drawn was with a row of dominoes. As Eisenhower observed, 'You knock over the first one, and what will happen to the last one is a certainty that it will go over very quickly.'[6]

The domino theory was based on an erroneous assumption. Ho Chi Minh might have been a communist, but he was also a nationalist. His administration looked to the Chinese and Soviets for support but after the long and bloody struggle for independence the last thing it wanted was to be subsumed by them. The failure to understand that fact led to a further inability to comprehend why Ho commanded support on both sides of the border. As Washington would learn to its cost, many ordinary Vietnamese who had little or no interest in communism still championed Ho because he promised to protect them from colonial intruders, be they Chinese, French, Japanese, Soviet or, indeed, American.

Containment of communism in Southeast Asia was nevertheless the reason why the United States refused to sign the Geneva Accords of 21 July 1954. Rather than risk a national election that could result in Ho assuming leadership of the entire country, the Eisenhower administration attempted to strengthen the vitality of the regime in the South Vietnamese capital Saigon with a transfusion of more than $1bn.[7]

For a short time, it seemed to work. Saigon shopfronts filled with displays of American consumer goods, though only a prosperous elite could afford to pay for them. What the impoverished peasant population outside the towns and cities needed was land ownership. But the politician in whom Washington placed its hopes proved to be an obstacle to reform. Ngo Dinh Diem had been appointed prime minister of South Vietnam in June 1954. Diem was not only a devout Catholic, which set him apart from much of the population, but also a brutal autocrat. To consolidate his control of the republic he called a referendum, winning a 98 per cent share of the vote that was a less than convincing endorsement of the electoral process. Diem used his power to impose absolute rule. He forcibly relocated thousands of peasants into what later became known as strategic hamlets under close government control. Political dissidents were deported, imprisoned and put to death. Diem did everything to undermine the democratic nation that the United States was attempting to build but there seemed no choice but to back him. As Lyndon Johnson would later remark, 'Shit, man, he's the only boy we got out there.'[8]

Ho Chi Minh was no less ruthless in consolidating his control of North Vietnam. He too incarcerated and put to death thousands of his own people including peasants who posed no political threat, imposed restrictions on press freedom and instituted indoctrination programmes. In contrast to Diem though he ruled not only with the iron fist but also the open hand, launching a land reform programme to relieve the country of food shortages and put an end to the power of the old feudal elite. Ho was a leader to fear but one whose power was planted firmly in the grassroots support of the Vietnamese people on both sides of the 17th parallel.

Washington was as determined to bring down Ho as it was to bolster Diem. In September 1954 US Secretary of State John Foster Dulles led the establishment of the Southeast Asian

Treaty Organization whose eight member nations pledged to the collective security of the region from communist aggression. The CIA also pursued a campaign to subvert the Viet Minh government by 'all available means'.[9] The situation was tense but without prospect of war. Viet Minh leaders were busy nation building in North Vietnam. Not only would their hope for a unified republic have to wait, but most also believed the way ahead was through elections not armed fighting.

The impasse did not last long. Determined to maintain power, Diem would not negotiate with Hanoi about a peaceable solution to the division of Vietnam. The Viet Minh in turn started construction of a secret route into South Vietnam that came to be known as the Ho Chi Minh Trail. It also collaborated with southern dissidents in an assassination campaign targeting officials sent by Saigon to impose political control on the countryside. In December 1960, the insurgents established a new organisation to coordinate their uprising against the hated Diem regime. The National Liberation Front of South Vietnam (NLF) – the Viet Cong, as Americans would call it with a derision that later turned to dread – had been born.

Just weeks before the removal vans arrived to help him vacate the White House, Eisenhower wrote to Diem. Praising him for his protection of South Vietnamese sovereignty, the president pronounced: 'Although the main responsibility for guarding that independence will always, as it has in the past, belong to the Vietnamese people and their government, I want to assure you that for so long as our strength can be useful, the United States will continue to assist Viet-Nam in the difficult yet hopeful struggle ahead.'[10] As his successor in the Oval Office would discover, what had seemed hopeful would increasingly come to seem hopeless.

*

John F. Kennedy was still a senator for Massachusetts when he declared South Vietnam 'the cornerstone of the Free World in Southeast Asia.'[11] On becoming president in January 1961, he added fresh mortar to keep that faltering foundation in place. Committed to the fight against communism, Kennedy was convinced his administration must take a stand in Vietnam. Bruised by his earliest encounters with Soviet Premier Nikita Khrushchev and the botched Bay of Pigs overthrow of Cuban leader Fidel Castro, he believed the reputation of his administration was on the line. 'Now we have a problem in trying to make our power credible,' he told *New York Times* journalist James Reston, 'and Vietnam looks like the place.'[12]

In autumn 1961 Kennedy sent his personal military adviser General Maxwell Taylor to assess the situation in Saigon. He returned to Washington bearing disturbing news. Unless the US committed ground troops, South Vietnam would succumb to communist overthrow. The president worried about acting unilaterally without the support of US allies, about the ability of American troops to adapt to jungle warfare, about the threat of provoking a military response from the Chinese. Send 8,000 American soldiers into action, as Taylor suggested, and how long before he was forced to increase those by an incalculable factor? 'It's like taking a drink,' he mused. 'The effect wears off, and you have to take another.'[13]

Nor though could he allow South Vietnam to fall on his watch. So in late 1961 Kennedy launched Project BEEF-UP, an aid programme intended to transform the weakling Saigon government into a muscular political and military force. Within a year, the number of advisers tripled from 3,000 to 9,000.[14] They also became more directly involved in counter-insurgency against the North Vietnamese. The Green Berets trained Republic of Vietnam troops, the CIA rolled out its Civilian Irregular

Defense Group programme and, with most lasting impact, the Air Force launched Operation Ranch Hand, spraying huge swathes of the countryside with herbicides to deprive enemy fighters of food and deep jungle cover.

It was not enough.

On 2 January 1963, the NLF inflicted heavy casualties on South Vietnamese forces at Ap Bac, a village thirty-five miles southwest of Saigon. The US had trained the South Vietnamese soldiers who outnumbered the enemy four-to-one, armed them with artillery and helicopters, but still they had lost the battle. Three Americans were among the dead, their loss sounding the first discordant note in the harmonious relationship between the media and the Kennedy administration. Ap Bac was only the beginning of a broader offensive in which the NLF would take control of 2,600 of the 3,700 strategic hamlets intended to pacify the South Vietnamese countryside.[15]

Still though, there was little sense that the country was moving slowly and inescapably towards military conflict. Kennedy remained unconcerned that increased intervention would lead to the commitment of combat troops. When Undersecretary of State George Ball expressed his worries, the president blithely dismissed him. 'George,' he teased, 'you're supposed to be one of the smartest guys in town, but you're crazier than hell. That will never happen.'[16]

For all the aid that was flowing into the country, South Vietnam was nonetheless becoming less stable. The challenge that the Kennedy administration faced came not only from a foe they were attempting to repel but the friend they were fighting to defend. Diem was becoming increasingly despotic, unresponsive to pressure from Washington that he win the fealty of his people through reform rather than repression. On 8 May 1963, Buddhists in the city of Hue defied the law by taking to the streets for a religious celebration. Government troops responded by firing shots into the crowd. Nine people died, two of them children crushed under the wheels of armed personnel carriers. Protest escalated, culminating on 11 June in the appalling spectacle of Buddhist monk Thich Quang Duc setting himself on fire on a busy Saigon street. The government was unmoved. 'If the Buddhists wish to have another barbecue,' commented Diem's wife Madame Nhu, 'I will be glad to supply the gasoline and a match.'[17]

South Vietnam was in chaos. Diem was deaf to demands for reform, aid money was disappearing into the pockets of corrupt administrators, government soldiers were shooting their own civilians and across the country a disaffected populace turned towards Ho Chi Minh for salvation. Washington seldom seemed to remember the war, the press had said. Now it was impossible to forget. By August, White House officials were discussing whether to support a possible military coup to depose Diem. Momentum waned, but by late October the issue was back on the agenda. Opinion was divided. The time for speculation was in any case over. On 1 November army officers led by General Duong Van Minh stormed the presidential palace in Saigon. Captured as they attempted to escape, Diem and his brother were bundled into the back of an armoured personnel carrier and sprayed with bullets at point-blank range.

Kennedy was in the White House Cabinet Room when a staffer rushed in with a telegram. The president was shaken. Diem and his brother were supposed to be exiled, not assassinated. What now? Uncertain as to what course of action the United States could or should take, the president ordered a 'complete and very profound review of how we got into this country, what we thought we were doing, and what we now think we can do'. He was still waiting for that report when he travelled to Dallas, Texas, on 22 November.[18]

We can speculate ceaselessly about whether Kennedy would have avoided military intervention in Vietnam, but will never know for certain. What we can be sure of is that the situation in South Vietnam had gone from bad to worse. Following the assassination of Diem there were six further changes of government in Saigon between November 1963 and June 1965. Rival factions were too busy fighting among themselves to coordinate strategy against their common enemy. North Vietnamese army units penetrated deeper below the 17th parallel, capturing control of more than half the countryside of South Vietnam. Kennedy had shown a lightness of step in foreign policy, improvising his moves rather than marching in time to the militaristic beat of advisers. That had most impressively seen him resolve the Cuban missile crisis through negotiation. He had performed another dance with Vietnam, increasing support for Saigon without committing combat troops. As South Vietnam faltered, however, so the space for political manoeuvre narrowed. Death spared Kennedy a decision that would torment and tarnish his successor.

He sits alone at the table, spectacles in one hand, face lowered into the other as he listens intently to a tape recording by his son-in-law, Captain Charles Robb of the US Marine Corps. Behind him a bust of his predecessor seems with its serene features to mock him silently.[19]

This photograph taken in the White House by presidential photographer Jack Kightlinger tells us how heavy the weight of the conflict fell on the shoulders of the man who succeeded Kennedy. It was a burden that to some measure he inherited but to another brought on himself.

Johnson lacked experience in foreign policy and leaned on the advice of national security advisers whom he largely inherited. There were several reasons why he was so willing to heed their words that the US must intervene militarily in Vietnam rather than risk withdrawal. First was his uncritical commitment to the domino theory. Second was a conviction that his political opponents would seize on any apparent softness towards communism to undermine his ambitious domestic reform agenda. Third was a feeling of personal insufficiency, a fear of being perceived as unequal to the responsibilities of president that haunted him in the small hours.[20]

He moved cautiously at first, apprehensive that increased intervention could undermine his chances in the presidential election of November 1964. By the time Johnson obliterated his opponent Barry Goldwater, however, he had already succumbed to the lies and deception that became the hallmark of his handling of the war.

On 5 August 1964, Johnson submitted a resolution to Congress seeking approval to retaliate against a reported attack by North Vietnamese torpedo boats on two American destroyers. According to the official narrative, the incident was an unprovoked assault on vessels in international waters. Little of that was true. The US ships were conducting covert reconnaissance close to the North Vietnamese coastline, and in the case of the second destroyer were not even the victim of an attack. Rather than enemy torpedoes, what the radar systems had likely sensed was an unusual weather condition. 'For all I know,' the president privately confessed, 'our Navy was shooting at whales out there.'[21] It didn't matter. Johnson persuaded Congress the episode in the Gulf of Tonkin was a wanton assault. The result was a resolution that authorised him 'to take all necessary measures to repel any armed attack against the forces of the United States and to prevent further aggression'. Less than an official declaration of war, it was more than enough to license military escalation on whatever scale the administration decided.[22]

With the country having decided to go 'All the way with LBJ' in the presidential election, it was no longer a matter of whether but when intervention would come. The North Vietnamese were sending more and more troops south, South Vietnamese soldiers were deserting in droves while new recruits swelled the ranks of the Viet Cong, the Strategic Hamlet programme was collapsing and the US was caught in a cycle of propping up one ailing administration in Saigon after another. National Security Advisor McGeorge Bundy spelled out the situation: 'without new US action defeat appears inevitable – probably not in a matter of weeks or perhaps even months, but within the next year or so.' Johnson understood the risks but believed he had run out of options. It was time to act.[23]

The catalyst came before sunrise on the morning of 7 February 1965. Viet Cong insurgents breached the perimeter fence at a US military base at Pleiku in the Central Highlands of South Vietnam, firing mortar rounds and detonating charges. The attack killed eight men and wounded more than a hundred others. Three days later, the Viet Cong inflicted further casualties in a raid on a US Army billet in the coastal city of Quy Nhon.

These incidents provided the pretext for a decision that the president had already taken. 'Pleikus are like streetcars,' asserted McGeorge Bundy. If Washington had not jumped aboard this opportunity to take military action another one would soon have come along.[24] There was near consensus among civilian and military advisers for the launch of air strikes against the North Vietnamese. No one was entirely certain what they would achieve, the most optimistic prediction being that Hanoi would be pressured to the negotiating table within six months, but Johnson believed 'doing nothing was more dangerous than doing something'.[25] Only Undersecretary of State George Ball demurred. 'Once on the tiger's back,' he warned, 'we cannot be sure of picking the place to dismount.' That destination would be national division and defeat.[26]

On 2 March 1965, nineteen A-1 Skyraider aircraft flew the first mission of Operation Rolling Thunder, a sustained aerial bombardment campaign against North Vietnam. Six days later came the first commitment of ground troops when 3,500 US Marines stepped from landing craft onto the shore at Da Nang. The United States was at war.

Not that the broader public was entirely aware. The White House did not admit immediately to the transformation of strategy to a military offensive led by American forces. Air strikes on North Vietnam were restricted to immediate retaliation for the assault at Pleiku, the president told the public, rather than a relentless bombardment. Johnson misrepresented the truth at every turn. He could have declared a national emergency to secure congressional endorsement of military intervention and the tax increases needed to pay for it, could have mobilised public support by providing a clear rationale for his change of policy, but instead he dissembled. Troop commitments increased without public awareness or congressional approval. 'We are not about to send American boys nine or ten thousand miles away from home to do what Asian boys ought to be doing themselves,' Johnson reassured an audience at Akron University in October 1964. Only they were and would be swelling the numbers already there.[27]

Johnson saw escalation as the solution to a war that was not going to plan. He and his advisers assumed that the massively superior firepower of US forces would win a swift victory. It was a serious miscalculation. The American military failed to impose dominance either from the air or on the ground.

Officials had been unsure from the outset what Operation Rolling Thunder would achieve. The answer was not much.

North Vietnam had very few industries essential to the war, and those it did possess were relocated to rural areas away from the urban centres targeted by American bombers. As investigative teams sent to North Vietnam would later attest, the pounding from American bombers had little impact on the resilience of the civilian population. People heeded the government slogan to 'call the shelter your second home', taking cover at the sound of air raid sirens inside one of the thousands of concrete tubes sunk into the ground along urban streets. Air assaults on the infiltration routes into South Vietnam were barely more effective. Repair crews were so effective at repairing the damage done by shells to roads and buildings that the number of Viet Minh soldiers stealthily crossing the 17th parallel actually increased from 1,500 soldiers a month in 1965 to 45,000 the following year. James Thomson of the National Security Council conceded the futility of US strategy. 'We could bomb them back into the stone age. They will disappear into the jungle and they will wait us out. Because they know something we know deep down, and they know that we know, which is that some day we're going to go home.'[28]

The prevailing opinion, however, was not that the strategy was wrong but that it could be better implemented. There was a temporary cessation of bombing in December 1965 and January 1966, intended to allow for the opening of negotiations with Hanoi. The failure of that diplomatic initiative unleashed the full fury of the American military. Johnson had at one time boasted that US pilots 'can't even bomb an outhouse without my approval'.[29] But by June 1966 he had authorised a massive expansion of the air campaign. Within a year, the number of bombing runs on North Vietnam increased from 79,000 to 108,000, and with them came an indiscriminate widening of the range of targets. South Vietnam was hit even worse in a desperate attempt to purge the country of enemy infiltrators.[30]

The war on the ground also became more intense. When Johnson assumed office in November 1963 there were 16,000 American troops in Vietnam. By the time in January 1968 he announced he would not seek a second term in office, there were more than half a million. And the casualties were also rising rapidly, with almost 14,000 soldiers killed in action by 1967.[31] The technological might of the American war machine afforded no advantage in a war fought against an unconventional adversary. There were no battlefields in Vietnam of the sort that US soldiers were trained to fight on. Enemy soldiers had the element of surprise, appearing from and disappearing into the dense jungle, an elusive but omnipresent threat. Traditional battle tactics were, in the words of one American journalist, 'like a sledge hammer on a floating cork'.[32] Unable to control when, where or how to fight the war, American military command resorted to more militant action. US soldiers took the fight to the enemy by launching search-and-destroy missions on their suspected bases. Acting at times on inaccurate military intelligence, troops stormed villages with little concern for the civilians caught up in the crossfire. In a war without any identifiable front, the only means by which the US military came to measure progress was not the lines on a map but how many enemy combatant lives it took. The Russell tribunal would later expose the tragic impact of this pressure to increase the body count.

Yet for all the ferocious firepower unleashed in Vietnam, the predominant belief of the American people was that Washington had done too little to win the war. In November 1967 a survey revealed that two-thirds of the public were of the opinion that 'the military has been handicapped by civilians who won't let them go all out'.[33]

*

From the start, there were those in the US who read newspapers, listened to radio, watched television and did not believe the stories being told. Their numbers were relatively small during the early years of American escalation, but would swell in time. They comprised the usual suspects resented and ridiculed by much of mainstream society: lefty and fellow-travelling artistes, clergymen and college professors. Then there were the students, motivated by moral revulsion, mistrust of the establishment and for men aged eighteen or over the reality of the military draft. The first teach-in, a participatory forum aimed to mobilise opposition to the war, took place at the University of Michigan between 24 and 25 March 1965 and from there spread to campuses across the country. More dramatic was the ceremonial burning of conscription papers that started with students from the University of California, Berkeley who on 5 May 1965 marched on their local draft board bearing a black coffin before setting their draft cards on fire. By then students were also starting to coordinate their protests, coming together in their thousands for the first march against the war, held on 17 April.

Most Americans nonetheless rallied around the flag. There were criticisms in the media of the tactics being used by American forces, not least the saturation bombing of enemy targets. Those publications sceptical of the purpose of the war itself were few, however, most of them for purchase by subscription rather than displayed on news-stands. Much of what was reported continued to rely on the positive statements made by officials from the White House, Pentagon and State Department.

Opposition to the war was not only stirring in the United States, however. Around the world, activists started to take to the streets during 1965. In Tokyo they formed human chains that made it harder for riot police to disperse them; in Rome they braved the evening chill of early winter on a solemn torch-lit march bearing banners urging peace; in Paris they assembled around the Luxor Obelisk in the Place de la Concorde to protest the American bombing campaign. There were other demonstrations in capital cities around the world, from Copenhagen and Stockholm to Manila and Nicosia.[34]

And then there was London. Britons were divided about the war. A poll conducted in December 1965 found, consistent with other surveys throughout the year, that 27 per cent of respondents approved of American military action in Vietnam, 37 per cent disapproved and 36 per cent were undecided.[35] That division was not simply between young and old or left and right, as disputes between students on university campuses and within the ranks of the governing Labour Party showed. And even among those who opposed the war there were differences of opinion, some of them ideological, others tactical. The more radical focused their ire on the modernist US Embassy building with its rooftop aluminium eagle perched above the plane trees of Grosvenor Square. There in October 1965 came the first clashes with police, who manhandled passive protesters into the back of Commer personnel carriers.[36]

Some of the most public faces of protest were those of celebrities. In photographs of a demonstration in Trafalgar Square during May 1965 you will see the American folk singer Joan Baez at the pedestal of Nelson's Column, taking aim at her country's foreign policy with a loaded guitar. So too more home-grown talent such as the Scottish troubadour Donovan, who that year released a number of peace songs including 'The War Drags On'.[37] And there too is the actress Vanessa Redgrave, who would become a celebrity icon of the anti-war movement, immediately identifiable in later photographs with a white headband that is a traditional Vietnamese sign of mourning. It was Redgrave whom representatives of the North Vietnamese government approached with an invitation to visit their country, to see for herself the impact of American military action. But personal circumstances prevented it. 'I was a new young mother and I told them I couldn't go.'[38] The actress did, however, have other influential friends committed to the anti-war movement. One in particular was a distinguished elderly gentleman whom she had befriended at a celebration of his ninetieth birthday in London's Festival Hall in May 1962. The two were close enough that she became a sponsor of the peace foundation that he established soon afterwards.

His name was Bertrand Russell.

2

THE PASSION AND THE PITY
OF BERTRAND RUSSELL

The life of Bertrand Russell spanned nearly a century that started with the invention of the electro-motograph and ended with the first moon landing. As an infant he sat on the knee of Queen Victoria, ruler of the vast British Empire. By the time he reached his last years, five other monarchs had ascended the throne and the empire was no more. When Russell made an improbable cameo appearance in the Bollywood romance *Aman* in 1967, he was featuring in a medium that had not existed at the time of his birth, screened for audiences in a country that had long since won its independence.

More than a half-century after his death, our image of Russell is like that of Charles Darwin and Albert Einstein, cast in perpetual old age so that is almost impossible to picture their younger selves. Besuited, with a cloud of white hair atop a bony face, a pipe stem seldom far from his mouth, it is a benevolent stereotype. Yet Russell was for much of his life a divisive figure, revered by many, reviled by others. One of the most eminent philosophers of the twentieth century, he was also among its more radical social and political critics. He wrote on almost every aspect of the human condition, from education to marriage, the decline of religion to the rise of modern science. 'Russell's books should be bound in two colours,' wrote his former student

Ludwig Wittgenstein. 'Those dealing with mathematical logic in red – and all students of philosophy should read them; those dealing with ethics and politics in blue – and no one should be allowed to read them.'[1]

Aristocrat or anti-establishmentarian? Worldly sage or unworldly fool? Rationalist or conspiracy thinker? What the members of the public thought of Russell depended on whether they were attracted to or affronted by his controversial opinions and behaviour. Russell was not so much one personality as someone who contained contradictions within himself, a man who espoused his love for the entire world but failed to remain faithful to one partner.

A committed atheist who placed his faith in the increasingly fragile world around him, Russell also possessed the patrician self-confidence to act as its self-appointed protector. 'Three passions, simple but overwhelmingly strong, have governed my life,' he wrote in the prologue of his autobiography. 'The longing for love, the search for knowledge, and unbearable pity for the suffering of mankind.'[2] It was the latter, fuelled by a fear that the recurring conflicts of the twentieth century could result in global catastrophe, which made him a persistent critic of international affairs and eventually led him into a collision course with the United States government.

Bertrand Arthur William Russell was born on 18 May 1872. His was a childhood blessed with wealth and privilege – and haunted by profound loss and loneliness. Ravenscroft, the Russell family home in Monmouthshire, sat in a spacious estate surrounded by woodland. Bertrand's parents, Viscount and Viscountess Amberley, were political radicals whose opinions on such issues as birth control and women's suffrage challenged the prevailing opinion of Victorian Britain.

By the time he reached his fourth birthday, Bertrand had lost both of his parents – his mother to diphtheria, his father to bronchitis – and his sister Rachel. He and his older brother Frank were placed in the care of their grandparents at their home in Pembroke Lodge, a rambling Georgian mansion in Richmond Park. Bertrand had not lived there long when his grandfather, former Prime Minister John Russell, passed away, leaving him and his brother under the supervision of their grandmother. 'Deadly Nightshade', as they called her, was the embodiment of Scottish Presbyterianism. The puritanical Countess Russell was intolerant of alcohol and anything other than the plainest food and 'until the age of eighty never sat in a comfortable chair until after tea'.[3] Frank escaped the strictures of Pembroke Lodge when he was sent to Winchester College. Bertrand, however, was home-schooled. Many of his days were spent in solitude, wandering the eleven acres of garden around the house. His sleep was interrupted by nightmares of being trapped behind a pane of glass that separated him from the world and of succumbing to the madness that had led to his uncle being incarcerated in an asylum.

Bertrand won salvation not through his grandmother's religion but the revelatory power of mathematics. When Frank introduced him to Euclidean geometry at the age of eleven, he found his passion. Logic and reason rather than religious dogma became the means by which Bertrand believed he could uncover the meaning of life. Asked in later years how he would explain himself to the Almighty if there was an afterlife, Russell replied that he intended to ask God why he had not offered more evidence of his existence.

The shy and solemn adolescent left the confines of Pembroke Lodge for Trinity College in Cambridge in October 1890. He graduated three years later with a first-class degree and was duly elected to an academic position as a fellow of the college. Cambridge afforded him more than a scholarly career. Russell made lifelong friends with members of the Apostles, a Saturday-night debating society that welcomed him within its intellectual ranks. He also found a less abstract form of devotion when he met Alys Pearsall Smith, an American with an ardour for social activism stemming from her Quaker faith. When Bertrand proposed to Alys, his family warned that any children they had would be threatened with the family curse of insanity. Russell's family did persuade him to separate from Alys, in pursuit of a 'brief and inglorious diplomatic career' as an honorary attaché to the British ambassador in Paris, but he could not be deterred for long.[4] On 13 December 1894 he and Alys married. The National Portrait Gallery has a photograph of the newlyweds, both of them looking uncomfortably stiff and gazing in different directions, a portent of their marriage's fate.

Russell established a formidable reputation as a philosopher. First came *The Principles of Mathematics* (1903), in which he attempted to prove that mathematics and logic are one and the same. Second was the monumental three-volume *Principia Mathematica* (1910–13), co-written with Alfred North Whitehead, a work that Russell mused only half a dozen individuals read – and fewer still understood.

At this point in his life, Russell was focused on his academic career and had little interest in politics. His conversion to the cause of world peace was incremental, and his first steps on the path came during the Boer War of 1899 to 1902. Before the war he believed that imperialism could be beneficial to both coloniser and colonised, assuming the altruistic intentions of European powers to impart their civilisation to the rest of the world. The war, however, disabused Russell of that belief. Uncritical at first in supporting his country's suppression of the

Boer insurgency, he became appalled by the tactics pursued by the British military, destroying farms and livestock and forcibly interning civilians in overcrowded and insanitary concentration camps. It was a formative moment in the development of his political consciousness. In coming to champion the cause of a colonised people fighting for liberation from imperial rule, Russell had reached a conviction that would find its fullest force more than half a century later.[5]

In 1907, Russell made the decision to run for public office. As the Liberal Party candidate in the Wimbledon by-election, he aroused anger and ridicule for his advocacy of women's suffrage and lost decisively.[6]

Four years later Russell accepted further defeat when he left his loveless marriage with Alys. He had already become embroiled in a long affair with the married aristocrat Lady Ottoline Morrell. His philosophical powers of logic appear to have counted for little when it came to matters of the heart.

It was during the First World War that Russell forged his identity as a peace activist. In his words, the conflict 'changed everything for me'.[7] The philosopher would insist for the rest of his life that certain threats to the peace and security of the world warranted an appropriate military response. The declaration of war by the Central Powers in 1914 was not one of them, however.

Russell believed from the outset that Britain should remain neutral. The very foundation of European civilisation was at risk, he warned. Better, he insisted, that Germany secure its invasion of Belgium with relatively little loss of life than the war escalate and claim the lives of millions.

In January 1916 the British government introduced conscription through the Military Service Act. At the age of forty-three, Russell was two years too old to be called to fight for king and country. His support of the pacifist movement nonetheless led to his becoming a member, and later chairman, of the No-Conscription Fellowship. Russell championed its cause with gusto, writing more than fifty articles for its magazine *The Tribunal*, assisting the appeals of conscientious objectors and paying visits to those serving prison sentences.

Russell's activism set him on a collision course with the authorities. In April 1916 he produced a pamphlet with the title 'Two Years Hard Labour for not Disobeying the Dictates of Conscience', a protest at the harsh sentence handed down on St Helens schoolteacher Ernest Everett, the first conscientious objector imprisoned under the new conscription law. Published anonymously, the pamphlet portrayed Everett as a martyr 'fighting the old fight for liberty'. The powers that be were not pleased with what they interpreted as sedition. Police harassed the pamphlet's distributors, raiding their offices, arresting and imprisoning them. Russell could not allow others to be punished for his work. On 17 May 1916 a letter appeared in *The Times*. '*Adsum qui Feci*', it declared, 'Here I am. I did it.' Russell concluded his confession with a declaration that 'if anyone is to be prosecuted, I am the person primarily responsible'.[8]

The authorities were more than willing to oblige. Prosecuting Russell under the Defence of the Realm Act provided the Foreign Office with the opportunity to deny him the passport he needed to travel to the United States. Russell had intended to cross the Atlantic in the hope of persuading President Woodrow Wilson to pressure the Allies for a negotiated peace. On 5 June 1916, Russell appeared before the lord mayor of London in the Palladian splendour of Mansion House. Found guilty of undermining military recruitment and discipline, he received a fine of £100, roughly £7,000 in today's money, plus court costs. Refusal to comply would, he was informed, result in imprisonment for sixty-one days.[9] Seeing an opportunity to become a martyr to the cause, Russell declined to pay the fine. However, he was denied his willing victimhood when friends intervened, selling some of his books to raise the money. However, they could not prevent his dismissal from Trinity College.[10]

Russell had made himself notorious. One incident the philosopher later recalled involved a mob surrounding the Brotherhood Church on Southgate Road in London, where he was due to deliver an anti-war lecture. The crowd burst into the chapel and began to assault Russell using wooden boards armoured with rusty nails. One of his fellow pacifists demanded that the police intervene. 'He is an eminent philosopher,' she protested when they did nothing. 'He is famous all over the world as a man of learning,' she persisted. Still no response. 'But he is the brother of an earl,' she proclaimed. Immediately the officers rushed to protect him.[11]

Russell remained determined to voice his dissent, and the authorities were no less resolved to silence him. There followed a game of cat and mouse between the two. With no source of income, Russell planned to earn some money from a public lecture series on the 'philosophical principles of politics'. When the War Office sought reassurance from him that he would not use the tour to promote the pacifist cause, Russell declined to do so. Whitehall immediately banned him from all war-time-restricted areas. In a letter published by the *Manchester Guardian*, Russell ridiculed this infringement of his freedom of speech, pointing out the difficulty of determining where personal opinion crossed into political subversion. 'May I say that I consider homicide usually regrettable?' he wrote. 'If so, since the majority of homicides occur in war, I have uttered a pacifist sentiment.'[12]

The game continued with Russell sidestepping the tackles of

his opponent. Delighted with the nimbleness of his own foot-work, he boasted to Ottoline Morrell that 'there is a lot of sport to be got out of the matter'.[13] He was nonetheless earnest in his intention to bring the war to an end. A German offer of peace negotiations in December 1916 met with a firm refusal from the British and French governments who were intent on the uncon-ditional surrender of their enemy. Russell penned an open letter to Woodrow Wilson, proclaiming that he would perform a service to the world greater even than Abraham Lincoln abol-ishing slavery by brokering an accord between the Allied and Central Powers. A sceptical *New York Times* dismissed the missive as 'so out of harmony with those coming from other authorities that their acceptance as true will be, to put it gently, not quite unanimous'.[14]

It was an article on the German peace offer published by *The Tribunal* in January 1918 that brought Russell's dance with the British government to an end. If the Allies did not accept the proposal soon, he warned, the people of Europe would be pushed to the point of starvation. 'The American garrison which will by that time be occupying England and France,' continued Russell, 'whether or not they will prove efficient against the Germans, will no doubt be capable of intimidating strikers, an occupation to which the American army is accustomed when at home.' The philosopher had crossed the line he had claimed was so hard to draw. On 9 February 1918 he appeared before Bow Street Chief Magistrate Sir John Dickinson, charged with threaten-ing the military alliance between Britain and the United States. Leaning forward on his high chair, the frock-coated magistrate denounced Russell for having 'lost all sense of decency and fair-ness' by choosing 'to insult by a deliberate and designed sneer the Army of the great nation which is so closely allied to us by ties of affection and kindred'. Dickinson sentenced the philosopher to six months' incarceration in the second division, the prison tier for serious criminal offenders.[15] On appeal, his reputation as a person of previous good character led to his serving the sentence in the first division, which provided a larger cell, meals prepared outside the prison and regular visits. Russell lamented the lack of tobacco, but the philosopher had succeeded in publicising his cause, with little personal sacrifice. By the time of his release in September 1918, with the war all but over, he had read hundreds of books and written thousands of words. Later he would rue the relative comfort of his incarceration while younger men continued to fight and die on the battlefield. As he wrote in his autobiography, 'I saw that all I had done had been totally useless except to myself.'[16]

Russell travelled extensively after the war. He was a member of a British government delegation that visited the Soviet Union in May 1920, an experience that soured his enthusiasm for the Bolshevik Revolution of three years earlier. Russell had come to Soviet Russia as a supporter of the revolution, he wrote in *The Practice and Theory of Bolshevism*, but left doubting 'the wisdom of holding a creed so firmly that for its sake men are willing to inflict widespread misery'.[17]

Back home, Russell became a public figure whose reputation went far beyond the cloisters of academe. He married his second wife, Dora Black, in September 1921 and the couple invested much of their time and energy in the progressive Beacon Hill School, its curriculum based on their humanist values. Russell also stirred transatlantic controversy following the publication in 1929 of *Marriage and Morals*, which decried the stifling conformity of Victorian values and advocated a more liberated attitude towards romantic love. There were international bans on the book and cancellations of public lectures in the United States following an outcry from religious groups.[18] Open marriage proved easier to sustain in principle than in practice – the Russells acrimoniously divorced in November 1934, and Russell married again little more than a year later.[19]

Russell's pacificism had caused controversy during the First World War. His reaction to the rise of Nazism during the 1930s was more consistent with British prevailing opinion. Russell shared the common conviction that Britain should not pursue a policy of rearmament to contain the expansionist ambitions of Hitler's government in Germany.[20] Following the failure of appeasement and declaration of war in September 1939 he supported the Allied cause, describing his position as one of 'relative political pacifism', a belief that armed conflict was a necessary last resort to forces that threatened world peace.[21]

Even though he more or less espoused political orthodoxy on the war, Russell could not stay out of trouble. When war broke out in Europe he was on the other side of the Atlantic. He led an unsettled existence in the United States, moving from teaching positions at the University of Chicago to the University of California, Los Angeles and then City College New York. Russell had long been a cause of irritation to the more puritanical members of American society. He had upset advocates of Prohibition during the 1920s. But it was his opinions on sex and marriage that really fuelled the fire of moral outrage. Concerned parents filed a lawsuit to prevent Russell from teaching their children, on the grounds that he was 'lecherous, salacious, libidinous, lustful, venerous, erotomaniac, aphrodisiac, atheistic, irreverent, narrow-minded, untruthful, and bereft of moral fiber'. The philosopher lost his position and returned once more to Trinity College.[22]

On Boxing Day in 1948, millions of Britons tuned the family wireless to the BBC Home Service. 'We present the Reith

Lectures,' intoned the announcer in received pronunciation, 'an annual series of broadcasts named in honour of the BBC's first Director General.' Inspired by the Reithian principle to inform and educate, the programme promised 'a stimulus to thought and a contribution to knowledge'. The speaker invited to launch this centrepiece of public broadcasting was Bertrand Russell. Already a familiar voice to audiences for his regular appearances over the airwaves, the philosopher won universal acclaim for his lectures on 'Authority and the Individual'.[23]

In broadcasts that were intimate and authoritative, Russell had mastered a medium of modern communication. In the process, he had become a public intellectual familiar even to those who never so much as opened a philosophy book. Now in his seventies, the changing nature of society had turned the ageing iconoclast into something of a conformist. The Labour government of Clement Attlee elected by a landslide in July 1945 pursued policies in keeping with his socialist principles. His hostility towards the Soviet Union was consistent with political orthodoxy at a time of escalating Cold War, and nor were his views on sex and marriage as scandalous as they had once been. Published in 1946, Russell's *A History of Western Philosophy* had become an international bestseller. He was in demand as a public speaker, touring the United States and Australia in 1950 and 1951. His private life too had become happier following his divorce from his third wife Patricia Spence in 1952 and marriage to Edith Finch three years later.

In December 1950 Russell was awarded the Nobel Prize in Literature. Camera bulbs flashed in the Stockholm Concert Hall as the smiling philosopher, dressed in finest black suit and white tie, received his medal from King Gustaf VI. The citation lauded him as a champion of 'humanitarian ideals and freedom of thought'.[24]

The former prison inmate and offender of moral sensibilities had finally become honourable, but it was not to last. 'I have always held that no one can be respectable without being wicked,' Russell mused, 'but so blunted was my moral sense that I could not see in what way I had sinned.'[25]

On the morning of 6 August 1945, the American B-29 bomber *Enola Gay* dropped a five-ton bomb above the Japanese city of Hiroshima. Codenamed 'Little Boy', the weapon detonated in a flash of light and heat at a height of 2,000 feet, killing 80,000 people. Three days later, a second bomb fell 250 miles southwest, on Nagasaki. Once more it obliterated everything in the immediate area of impact, killing another 40,000 men, women and children.

The atomic bomb confirmed for Russell the fear he had held since the First World War that the machinery of modern warfare threatened the future of the human race. Hiroshima and Nagasaki showed how scientific progress had transcended moral reason. 'One is tempted to feel,' Russell wrote, 'that Man is being punished, through the agency of his own evil passions, for impiety in inquiring too closely into the hidden secrets of Nature.'[26] The threat of imminent catastrophe led to Russell giving a rare speech in the House of Lords in November 1945. He had inherited an earlship following the death of his brother Frank fourteen years earlier, but never used the chamber as a platform for his political opinions. Now he rose to share his nightmarish vision of a world reduced to 'heaps of rubble and corpses all around'. To avert this disaster, atomic power should be placed under the control of an international authority, he said. At first Russell saw the Soviet Union as the greater menace in the escalating nuclear arms race with the United States. He even flirted with the idea that Washington should launch a pre-emptive strike against Moscow, a position from which he hastily distanced himself.[27]

As the Cold War intensified, Russell became a prolific campaigner for nuclear disarmament. One of his most famous statements was a manifesto co-authored with Albert Einstein published on 9 July 1955 that called on world leaders to resolve their differences peacefully. Russell followed this two years later by co-founding the Pugwash Conferences on Science and World Affairs, a forum for expert testimony on the threat to world security posed by nuclear testing and war.[28] Interviewed for the BBC television programme *Face to Face*, Russell was in turn thoughtful and witty. But when the presenter John Freeman asked him about nuclear disarmament, he went on the attack. 'I can't bear the thought of many hundreds of millions of people dying in agony only and solely because the rulers of the world are stupid and wicked,' seethed Russell. 'I can't bear it.'[29]

In February 1958, Russell became one of the co-founders and first president of the Campaign for Nuclear Disarmament. On 20 September 1959, 12,000 demonstrators congregated in Trafalgar Square. Flanked on either side by the stone lions surrounding the base of Nelson's Column, Russell saw everywhere the iconic semaphore symbol of CND. His young audience applauded enthusiastically as he denounced 'the politics of Bedlam' practised by a British government that prioritised its nuclear arsenal over the safety of its citizens.[30]

Russell was in truth not a great orator. On the page his prose still possessed a smart and lively step, but in public he was more flat-footed, reading the words without rhythm or resonance. It did not matter. The mere presence of this intellectually towering elder statesman on the front lines of the peace campaign was enough to arouse derision and anger in some but hope and inspiration in others. As a profile in the *Observer* put it, there were those who dismissed him as senile, his action proof 'how silly a clever man can be', but millions more were in awe of the indefatigable determination of a man in his late eighties 'to risk abuse, imprisonment and even death' in warning the world of the nuclear threat.[31]

Death would have to wait, but the abuse was constant and the imprisonment not long in coming. Impatient with the momentum of the disarmament campaign, in October 1960 Russell resigned the presidency of CND to help form the Committee of 100. This new organisation attempted to pressure the government through acts of civil disobedience, including a sit-in at the Ministry of Defence in February 1961 motivated by the installation of a Polaris missile base at Holy Loch on the Firth of Clyde. On 6 August, the Committee held a rally at London's Hyde Park to commemorate the anniversary of the Hiroshima bombing. Police interrupted the demonstration, appropriating a microphone that Russell had used to address fellow activists. In heavy rain, the philosopher and his wife Edith proceeded to lead a march to Trafalgar Square, where Russell took to a microphone without interference. The following month, the Russells were returning home from an afternoon drive when they encountered a motorbiked police sergeant at their front door. They had been charged with a disturbance of the peace.

So in September 1961 Russell found himself where he had stood more than forty years earlier, on trial at Bow Street Magistrates Court. Called to stand before Magistrate Bertram Reece, Russell produced a sheaf of typewritten pages from his pocket, on which he had prepared a speech. Peering over his small round spectacles, he looked towards the magistrate.

'May I proceed?' he asked.

'No, you may not,' replied Reece.

The magistrate found Russell, Edith and other members

of the Committee of 100 guilty, imposing a sentence of two months' imprisonment on the philosopher. At this there were shouts of 'Shame!' and 'Fascism!' from the public gallery. Defence counsel provided medical evidence that reduced the sentence to a week. With Edith receiving the same sentence, the Russells were led to a Black Maria bound for Brixton Prison. In the dirt on the vehicle, someone had scrawled 'Ban the bomb' with a finger. While he served his sentence, Russell received a £1 fine for his prohibited use of the microphone.[32]

Again, Russell divided public opinion. The letters page of the *Daily Mail* clashed with the newspaper's editorial line; a reader from Devon protested that the philosopher was 'trying to keep us all alive', while columnist Pearson Phillips denounced him for believing his noble birthright entitled him to an outspoken voice in public affairs. 'It's his looking down, not the sitting down, I resent', wrote Phillips. Here was evidence of how Russell turned conventional politics upside down, a champion of the radical left criticised in class terms for his aristocratic arrogance by the political right.[33]

The prison sentence may have been mostly symbolic, but Russell was determined that he must do what he could to warn the world that it was close to nuclear annihilation – and closer, possibly, than even he realised.

The aerial photographs taken by the U-2 spy plane sounded the alarm. Soviet Premier Nikita Khrushchev had carried out his threat to 'throw a hedgehog down Uncle Sam's pants'.[34] The Soviet Union had installed ballistic missile bases in Cuba, ninety miles from the southeastern shore of the United States. Cuba was an obsession of President John F. Kennedy. The island had long been an important strategic asset to the United States, both as a trading hub and a naval base. That all changed on New Year's Day

1959, when an armed insurgency led by Fidel Castro overthrew the corrupt military regime of Fulgencio Batista. Kennedy had barely got his feet under the desk in the Oval Office before he approved a covert CIA operation to overthrow the new Marxist government on his country's doorstep. But the attempted invasion by Cuban exiles in April 1961 was a humiliating failure, the insurrectionists pinned down by enemy fire and forced to surrender at the Bay of Pigs where they had landed. The Kennedy administration, however, only hardened its resolve to remove Castro. The CIA conspired to take down the Cuban leader by means ranging from poison pens and exploding cigars to contaminating his scuba diving suit and spraying his broadcasting studio with psychedelic drugs.

While Kennedy was scheming to topple Castro the Soviet Union seized the opportunity to strengthen its tactical foothold in Cuba. In a televised broadcast of 22 October 1962, the president announced to the American people the discovery of Soviet missile bases on the island. The United States would meet this challenge first with a naval blockade of Cuba to prevent Soviet vessels transporting any further missiles and second with a demand for the removal of those weapons already installed. Should the Soviets launch one of the missiles against any nation in the West, he warned, it would be regarded as an act of war 'requiring a full retaliatory response'. Faced with the existential threat of nuclear confrontation, the world held its breath and awaited Moscow's response.[35]

Thousands of miles away, Russell followed events with mounting alarm that the catastrophe about which he had long warned could be about to happen. He supported the Cuban Revolution as a popular uprising against a despotic regime and was critical of what he regarded as the hysterical overreaction to Castro from the United States. The installation of Soviet missiles on the island was a crisis of Kennedy's making, a defensive reaction to the abortive Bays of Pigs invasion and continued assault on its sovereignty. Rather than pull back, however, the president had engaged in a reckless act of brinkmanship.

For a desperate moment, Russell looked as though he would be proved right. The US blockade went into force on the morning of 22 October. Soviet vessels approached. A US destroyer prepared to intercept. Then, the sudden news that the Russian ships had not only stopped but turned around.

It was in this moment of impasse that Russell sent telegrams to the leaders of the duelling superpowers. 'Your actions desperate,' he scolded Kennedy. 'End this madness.' His tone with Khrushchev was more conciliatory, urging the Soviet premier to seek negotiation through the UN. Russell also contacted Castro with an appeal to dismantle the bases.[36] What is astonishing is that in the midst of a crisis that threatened a third world war, the statesmen thought it important to respond publicly to the philosopher. The Russian news agency TASS published Khrushchev's 'sincere gratitude' to Russell and his agreement to engage in dialogue. Kennedy was more sour in his response. 'I think your attention might well be directed to the burglar,' he wrote, 'rather than those who have caught the burglar.'[37] Russell had no role in the deal that ended the threat of global disaster, the Soviets agreeing to the gradual withdraw of their missiles from Cuba in return for an American commitment not to invade. He could, however, take satisfaction from the fact that the resolution was along similar lines to those he proposed. More than that, though, he had proven himself as a spokesperson for concerned private citizens around the world, pressuring its most powerful leaders to account publicly for their actions.

*

'From Dallas, Texas, the flash, apparently official: President Kennedy died at 1 p.m. Central Standard Time, 2 o'clock Eastern Standard Time, some thirty-eight minutes ago.' CBS news anchor Walter Cronkite removed his glasses and peered up from his script to the studio clock. Momentarily lost for words, 'the most trusted man in America' fought back tears and cleared his throat before continuing the bulletin in a voice, usually so authoritative but now quivering with emotion. While his whereabouts were then unknown, it was assumed Vice President Lyndon Johnson was about to take the oath of office.

With this dramatic broadcast on the CBS network, millions of Americans learned what the entire world soon knew. John F. Kennedy had been the victim of an assassination, shot as he sat in the back seat of an open convertible travelling through downtown Dallas. As the presidential motorcade passed through Dealey Plaza there was a sudden sound of gunfire. Two bullets fired from the sixth floor of the Texas School Book Depository struck Kennedy, one in the base of his neck, the other in the back of his head. In less than thirty minutes the police circulated a description of a suspect. Shooting dead one officer who had identified him, the assailant fled into the darkness of the Texas Theatre. Responding to a tip-off, police converged on the cinema and apprehended the perpetrator. Taken to City Hall, he was identified as Marine veteran Lee Harvey Oswald. The following day, police prepared to transfer him to the county jail. As cameras rolled, local club owner Jack Ruby stepped out of a crowd, pulled a handgun and shot the prisoner in the abdomen at close range. An ambulance rushed Oswald to the same hospital where surgeons had tried to save the president. Once more it was too late.

The case, however, was not closed. Over time more and more questions would be asked of the official account of events provided by the twenty-six-volume report of the President's Commission on the Assassination of President Kennedy. The conclusion of the Warren Commission, that a lone gunman had murdered the president, came under relentless criticism from conspiracy theorists who attributed the assassination to ceaseless combinations of Washington elites, foreign powers and organised crime.

One of the earliest sceptics was Russell. The philosopher was far from an admirer of the fallen president. But a meeting with Mark Lane, a lawyer hired by Oswald's mother to clear his name, convinced him there was more to the story than the public was being told. Guided by the same search for truth that informed his greatest philosophical works, he set out to uncover what had really happened in Dealey Plaza.[38]

Russell's scepticism led to him becoming one of the prime movers of the Who Killed Kennedy Committee. The committee was an important development in Russell's public campaigning, a precursor to the war crimes tribunal in attempting to use the celebrity of its members to mobilise public opinion against the Washington political establishment. Those who added their name included author J. B. Priestley, film and theatre director Tony Richardson and Labour MP Michael Foot.[39] However, the committee never actually convened. Russell penned its only important statement, '16 Questions on the Assassination', which accused the Warren Commission of consisting entirely of members of the Washington elite, with a vested interest in covering up a possible conspiracy from within the political establishment to shoot the president. Evidence was being concealed and manipulated, he warned, to construct a preconceived narrative that Oswald had acted alone. Russell raised some important issues, but he was himself drawing conclusions without being in possession of all the facts, dismissing the Warren Commission before it had published its report. It was a lesson Russell should not have had to learn: like academic philosophy, political argument needed reasoning based on evidence not speculation.[40]

The committee anticipated the war crimes tribunal in another, more ominous, way. Reaction from the other side of the Atlantic was derisive. In what would later become a consistent media tactic of deflecting the substance of his accusations through criticism of his character, *Time* magazine went so far as to belittle Russell as 'that sometime philosopher'.[41]

'I dislike being thought to be silly.' Bertrand Russell was a man in earnest, his hope for the world tempered with disappointment and, as he approached the end of his life, anger. For much of the twentieth century he had campaigned for peace but seen the world come closer than ever to destruction. His resolve was nonetheless unbroken. Russell had long since abandoned his faith in God, but the religious fervour of his grandmother retained an enduring influence in an almost messianic desire to save the human race from itself. For all his concern about being ridiculed, as he reached his tenth decade, he would launch one of his last and most controversial public campaigns, risking his health, his reputation and his family. Russell was determined to end the Vietnam War.[42]

3

ANGRY DOVE

John Bertram Oakes, the editorial page editor of *The New York Times*, was unprepared for the letter awaiting him one morning in April 1963. 'The United States government is conducting a war of annihilation in Vietnam,' it proclaimed. Washington 'has suppressed the truth about the conduct of this war, the fact that it violates the Geneva agreements concerning Indochina, that it involves large numbers of American troops, and that it is being conducted in a manner reminiscent of warfare as practised by the Germans in Eastern Europe and the Japanese in South-east Asia'. These tactics, according to the letter, included the use of chemical weapons intended to wipe out the crops and livestock on which the peasant population of Vietnam subsisted and force them to submit to the brutal regime in Saigon. The American people had to learn the truth so that they could hold their own government accountable for the crimes it was committing. Having spoken truth to power, the author signed off with a single name that established his identity: 'Russell'.[1]

The *Times* responded with a scathing assault on the philosopher. For a man supposed to possess one of the most brilliant intellects in the world, Russell had shown a remarkably 'unthinking receptivity to the most transparent Communist propaganda'. His criticism of US foreign policy and of how the newspaper covered it was full of 'distortions or half-truths'. The

Times was not unprepared to criticise American intervention in Vietnam, especially Washington's support for the unpopular and oppressive government of Ngo Dinh Diem. But it also believed that US advisers were bringing 'a great deal of good' to the country. Their sanctioning of chemical weapons occurred only in the case of clearly identified military targets. If innocent civilians were becoming casualties, this was the unintended consequence of all wars. To imagine otherwise was to live in 'never-never land'.[2]

If Oakes believed this would end the matter, he was mistaken. Russell wrote again to the newspaper, challenging it to refute the substance of his accusations. The *Times* claimed that he had accepted as fact the falsehoods propagated by the communist insurgency against Saigon. In a powerful retort, Russell pointed out that one of his principal sources was the very same newspaper that had charged him with misrepresenting the truth. In an instance of the left hand seeming not to know what the right was doing, the *Times* was running stories about atrocities in Vietnam that contradicted its own editorial line on the war.[3]

Russell's feud with *The New York Times* was one front in a larger war of words with the media, on both sides of the Atlantic. That first letter warning of 'a war of annihilation' set the tone. Russell blended hard fact and logical reason with rhetorical excess, forensically exposing uncomfortable truths about Vietnam that the mainstream press downplayed or disregarded. But flourishes such as his comparison between the suppression of the Vietnamese and the brutal tactics of Axis forces during the Second World War were not only imprecise but also bound to antagonise the very people he hoped to persuade.

If you were to commission a documentary about the British anti-Vietnam War movement, there is a chance that it would look like this: Sunday morning, 27 October 1968. Pallid sunlight shines through the leafless plane trees surrounding London's Grosvenor Square. Atop the grillwork exterior of the US Embassy Chancery, a gilded eagle spreads its wings and surveys the scene below. What it sees is chaos. Thousands of demonstrators surge towards a police cordon around the building, breaking through its ranks and trampling across a carefully tended lawn. Cameras record images of mounted police charging protesters, officers on foot patrol pushing and swinging punches. The soundtrack accompanying these images is the Rolling Stones' 'Gimme Shelter', Mick Jagger declaiming, 'War, children/ It's just a shot away'.

A less obvious choice would be black-and-white footage of earnest young men and women sitting on uncomfortable folding chairs, shivering in duffle coats and scarves as they listen to an elderly man with a cloud of white hair denouncing the US war machine. There is no soundtrack, only the stark words of the speech punctuated by applause. Far less dramatic, this occasion is more characteristic of how the British anti-war movement developed during the 1960s, what little newspaper coverage there was restricted to the inside pages rather than splashed as a headline story. And in a movement characteristically associated with a younger generation rising to political maturity, it places front and centre the nonagenarian Bertrand Russell.

Senescence did little to impede Russell from becoming a leading voice of opposition to the Vietnam War. On the contrary, it imbued him with a sense of urgency to see a world freed from the military confrontations that threatened its very existence. Russell was one of the earliest public figures to raise the alarm about the Vietnam War; his moral condemnation of the conflict contrasted with the equivocation of an establishment that at most criticised aspects of US strategy but not its actual purpose.

Vietnam was not Britain's war. Neither the British people nor their government had any vested interest in the internal politics of a country more than 6,000 miles away. There were no important ties, either historical or contemporary, between the two nations. Vietnam had not been a part of the British Empire nor was it a principal trading, diplomatic or military partner. The conflict that plagued the country had no impact on the daily lives of Britons in terms of the purchasing power of the pound in their pockets.

Yet the plight of the Vietnamese people following the end of the Second World War captured the imagination of many on the British political left. In Ho Chi Minh they saw a resistance leader of an oppressed people in their own tradition of heroic figures, real and mythical, from Wat Tyler to Robin Hood. Ho and his Viet Minh forces were fighting to liberate an impoverished peasantry from French colonial overlords whose capitalist imperialism plundered the country of its resources and impeded hopes for independence. Activists on the British left therefore felt a sense of solidarity with the Vietnamese as foot soldiers in a larger fight to liberate the subjugated masses around the world. Their romantic impression of the nationalist insurgency against the French is captured in a protest anthem composed by Ewan MacColl, the troubadour at the forefront of the 1950s British folk revival. MacColl wrote 'The Ballad of Ho Chi Minh' in celebration of the overthrow of French colonial rule in 1954. Sung in his quavering baritone, the lyric rhapsodises:

From Viet Bac to the Saigon Delta
Marched the armies of Viet Minh
And the wind stirs the banners of the Indochinese people
Peace and freedom and Ho Chi Minh.

The same spirit of political solidarity shaped the creation of the British–Vietnam Committee. Founded in 1953, a year before the Battle of Dien Bien Phu broke French imperial hold on Indochina, the committee held public meetings, published reports and, with the increasing Americanisation of the conflict, staged the first protests outside the US Embassy in London's Grosvenor Square. Its members may have adhered to an idealised image of Ho Chi Minh constructed from afar, but they also gained a greater appreciation of what was happening on the ground in Vietnam. Honorary secretary Hilda Vernon travelled to Hanoi in July 1962, accumulating evidence that served as the basis for a series of publications in which she documented the massive increase in the US targeting of strategic villages. Vernon not only cut through the unduly optimistic forecasts from Washington about the advances being made against the National Liberation Front but also warned that propping up the unpopular Diem regime was the surest means of dragging the United States deeper into an unwinnable war.[4]

Vernon's commentary caught the eye of Russell. The two corresponded on Vietnam, an experience for the philosopher that inspired his first public statements about the military and political turmoil in the country.[5] Russell was not a neutral observer of the Vietnam War. To him, Ho Chi Minh was a heroic nationalist attempting to unite his people in a nation free from a century of colonial rule. He was a David to the Goliath of the United States that was intent on imposing its domination over the country. Washington must withdraw immediately and allow a 'popular national revolution' in which the Vietnamese would become masters of their own fate.

The philosopher levelled a series of charges in his indictment of the US government. First, its support of a corrupt and brutal regime in Saigon defied the democratic will of the

Vietnamese people. Washington had cynically reneged on the Geneva Accords, refusing to hold nationwide elections and thereby making permanent the partition of Vietnam. What the Vietnamese wanted was their independence; what they had was a southern half of the country under de facto colonial control through a puppet regime whose strings were pulled by the United States. Second, Washington colluded with the Saigon government in consolidating dominion over South Vietnam through the ruthless suppression of the peasant population, which included the use of chemical weapons. Third, the aggressiveness of US foreign policy threatened to provoke a nuclear confrontation with China and the Soviet Union.[6] Vietnam once more raised the spectre that haunted Russell, his waking nightmare of a world turned to ash. The headline accompanying a Pathé News clip of the philosopher addressing students at the London School of Economics in February 1965 captures that profound alarm: 'Earl Russell Sees World Suicide Over Vietnam'. In a crowded lecture theatre, students standing in the aisles to listen, the philosopher evoked the Cuban missile crisis in warning that, 'Once more, America summons mankind to the brink of nuclear war. Once more, America is willing to run the risk of destroying the human race rather than bow to the general will.'[7]

What, though, did Russell propose to do to prevent the Vietnam War consuming all mankind? The tone of his letters to newspaper and magazine editors was one of urgency. The world could not wait: could not wait for the outcome of the US presidential election contested by Lyndon Johnson and his Republican opponent Barry Goldwater, could not wait for more innocent civilians to die through the cruelties of the Saigon government, could not wait for the world to end in destruction. One missive to *The Times*, written with Labour MP William

Warbey in July 1964, spelled out a plan of action: an immediate ceasefire and reconvening of the Geneva Conference to negotiate a peaceful settlement that restored national sovereignty to the Vietnamese. Russell repeated his proposals in a strongly worded statement to the US Embassy in London the following month.[8] He stepped up the pressure on diplomatic staff around the world by calling for demonstrations in every city where Washington had an embassy building. Russell also raised funds, wrote pamphlets and participated in protest activities through his own Peace Foundation, founded in 1963, and the Vietnam Solidarity Campaign, which he helped launch three years later.

Russell was almost as critical of the British government for escalating the Vietnam War as he was of the powers that be in Washington. In his mind, anything other than unequivocal opposition amounted to collusion with US imperialism. The British government had actually proffered little practical support for American intervention. Prime Minister Harold Macmillan had made it a priority to repair relations between London and Washington following the tensions caused by the Suez crisis of 1956, the Edwardian patrician forming a close partnership with his suave young counterpart, John F. Kennedy. Macmillan wanted to prove faithful without committing himself entirely to US foreign policy, offering diplomatic support while resisting pressure to participate militarily in the war. His decision to send a small police advisory mission to Vietnam was a minor concession intended to appease the Americans with as little financial or political cost as possible to Britain. Failing health, economic woes and the fallout from the sex and spying scandal that forced the resignation of Secretary of State for War John Profumo led Macmillan to retire in October 1963. His successor, Alec Douglas-Home, survived only a year in office before being defeated by Harold Wilson's Labour Party in the general election of

October 1964. Russell hoped that the change of government would mean a reassessment of the situation in Vietnam, a hope that soon turned to disappointment.

In April 1965 the satirical magazine *Private Eye* ran a scabrous front-cover cartoon by Gerald Scarfe that showed a servile Wilson on his knees pulling at the trousers of Johnson so he could kiss the presidential buttocks. 'I've heard of a special relationship,' remarks the Texan, 'but this is ridiculous.'[9] For all its grotesquery, the cartoon conveyed a core truth about the power dynamic between the two politicians. Theirs was never an equal partnership, nor an easy one. Wilson tried to win over Johnson through charm, persuasion and persistence. What he received in return was coolness, warmed by flashes of anger.

Like Johnson, Wilson inherited a commitment to support the containment of communism in Vietnam. Unlike the president, he did not see escalation as the solution. The prime minister was caught between conflicting interests. On the one hand, the Johnson administration wanted the war to be an international rather than unilateral action and applied relentless pressure on Wilson to provide military support. As little as a 'platoon of bagpipers would be sufficient' to offset the perception of critics that the United States was empire building in Southeast Asia.[10] Wilson had come to power with the British economy buckling under an £800bn balance of payments deficit that necessitated US financial aid to avert a currency crisis. Washington officials used the threatened withdrawal of economic support as leverage for the British government committing troops in Vietnam. Averting the devaluation of the pound was a crucial priority for the prime minister. However, there was widespread opposition to the Vietnam War within the Labour ranks, not only among grassroots members and rebellious backbenchers but also in Wilson's Cabinet. When his Minister of Technology Frank

Cousins confronted him on why he failed to stand up more forcefully to Washington, Wilson responded, 'Because we can't kick our creditors in the balls.'[11]

The prime minister's innate political pragmatism led him to try appeasing both sides. He provided rhetorical support to the US war effort but refrained from sending British soldiers to fight, yet his attempt to placate his party and the president pleased neither. A frustrated Johnson flew into 'an outburst of Texan temper' during a telephone call in February 1965 when Wilson proposed coming to Washington to discuss the dangers of escalation. No less furious were the Labour members who at the party conferences of 1966 and 1967 voted to renounce government policy on the war.[12]

Removed from the machinations of politics, Russell saw the war in purely moral terms. What was happening in Vietnam was an abomination and Wilson should put principle ahead of pragmatism. Tensions between the philosopher and 10 Downing Street sharpened during the late summer of 1965, when the Home Office refused a request from Russell to grant visas to representatives from the North Vietnamese government. Russell saw this as a deliberate attempt to prevent the British public from hearing an alternative perspective on the conflict.[13] His simmering hostility towards Wilson had reached boiling point. On 14 October, Russell concluded a speech on the war at the Mahatma Gandhi Hall in London's Fitzroy Square by tearing up his Labour Party membership card.[14]

Russell had long been a controversial public figure, hailed by some but hated by others. His invectives provoked a backlash in a way not seen since his pacifist campaigning during the First World War. In the United States, one of the most widely syndicated retorts came from former federal government official

Stephen J. Spingarn, who reprimanded Russell for criticising US military forces while ignoring the thousands of South Vietnamese civilians killed by the Viet Cong.[15]

Political critics on both sides of the Atlantic claimed that Russell was 'anti-American'. If that was the case, he was hardly the first or last Englishman to hold such animus towards the United States. Russell was not immune in earlier life to the cultural snobbery about the United States endemic among the English elite, later confessing of his first transatlantic lecture tour that his parochialism had blinded him to the freedoms of American life. Like many a turn-of-the-century aristocrat, this conceit did not prevent him from marrying an American. Russell's appreciation of the United States improved with successive visits, even though his attempt to establish an academic career there proved unsuccessful. He was also a supporter of the 'special relationship' between Britain and the United States, both during the Second World War and the early Cold War containment of the Soviet Union. His attitude did sour during the 1950s, however. As with others on the left of British politics, he was critical of the domestic conformity of Cold War America, including the repression of civil rights and liberties by anti-communist witch-hunters and opponents of the civil rights movement. The death of Stalin in 1953 simultaneously softened his hostility towards the Soviet Union, and Russell championed what he saw as the progressive reforms of the new premier, Nikita Khrushchev. The Cuban missile crisis further affected his perception of the balance between the competing superpowers, the restrained statesmanship of Khrushchev contrasting, according to his interpretation of events, with the belligerent recklessness of Kennedy. By the 1960s Russell had come to believe that it was not the Soviet Union but the United States whose aggressive foreign policy posed the greater danger to global security.

Yet to characterise Russell as 'anti-American' obscures more than it illuminates. To criticise some aspects of American culture and policy is not to condemn the country in its entirety. Branding him 'anti-American' was a means to dismiss his opposition to the Vietnam War on the basis of his personal prejudices without addressing the substance of his arguments. His public statements on the war often sacrificed reason for angry rhetoric, language that allowed his detractors to accuse him of a pathological loathing of the United States.

American hostility towards Russell was only to be expected, but anger towards him also raged closer to home. The philosopher was certainly ahead of public opinion in his opposition to the Vietnam War. Gallup conducted the first survey of British attitudes towards the conflict following the Gulf of Tonkin incident of August 1964. Forty-one per cent of respondents approved of US military action, and not until June 1965 did public disapprobation poll consistently ahead. Anti-war sentiment was strong among the more radical elements of the British left, but there was no consensus of opinion even among the literary and artistic circles in which Russell moved. A cluster of public figures, led by the novelist Kingsley Amis, voiced their unequivocal support for the US war effort. They denounced detractors for spouting crude anti-American propaganda that 'accords better with emotional habit than with any real concern for either truth or humanity'.[16]

Russell was an irritant to a British public that was unaware, indifferent or ambivalent about the war. He was at best a senile old fool, wrote correspondents from around the country, at worst a liar whose words were an abuse of the freedom of speech and an affront to the Anglo-American relationship that had sustained world peace since the Second World War. In the words of one letter writer from suburban Surrey to the *Telegraph*, much of the public 'regard his activities as constituting a disgrace to this country'.[17]

Russell's feud with the press was epitomised by an angry exchange of words between the philosopher and *Observer* correspondent Dennis Bloodworth. Bloodworth had been to Vietnam but seen little evidence of the claims being made by Russell. He conceded that the strategic hamlets in which the Diem regime rehoused South Vietnamese civilians to separate them from the Viet Cong were a 'great inconvenience', though far from the cause of any further suffering, and dismissed any suggestion that the United States sanctioned the use of anything more harmful than 'weed killer'. Bloodworth accused Russell of being a communist propagandist, yet the failure of his own reporting to reveal the existence of Operation Ranch Hand, the spraying of herbicides over huge swathes of the Vietnamese countryside to deprive the Viet Cong of food and protective cover, made him an apologist for the sanitised press releases coming from the US State Department.[18]

It was not only the press and members of the public who were hostile towards Russell. His daughter Katharine despaired of him. Proud of the respectability he had attained as a public intellectual, she was alarmed at the way he tore that reputation apart with his virulent criticism of nuclear weaponry and the war. It seemed to Katharine that his contrarian spirit 'felt comfortable only in opposition'. He had, she admitted, become an embarrassment to her.[19]

So why did he carry on his crusade? Why place his already seriously faltering physical health at further risk? Why smear the revered public status that it had taken a long lifetime to attain? Why spend his own wealth on a cause in which he had no personal investment?

Because he believed it was right.

Katharine sympathised with her father's implacable moral conviction even when it caused their estrangement. 'He felt himself responsible for the welfare of mankind,' she wrote, 'driven by his wisdom to cry out like a prophet, hoping yet to save the children of Israel from the destruction their folly and wickedness deserved.' Her language reflected the Christian faith she followed, one which her father had long since abandoned. Yet it articulated the almost religious fervour of his mission.[20]

For all his physical frailty, Russell withstood public criticism with ease, insulated by the protection afforded by his aristocratic birth and the strength of his moral self-righteousness. Indeed, he only became bolder in his determination to expose the excesses of the war. Russell was further buoyed by some influential friends and admirers. In June 1966, he received a knock on the door of his Chelsea residence. 'Could I meet Mr Russell?' asked the caller. He could. During the course of two visits, the young man learned for the first time 'what had been going on Vietnam'. Excited, he later told his friend about the conversations with the philosopher. And so Paul McCartney and John Lennon formed their critical opinion of the Vietnam War.[21]

By the time The Beatles came calling, Russell had long been pondering the power of celebrity, including his own, to influence public attitudes on Vietnam. Plans first conceived the previous winter were being put in place for his most audacious gambit against the war. With a further turn of the seasons he was ready.

The mood in the room was sombre. It was Wednesday 16 November 1966. Outside, early winter sunshine dried morning rain from the streets of Westminster. Inside Caxton Hall, the Victorian building that served as a venue for everything from celebrity weddings to fringe political meetings, reporters were becoming impatient. Bertrand Russell was late.

Half an hour later than scheduled, the philosopher shuffled to his seat in the wood-panelled room and falteringly read a prepared statement. He recalled how he had first written to *The New York Times* three years earlier, warning of the atrocities being committed in Vietnam. In the time since, all that he heard about the conflict had confirmed his worst fears: 'The western press has recorded, frequently without consciousness of the full implications, a record of acts which force one to look back twenty years for anything comparable in our collective experience.' Russell had therefore determined to convene a tribunal that would document the scale of war crimes being committed by American military forces and present the facts to the world. Its members were to include some of the greatest intellectuals of their age, men and women from around the world renowned for their integrity and insight. With that, he was gone, leaving the members of the tribunal who had gathered to answer questions.[22]

Notwithstanding the late start, the press conference passed relatively smoothly. But the path to the announcement of the tribunal had been long and arduous. Russell and his associates had been met with many logistical challenges. How would the tribunal be funded? Where would it be held? What was it intended to achieve? And who, given Russell's age and physical frailty, would he appoint to preside over its investigation? The person selected for this crucial role was the French philosopher Jean-Paul Sartre.

4

FREEDOM FIGHTERS: JEAN-PAUL SARTRE AND SIMONE DE BEAUVOIR

When Bertrand Russell's 900-page *History of Western Philosophy* appeared in 1946, there was no mention of Jean-Paul Sartre. In fairness, the Frenchman was still on his ascent into the intellectual stratosphere. The two men were nonetheless very different in their political and philosophical thought. Russell repudiated the Marxism embraced by Sartre. Sartre in turn was scornful of the liberal humanism espoused by Russell. Both men occupied an anomalous status that made them a part of the intellectual and cultural establishment, but also separate from it. Yet while Russell was a willing recipient of the Nobel Prize for Literature in 1950, Sartre spurned the same honour fourteen years later. Interrupted at lunch on the Parisian Left Bank, the philosopher responded to news of the award by pronouncing he did not want 'to be transformed into an institution'.[1] Almost twenty years younger than Russell had been when he won his Nobel, Sartre had less immediate reason to ponder how posterity would remember him, but his was also the more unsentimental heart. Yet for all these dissimilarities, there was a close connection between the philosophers. Neither Russell nor Sartre was content with abstract intellectualism. Their public role as they saw it was to work for the betterment of humanity. In this they spoke out separately on the same issues, from violations of the rights of one individual to the global threat of nuclear Armageddon. What Russell saw in Sartre therefore was a man of conscience willing to brave public outrage by exposing the uncomfortable truths of the Vietnam War.[2]

Jean-Paul Charles Aymard Sartre had been born into a bourgeois Parisian family on 21 June 1905. Fifteen months later, his naval officer father died of tuberculosis and his widowed mother moved with her infant son into his grandparents' home. Sartre claimed in adulthood that the loss of his father was the 'greatest piece of good fortune' because it liberated him from paternal expectations.[3] Even so, young 'Poulou' was a pampered child, his mother cherishing the curls she let grow above his delicately featured face. Anne-Marie Sartre could not protect her son, however, when at the age of four he developed leucoma and lost the sight in his right eye. Other children might crave to discover the world outdoors, but Poulou became more introspective. 'Books were my birds and my nests,' he later wrote, 'my pets, my stable and my open fields.'[4]

The comfortable childhood of the precocious bibliophile was interrupted when his mother remarried in April 1917. Sartre liked neither his stepfather nor the school in the coastal town of La Rochelle to which the family moved. He endured both for three years before returning to Paris in the autumn of 1920 as a boarder at the Lycée Henri IV. From there he enrolled four years later at the prestigious École Normale Supérieure. A brilliant student, he somehow succeeded in failing his exams during the summer of 1928, rectifying matters the following year when he received first place for the *agrégation* in philosophy. Before he could begin an academic career, however, military service beckoned. He spent nearly eighteen months from November 1929 training as a meteorologist, his restless mind elsewhere while he watched weather balloons move aimlessly on the wind. Sartre offset the monotony of military routine by filling his days with reading and writing. In March 1931 he discarded his soldier uniform for the tweedier threads of a provincial schoolteacher in Le Havre, endearing himself to pupils by singing songs from operettas and competing with them at cards and ping-pong.

The fabled story of how fate rescued Sartre from a future in small-town classrooms revolves around apricot cocktails at a bar on the rue Montparnasse. Sartre listened to his friend and fellow philosopher Raymond Aron discuss Edmund Husserl, the principal founder of phenomenology, the study of how human consciousness perceives observable objects and events. 'You see, my dear fellow,' beamed Aron, indicating his drinking glass, 'if you're a phenomenologist you can talk about this cocktail – and that's philosophy!'[5] Sartre was astonished by this pronouncement, which transformed his understanding of philosophy. It inspired him to study at the French Institute in Berlin between 1933 and 1934, where he focused his learning on phenomenology while around him the Nazis consolidated their control of political power. From there he returned to Le Havre but soon moved on to teaching positions, first in Laon and, finally, in the autumn of 1937, Paris. The following year saw the publication of what many critics still consider his greatest novel, *Nausea*. He followed it in 1939 with the short story collection *The Wall*, the title story of which is set during the Spanish Civil War, an early articulation of the political engagement integral to Sartre's life and career.

The formative influence that fused the intellectual with the activist was the Second World War. Stationed with a meteorological unit in Alsace, Sartre resumed his military career where he had left it, filling his days frantically writing. That personal freedom did not last. On 10 May 1940 German forces advanced through the Ardennes Forest in an invasion of France. Paris fell the following month. On 21 June, his thirty-fifth birthday, Sartre became a prisoner of war. He escaped from Stalag 12D in Trier by procuring a medical pass for an appointment with an ophthalmologist and then, having left the camp, not stopping until he reached Paris.

Sartre was critical of his fellow Parisians for their passivity during the Nazi occupation but his own role in the Resistance remains contested.[6] Although a member of the underground group Socialisme et Liberté, he spent more of his time teaching at the Lycée Condorcet and perpetually writing. His plays *The Flies* and *No Exit* were first performed in 1943 and 1944 respectively, and his definitive philosophical statement, *Being and Nothingness*, was published in 1943. At the heart of all human experience, asserted Sartre, is freedom. In a godless universe, there is nothing about our lives that is predetermined. Individuals define themselves continually through their own choices.[7] Only by accepting the freedom to determine our own lives and the impact we have on others can we live authentically, concluded Sartre; to do otherwise is to act in 'bad faith'. Following more than a decade of frustrated ambition, Sartre had become a sensation, a public intellectual par excellence. Whether holding court at the Café de Flore or writing amid the crowded bookshelves of his fourth-floor apartment on the rue Bonaparte, his pronouncements on any aspect of life were a matter for discussion in an infatuated French media.

Reading history backwards, it would be easy to plot a straight line connecting the points of Sartre's political career that led him to Russell's tribunal. Politically on the left, he retained faith in the communist regimes of China and the Soviet Union long after other leading intellectuals had lost theirs, convictions that have led critics to label him 'the paradigmatic anti-American' of the Cold War.[8] Sartre could certainly be highly partisan in holding the United States accountable for political abuses while ignoring greater crimes committed by the Soviet and Chinese governments. His relationships with the competing superpowers were, however, complicated. Far from uncritical of the Soviet Union, he fell out of favour with Moscow on several occasions. He was also an avid admirer of much about the United States, consuming its culture from childhood comic books to later passions for jazz music, cinema and literature. As with Bertrand Russell, the phrase 'anti-American' was a means to attack Sartre as a person rather than assess the substance of his political opinions, to see him as having been motivated by propaganda purposes rather than sincere moral conviction. In reality, there was an element of both in his decision to accept the presidency of the war crimes tribunal. Mapping the landscape of his political associations between East and West provides us with a sense of how and why he participated in the tribunal, of the prejudices he had of Americans – and they of him.

For all his later criticism of the United States, the first impression Sartre gained reading imported comic books as a child had a lasting impact. From the cinema screen to the printed page, American culture had a profound influence on him before the Second World War. The United States became more than a place of the imagination when he travelled to the country for the first time on a three-month tour in January 1945. Eager to escape the woes of wartime Paris, he boarded a transatlantic flight along with a small delegation of French journalists hosted by the US Office of War Information on a coast-to-coast tour of American home-front industries.[9] At first he found the experience overpowering. Disoriented from the long journey, the bright lights of New York City further unbalanced him. Without having experienced the deprivations of life in Nazi-occupied Europe, the American people acted as though they were unaware there was a war on.

Sartre and his fellow reporters enchanted the American press with their Gallic sophistication. 'One wishes these people could stay for a real visit,' gushed notorious gossip columnist Hedda Hopper after attending a Los Angeles reception for them hosted by suave French actor Charles Boyer. 'We could learn so much from them.'[10] Others, however, were more concerned about what the French visitors might learn about the United States. J. Edgar Hoover's FBI monitored their every move, focusing their attention less on the unfamiliar Sartre than the two female correspondents among the French entourage, Etiennette Benichon and Andrée Viollis, both of whom were known communist sympathisers.[11] Concerned with protecting state secrets, the FBI nonetheless placed all the reporters under constant surveillance. Whether Sartre was taking a train from Albany to New York City or making a long-distance phone call from Room 372 of the St. Anthony Hotel in San Antonio, the Bureau knew what he was doing. Staff acting as informants during his month-long stay at the Hotel Victoria in Manhattan documented the more-than-fifty occasions when the switchboard assisted him. Despite some calls to politically suspect persons, the FBI found nothing incriminating. Their file on Sartre, however, remained open for over twenty years.[12]

While the FBI was busy monitoring his private activities, Sartre made himself controversial through his own public statements. In an article published by *Le Figaro* on 24 January 1945, he accused French expats of colluding with the US State Department to publish stories intended to undermine the provisional government of Charles de Gaulle that had come to power following the liberation from Nazi military forces. The piece prompted a furious riposte from those Sartre had criticised who, in turn, claimed it was he whose 'lying and hateful' words were the real threat to Franco-American relations. Conscious of how reliant France was on the United States, *Le Figaro* issued a public apology, while Sartre insisted he had been misunderstood. True, he had criticised American policy towards his own country, but this was only 'from a spirit of deep friendship for the United States'. Was it not after all an openness to different opinions, a 'deep love for the freedom of thought', that defined the greatness of the American people?[13]

For all the mistrust of federal authorities and occasional contretemps in the metropolitan press, Sartre and the United States emerged from their first encounter with a warm mutual regard. Trading his tatty sheepskin coat for a sharp pinstripe suit from a Manhattan tailor, Sartre toured the country aboard an exclusively chartered US Army plane, meeting everyone from Hollywood film-makers to President Franklin D. Roosevelt, whose 'profoundly human charm' so impressed him. What he saw on the tour sharpened the romantic impression formed in France that the United States represented the future of mankind.[14]

Sartre returned to the United States in December 1946. The military cargo ship he voyaged aboard might have heralded little sense of occasion, but he set foot on American soil as a conquering hero. In the time since he first came to the country, he had become an internationally renowned author. Sartre spoke to crowded audiences not only at Ivy League universities but also from the stage of Carnegie Hall, while flattering profiles appeared in the pages of leading literary magazines.[15]

Even when he was no longer in the country, Sartre seemed to be everywhere in American culture during the late 1940s: across the printed page, in theatre productions and on cinema screens. This was a phenomenally prolific period in his writing career, with near-simultaneous translations of the many essays, novels, plays and philosophical works that spilled from his pen. His drama *No Exit*, which opened at the Biltmore Theatre on

Broadway the month before his return to the United States, won the Critics' Circle Award for best foreign play. Sartre was for a time unaware of the award because he refused to pay to collect the telegram sent by the prize givers.[16] But he was not oblivious to the plaudits for productions of other plays including *The Flies* and *Dirty Hands* (also translated as *Red Gloves*), nor the critical reception and commercial impact of books ranging from his polemical *Anti-Semite and Jew* to the novels in his unfinished Roads to Freedom series, *The Age of Reason* and *The Reprieve*.

Several reasons account for Sartre's powerful impact on the cultural zeitgeist of post-war America. The emphasis in existential philosophy on the role of the individual in shaping his or her own identity appealed to the idea of the American Dream, of a country without class barriers where the self-made person could rise from rags to riches. That notion had a particular resonance to a younger generation ambitious to form the post-war future. It was also a potentially powerful ideological tool in the nascent Cold War struggle against the Soviet Union. Refracted through the lens of American conservatism, existentialism provided a powerful retort to the Marxist doctrine of the Soviet Union.[17] The Cold War utility of existentialism gained further credence among American intellectuals when author David Zaslavsky denounced Sartre in *Pravda*, the official Soviet Communist Party newspaper, as pandering to a 'wealthy American bourgeoisie' hostile towards Marxism.[18]

In truth, Sartre had no intention at all of fighting for the United States on the ideological front lines of the Cold War. That much is clear from two of the plays he wrote while at the peak of his popularity with American audiences, *The Respectful Prostitute* (1946) and *Red Gloves* (1948).[19] The first of these dramas was a fierce indictment of the racism Sartre witnessed during his first trip across the Atlantic. *The Respectful Prostitute* dramatised that tension in a tale set in the American Deep South involving a white politician who covers up one act of racial murder by encouraging a mob to commit another, lynching a Black man they believe guilty of the first felony. Civil rights leaders enthusiastically endorsed a Broadway production in 1948, but authorities banned it from the stages of other cities. Federal officials also feared foreign enemies would use the play as anti-American propaganda, a worry that was affirmed when the play opened in Moscow.[20] Sartre further revealed that he was far from the anti-communist American critics had supposed in his response to a New York production of *Red Gloves*. Set in the fictional country of Illyria during the Second World War, the play tells the story of a young man who agrees to assassinate a political leader, only for those who hired him to adopt the policies of the slain man. Sartre learned that critics were hailing the Broadway adaptation as an attack on the absurdities of Soviet rule. Troubled by this interpretation, he asked his friend and fellow cultural icon Jean Cocteau to attend a performance while he was visiting the United States. Cocteau agreed but claimed his English was too poor to understand whether the play was a faithful adaptation. Sartre sued his publisher for authorising a version of the play that turned it into 'a vulgar common melodrama with an anti-Communist bias'.[21]

By the early 1950s the sharpening of diplomatic tensions between the Soviet Union and the United States impelled Sartre to take sides. On the evening of 28 May 1952, traffic police forced French Communist Party (PCF) leader Jacques Duclos to stop and get out of the car he was driving home. On the back seat they found a basket containing a pair of pigeons, which they accused him of having trained to take messages to his Soviet paymasters. Duclos pointed out that the birds were dead and protested that he was taking them home for his wife to cook. The police

ordered an autopsy on the fowl but failed to find the micro-
film they suspected was concealed in their stomachs. Duclos
remained in custody for a month, while the authorities continued their futile search for evidence that the birds were carrier
pigeons.[22] A furious Sartre swore his allegiance to the PCF in
the essay series 'Communists and Peace', the first instalment of
which appeared in the July 1952 edition of *Les Temps modernes*,
the literary magazine he co-founded with Simone de Beauvoir
and Maurice Merleau-Ponty after the war. He also became a
spokesperson for the broader communist cause, travelling to the
Soviet Union in May 1954 and reporting how its citizens shared
a sense of belonging unrivalled in any Western state. Years later,
he claimed that his public statements concealed private misgiv-
ings about the Moscow regime. 'I did it partly because it is not
considered polite to pour shit on your hosts as soon as you are
home, and partly because I didn't really know where I stood in
relation to both the USSR and my own ideas.'[23] If so, he proved
more than proficient in concealing the truth. In December 1955,
Sartre accepted an appointment as vice president of the Franco-Soviet Association, which had close ties with the Comintern.
Two months later, he addressed its members in a speech com-
memorating the Battle of Stalingrad that stressed the role of the
Soviet Union in securing Allied victory over Axis forces.[24]

Sartre caused further friction with the United States by
befriending some of its other ideological foes. The Chinese government hosted him on a tour in autumn 1955. It was an unusual
experience. The Chinese seem not to have entirely understood
their guest, assuming he was Russian rather than French and
insulating him from contact with ordinary citizens. A photograph of Sartre attending a parade in Peking shows him looking
a little lost among the crowd.[25] Interviewed on his return home,
he was nonetheless enthusiastic about the visit, proclaiming that

Mao Zedong had led a revolution that was firmly rooted in the hearts and minds of the Chinese people. In his prediction of a prosperous future for the country, Sartre proved a false prophet. Within three years Mao had launched the Great Leap Forward, a campaign to reform the agricultural economy of China that resulted in the starvation of millions.[26]

While Sartre became an apologist for communism, he was swift to condemn what he saw as the sins of the United States. Moscow aspired to improve all of humanity, he asserted, Washington only to promote its own interest. Sartre focused his ire on the anti-communist inquisition that convulsed American public life in the early 1950s.[27] One particular incident provoked his outrage. In March 1951 members of an atomic spy ring stood trial in a New York court, charged with conspiracy to commit espionage. The court found the defendants guilty and passed sentences of thirty years in prison on Morton Sobell and death by electrocution on Ethel and Julius Rosenberg. Sartre was far from alone in condemning the slender evidence on which the court reached its decision and the harshness of the sentences imposed, with even Pope Pius XII denouncing the use of the death penalty. The fate of the defendants also pulled Sartre for the first time into the same political orbit as Bertrand Russell, both philosophers demanding the court overturn its decision. Yet it was Sartre whose wrath rose to the more venomous assault on the United States for failing to honour its own liberal ideals. Far from being the leader of the free world, he fumed, the country had become 'the cradle of a new fascism'. Sartre could do nothing to spare the Rosenbergs from a 'legal lynching' in the electric chair, but he persisted for years in protesting the 'false evidence and false testimony' that convicted Morton Sobell.[28] Only long after the philosopher was dead did it become clear that the defendants really had betrayed their country.[29]

Sartre had placed his political faith in the Soviet Union, only to feel the sharp sting of betrayal. On 4 November 1956, Russian tanks rolled across the Hungarian borders to suppress a popular uprising against communist rule. The rebels could not withstand the might of Soviet forces, and 3,000 people died. When the fighting was over, tanks occupied a wounded city, flags hanging limp from ruined buildings and bodies strewn in the rubble-filled streets. Revolutionary leader Imre Nagy received a sentence of death by hanging from his Soviet captors. Protesters in Paris reacted by storming the offices of the PCF, smashing its windows and throwing burning papers into the streets below. Sartre wrestled with his conscience before concluding he had no choice but to denounce the brutal suppression of Hungarian democracy as a 'crime', and to dissociate himself from the 'disgusting lies' of the PCF in support of Moscow. He resigned from the Franco-Soviet Association and challenged any Russian author willing to debate him on the brutal tactics used by Moscow, but none had the courage.[30]

Critics would later claim that it was farcical for Sartre, a notorious anti-American, to preside impartially over the Vietnam war crimes tribunal. How dare he pronounce on the actions of an American military attempting to defend an impoverished and powerless nation from the same communist tyranny that he refused to condemn despite its murder, imprisonment and starvation of millions? They also pointed to his sympathy for Fidel Castro as further evidence of his hostility towards the United States. In contrast to his Chinese tour, photographs of the invited visit to Cuba in early 1960 portray a spirit of camaraderie between Sartre, Castro and Che Guevara. On his return to Paris, Sartre penned a series of articles published in *France-Soir* that championed the 'real revolution' that had restored power to a people who had endured decades of colonial rule and despotic corruption.[31] With friends like these, surmised American critics, it was obvious who Sartre saw as his enemy. As his tangled history with the Soviet Union nonetheless showed, Sartre was too fierce an intellect to serve as a crude propagandist for Moscow. Hostile as he could be towards the United States, his opposition to the war has to be understood in terms of a broader critique of Western power.

A mighty Western power imposing its superior military force on a nation seeking political independence, the dehumanisation of a foreign people, entire communities forcibly relocated, civilians tortured and raped, thousands killed. The Vietnam War resonated with Sartre because he had seen such brutal excesses before – and committed by his own country. At a time when most of France wanted to retain its colonial rule in North Africa, Sartre was a fearless advocate of decolonisation. During the Algerian War of Independence he defied public opinion, death threats and state censorship in denouncing the many atrocities committed by the French military. His later opposition to the Vietnam War was therefore the logical progression of a committed activism against all forms of colonialism.

The Algerian struggle for independence was one of the cruellest colonial conflicts of the twentieth century.[32] Pierre Mendès France, the premier of the Fourth Republic, pronounced the overwhelming feeling of his fellow citizens when he informed the National Assembly that Algeria was 'irrevocably French'. France had imposed its rule over the country since the military invasion of 1830. The French population was around 10 per cent of the total but controlled all aspects of a segregated society. By the early 1950s Algerian nationalists were ready to reclaim that power for their own people. Inspired by the French defeat at Dien Bien Phu, they formed the National Liberation

Front (FLN) in October 1954. The following month, the insurrectionists instigated a military campaign in the mountainous southern region of the country. There was a furious reaction in France. The government sent 20,000 troops across the Mediterranean. Overwhelmed by superior forces, the FLN abandoned conventional military tactics and turned to terrorism. In August 1955 it launched a series of bloody raids in the northeastern region of Constantinois. French soldiers retaliated by burning villages and executing suspects without trial. Thousands died or disappeared.

Algeria descended in a downward spiral of violence. In March 1956 the government declared a state of emergency. French military forces were ferocious in their efforts to destroy the enemy, forcibly relocating villagers they suspected of harbouring the FLN and torturing them for information. The FLN retaliated by calling a general strike and launching a bombing campaign using young women dressed in Western attire to plant explosive devices in bars and restaurants. The most serious urban offensive occurred in the capital city of Algiers. From September 1956 the Battle of Algiers raged for twelve months, during which the French military subjected prisoners to electric shock, waterboarding and sexual assault. Having secured control of Algiers, French soldiers reasserted colonial rule over much of the rest of the country.

The Arab insurgency might have been in abeyance, but trouble from another source was about to bring down the political establishment in Paris. On 13 May 1958, the National Assembly confirmed Pierre Pflimlin as the new French prime minister. Fearful that Paris would negotiate a settlement with the FLN that turned power over to the Arab population, French Algerians took to the streets of Algiers in protest. General Jacques Massu, who led the purge of the FLN from the capital, turned on the same officials he had protected, taking over the governor-general's offices from where he proclaimed the establishment of a Committee of Public Safety. The insurrectionists demanded the replacement of Pflimlin with an emergency government headed by General Charles de Gaulle. With the military on the point of staging a coup d'état, President René Coty invited the hero of the French Resistance to assume power. Within a week, de Gaulle flew to Algiers to calm the fears of insurrectionists, while also announcing his intention to implement reforms that would resolve the conflict.

The tide appeared to be turning towards a political settlement. In September 1959 de Gaulle announced his support in principle of Algerian majority rule. Feeling betrayed, defenders of French colonial rule mounted another attempted insurrection four months later. De Gaulle made another broadcast in which he appeared in full military uniform to demand the rebels' obedience. Back in France, opinion polls confirmed that a French public formerly opposed to Algerian independence now favoured self-rule. Forming themselves into the Secret Army Association, fanatical supporters of French Algeria mounted a series of bomb attacks in both Algeria and France – a final act of defiance. On 18 March 1962 the French government and representatives of the FLN signed the Évian Accords, guaranteeing the withdrawal of troops from Algeria. Referenda in France on 8 April and in Algeria on 1 July confirmed massive support in both countries for an end to hostilities. After seven years of conflict, and military and civilian losses in the hundreds of thousands, Algeria was an independent nation.

'I've always looked upon colonialism as an act of pure theft, the brutal conquest of a country and the absolutely intolerable exploitation of one country by another.' Sartre claimed to have reached this conclusion while a schoolboy. The adult philosopher framed his criticism of colonialism in existentialist terms. While every individual possessed freedom of action, the only way to live authentically was to make choices that impacted positively on others. Dispossessing another people of their own land, resources and right to govern themselves was a blatant act of bad faith that belied any authentic way of being. Supporting the fight for Algerian independence allowed the philosopher to give meaning to his choice of action.[33]

Sartre was in truth less consistent than he claimed. While he had recognised the racism of French colonial rule in interviews from the late 1940s, travelling through southern Algeria during the spring of 1950 he nonetheless showed scant regard for the political situation in the country.[34] The FLN was eighteen months into its long and bloody fight for independence before Sartre penned his first substantial piece on the conflict, 'Colonialism Is a System'. Published in the March 1956 edition of *Les Temps modernes*, the article contended that all French citizens were implicated in the 'misery and despair' of the Algerian people, since it was within their power to put a stop to it. The root cause of the problem, according to Sartre, was the inherent cruelty and corruption of colonialism. Since it was impervious to reform, it must be abolished. 'The only solution,' he wrote, 'will be revolutionary rupture and independence.' In recognising their responsibility to others, the French people would liberate not only Algerians but also themselves.[35]

It was only a matter of time before Sartre ran into trouble with a French government intolerant towards public criticism of the war. In February 1958, handwritten sheets penned by imprisoned French-Algerian journalist Henri Alleg were smuggled from his cell and published as *La Question*. The book documented his torture at the hands of the French military, and Sartre contributed a preface in which he wondered how a French people who endured the cries of anguish from prisoners of the Gestapo during the Occupation could now themselves be complicit in torture. If Sartre intended this as an act of provocation, he succeeded. Police confiscated copies of the book in a raid on the offices of its publisher and shut down the printing press of the newspaper *L'Express* after it ran several extracts. They could do little, however, about the 60,000 copies of the book that had already been purchased or the clandestine editions that soon followed.[36]

State censorship only strengthened Sartre's resolve to speak out in support of Algerian independence. In public meetings and on the printed page, he admonished the public for its collusion with the war, the political left for its moral indifference, and President de Gaulle for his slowness to formulate a political solution. He also signed the 'Manifesto of the 121', an open letter published on 6 September 1960 that supported Algerian nationalism, condemned the use of torture by the French army and encouraged conscripts to resist orders.

Sartre's outspoken opposition to the war made him a hate figure for many on the political right. The authorities imprisoned some of the dissidents responsible for the Manifesto of the 121 but spared him despite his demands that he also be charged, for fear of making him a martyr.[37] Prison was not the only form of censure, however. In October 1960, military veterans marched along the avenue des Champs-Élyseés to the Tomb of the Unknown Soldier where they relit the torch in honour of victims of the FLN, lining the pavement and raising their collective voices to shout, 'Death to Jean-Paul Sartre.'[38]

On 17 October 1961, thousands of peaceful Algerians took to the streets of Paris to protest the imposition of a curfew. The police reacted with astonishing brutality, shooting indiscriminately at demonstrators and drowning others in the Seine. A fortnight later, Sartre stood with others in a silent solidarity demonstration. He was a conspicuous presence at further protests in the months that followed. Public support for Algerian independence was mounting, but an impatient Sartre pushed beyond respectable opinion with his preface to *The Wretched of the Earth*, a book by French Afro-Caribbean political philosopher Frantz Fanon published in 1961. Sartre had come to share with Fanon a conviction that the inherent brutality of colonialism legitimated the use of force in its overthrow. Violence provided a means for colonised peoples to regain not only their political sovereignty, he contended, but also their personal identity, liberating them from their oppressed mindset. 'There is one duty to be done, one end to achieve,' he wrote, 'to thrust out colonialism by *every* means in their power.'[39] Public statements such as this made Sartre a target of the far right. On 7 January 1962 a bomb detonated on the rue Bonaparte in the apartment above the one Sartre shared with his elderly mother. Neither was at home, but the philosopher moved address soon afterwards.[40]

The episode had important repercussions. In his advocacy of political violence, Sartre was at polar opposites to the pacifism of Bertrand Russell – but his bravery in bearing the consequences of what he believed marked him out as more than a man of words. Russell and Sartre had already come into contact through their shared sympathy for the Cuban Revolution. Both were members of the Fair Play for Cuba Committee founded in April 1960 with a hope of easing the hostility of US government policy towards Havana.[41] Russell saw in Sartre a kindred spirit, and was inspired in June 1966 to approach him with the offer to preside over the Vietnam War crimes tribunal.

Ironically for Sartre, it was the war that hardened a heart that had been softening towards the United States. Interviewed by the theatre critic Kenneth Tynan in June 1961, he regretfully claimed to have no intention of again setting foot on American soil. He could not return, Sartre said, because 'to the extent that they were too violent, too full of over-simplifications, I would feel discontented'. He paused. 'Nevertheless, I used to like America very much. Very much indeed.'[42] Yet Sartre had been on the point of breaking his vow not to return the United States when the Vietnam War intervened. Having come out in support of Vietnamese independence from his own country during the 1950s, the philosopher was appalled by what he saw as the imperialist ambitions of the United States. By the spring of 1965, Sartre was poised to return to the country. The American authorities had debated whether to grant him a visa because of his communist connections but decided to do so because of the criticism that would come from blocking an internationally renowned personality.[43] Lecture tour theatres were booked, tickets sold and a flight to New York scheduled. Then Lyndon Johnson launched Operation Rolling Thunder. Sartre cancelled the tour. Citing opinion polls, his public statements made clear he would not come to a country whose population overwhelmingly supported what he considered cruel acts of military aggression. 'Where contradictory opinions thus have hardened,' Sartre stated, 'dialogue is impossible.'[44]

When the invitation from Bertrand Russell arrived in June 1966, there was no question who would be Sartre's first appointment to the panel. Wherever he travelled, whatever stage he stood upon, Sartre did so in the company of Simone de Beauvoir, who matched him in her accomplishments both as a philosopher and as a novelist. By the mid-1960s, they had been in a relationship for more than three decades that was at turns, and sometimes simultaneously, fulfilling, frustrating, amorous and intellectual. For all the emotional complications created by the openness of their relationship, they shared an intense and intimate life together. Working separately in the morning, de Beauvoir each day walked the short distance to Sartre's flat at 42 rue Bonaparte for lunch before the couple continued writing at nearby desks, hers relatively orderly, his a towering chaos of papers. Intimate yet self-contained, it was as if they were circles in an emotional and intellectual Venn diagram, with just enough overlap to sustain their complex relationship. On the Vietnam War they nonetheless spoke with one voice. 'I was utterly disgusted by the Americans' interference and their contempt for the Vietnamese people's right to self-determination,' stated de Beauvoir.[45]

Compassionate but uncompromising, she lived with a fearless defiance of social convention that embodied the existentialist belief in freedom as being what defines the human condition. No account of her life can tell it as well as she did in her own autobiographical series, *Memoirs of a Dutiful Daughter* (1958), *The Prime of Life* (1960), *Force of Circumstance* (1963) and *All Said and Done* (1972). That she had an enormous cultural and intellectual influence, redefining our understanding of womanhood through what she wrote and how she lived, is nonetheless evident in even the shortest retelling.

Simone Lucie Ernestine Marie Bertrand de Beauvoir was born on 9 January 1908 in the Parisian neighbourhood of Montparnasse. The first daughter of a bourgeois but financially faltering family, she was a pampered and precocious child who wrote her first fiction at the age of seven. Her later life was in some measure an act of rebellion from the strictures of a Catholic upbringing that led her to convent school and a calling towards taking the vows of a nun. Losing her religious faith as a teenager, she pursued an array of academic interests: mathematics at the Institut Catholique, literature and languages at the Institut Sainte-Marie and philosophy at the Sorbonne. It was while studying for the *agrégation* in philosophy at the École Normale Supérieure in July

1929 that she had a fateful encounter with another student. She was finely featured and fashionably attired. He was short and scruffy with a wandering right eye that added an asymmetry to his pockmarked face. They fell in love. 'Sartre corresponded exactly to the dream companion I had longed for since I was fifteen,' de Beauvoir later recalled. 'He was the double in whom I found all my burning aspiration raised to the pitch of incandescence.'[46]

Much has been written about the relationship spawned by this remarkable meeting of hearts and minds. Sartre and de Beauvoir never married, never lived together, never had children. Nor were they even devoted exclusively to one another, each of them having many other romances. In Sartre's words theirs was 'an essential love' that still allowed for 'contingent love affairs'.[47] Others have observed he and de Beauvoir were not the equal partners they appeared to be.[48] Their intellectual importance to one another however is indisputable. De Beauvoir graduated second in her class at the École Normale Supérieure, losing out only to Sartre, although their examiners later said she was the finer philosopher. They had by this time long since established the working partnership that withstood even the severest tensions, shaping their ideas and sharpening their prose through perpetual critical dialogue.

That mutual dependency endured despite the difficulties life posed following the completion of their academic studies. Their teaching careers took them to opposite sides of the country, Sartre at the mouth of the Seine in the English Channel in Le Havre and de Beauvoir 600 miles away in Marseille on the Mediterranean coast. Sartre's students became accustomed to his Friday dash from the classroom to the train station en route to a weekend rendezvous with de Beauvoir in Paris. By 1937 the couple appeared to have secured a permanent reunion through new positions in the French capital. Then came the war. Sartre's escape from a prisoner-of-war camp brought them back together. They found occasional relief from Nazi occupation holidaying in the nominally free region of southern France. First and foremost, though, they wrote. The war years were a watershed in both their careers. De Beauvoir's first novel, *She Came to Stay*, appeared on the stands of French booksellers in 1943. Further fictional works soon followed, first *The Blood of Others* in 1945 and then a year later *All Men Are Mortal*.

De Beauvoir became a literary celebrity in France, but she was still relatively unknown outside her native country when she embarked on a nationwide lecture tour of the United States. De Beauvoir shared with Sartre an enthusiasm for American culture, observing how the likes of Ernest Hemingway and John Steinbeck had informed her own literary style.[49] Seeing the United States in person both confirmed and confounded her expectations. For a Frenchwoman who had endured military defeat and enemy occupation, the power and prosperity of the United States was overwhelming. The tall buildings towering over city streets were monuments to the ambition of the earliest pioneers, she marvelled, the consumer products that crowded the shelves of even the humblest dime store a demonstration of industrial power and enterprise. Here in the United States 'it has taken less than two centuries to endow an immense continent with history and civilization, to integrate within humanity a vast portion of the earth: a humanist cannot but marvel at this magnificent triumph of man.'[50]

While there was much about the United States in which she delighted, de Beauvoir found some aspects of the country unpalatable. She sympathised with the plight of African Americans who had rallied to the flag during the war without being rewarded with the full rights of citizenship, and scorned the obsession with wealth. De Beauvoir recorded these impressions in *America Day by Day*, a road book of her travels published within months of her return home.

De Beauvoir rose to world renown with the publication in 1949 of her book *The Second Sex*. An instant bestseller, it was discussed as widely it was read. Women are not born subordinate, argued de Beauvoir; they become so because of how their role and status is defined by men. This is to undermine the freedom that all people, whether male or female, have to define their own identity. The existentialist tenet that 'existence precedes essence' applies to women as well as men. They must be able to give their lives meaning by determining who they are.

The Second Sex elevated de Beauvoir to the role of activist as well as thinker. She was still an important writer – her novel *The Mandarins* won the Prix Goncourt, the highest literary honour in France, in 1954 – but her notion of freedom and the need to use it with responsibility towards others also led de Beauvoir to take up the cause of oppressed people around the world. Compared to Sartre, she was at first less conspicuous on newspaper front pages as a political campaigner. The domestic and international turmoil of the 1950s transformed her situation. Alone or more commonly with Sartre, she became as much the subject as the author of editorial comment. The Algerian independence struggle was for her, too, instrumental in shaping political opinions that informed her decision to participate in the Vietnam war crimes tribunal: a sympathy for the poorer peoples of the developing world fighting to free themselves from colonial rule, a moral revulsion at the use of torture to force dubious confessions from political prisoners and a rage at the deliberate targeting of innocent civilians by military forces that would stop at nothing to win a war that should never have been fought. At a time when most of her fellow citizens held faith in a French Algeria, de Beauvoir was an ardent advocate of decolonisation, adding her name to the Manifesto of the 121.[51]

Having once remained beneath the radar of US authorities, her leftist politics also started to raise alarms across the Atlantic. De Beauvoir travelled with Sartre to China in 1955. Published two years later, her account of that tour, *The Long March*, praised Mao Zedong as the leader of a genuine grassroots revolution. As she asserted, 'the leaders lead the masses only upon condition they lead them where they have a mind to go'.[52] The American press went apoplectic, one reviewer branding the book 'crude and insulting party-line balderdash'.[53] Less confrontational than Sartre, de Beauvoir could also be seen as implicitly critical of the United States in her association not only with China but also many of its other ideological enemies. Broaden the frames of the photographs featuring Sartre, Castro and Guevara and there she is, inhaling the fumes from their fat Cuban cigars. Scroll through the alphabetical list of celebrities who demanded 'Fair Play for Cuba' in an April 1960 edition of *The New York Times* and there she is again, second from the top. Flick through the FBI file on Sartre for details of the flight he took via La Guardia Airport en route to Havana and there once more is her name listed – a fellow traveller in more ways than one.[54] Sartre might feature higher in US authorities' lists of foreign political suspects, but de Beauvoir was at the very least his known accomplice.

Russell, Sartre and de Beauvoir. All of them famous and formidable thinkers, with critical but complicated political opinions of the United States. Each individually had the moral and intellectual authority to influence public opinion about the Vietnam War. Through the tribunal they believed their collective voice would resonate with even greater power and persuasion. That would be amplified all the more by persuading other prominent activists, artists and intellectuals from around the world to participate. Recruiting the members of the tribunal would prove a challenge, retaining them even harder. As he gazed around the room at the illustrious figures who had gathered for the first planning meeting following the press conference in London, Russell could not help his enthusiasm for the enterprise being tempered by restless doubt. With a sense of humour that only slightly hid his seriousness, he turned to one of his aides. 'Which one,' he asked of his assembled guests, 'do you think will abandon us first?'[55]

5

APPOINTING THE PANEL

For more than a millennium, persons accused of a crime have had the right to a trial by jury in Britain. The practice predated its enshrinement in law, when rebel barons forced the despotic King John to sign the Magna Carta at Runnymede in June 1215. Believing that the credibility of the war crimes tribunal necessitated the appearance and procedure of a courtroom, Bertrand Russell was intent on honouring this core tradition of Western jurisprudence when he announced the provisional membership of the tribunal in August 1966.

From the moment that the names were first publicised, there was confusion about who would actually serve on the tribunal. Several of the people the philosopher invited said no. Some, like the German psychoanalyst Erich Fromm, contended, with some justification, that the tribunal's lack of formal status would allow critics to dismiss the legitimacy of its findings. Arthur Miller also declined. The American playwright's confrontation with McCarthyism during the 1950s had established him as one of the great liberal consciences of his nation. His appointment would have added substantial authority to the panel, but as his reply to Russell's invitation made clear, such was 'the differential in power between the United States and the rest of the world that world opinion, however important in the long run, is not the critical factor at this moment as compared with the sentiment inside this country'. The dramatist may also have feared a reprise of his encounter with anti-communist witch-hunters when the US government had denied him a passport.[1]

Such setbacks led to months of toing and froing between Russell and other potential tribunal members. By the time the philosopher had finalised the list, it had increased from twelve to over twenty (including Russell as honorary president). Recovering the identities of the men and women who eventually sat around the horseshoe table in Stockholm and Roskilde is surprisingly difficult. Even those who were there could not correctly recall. Simone de Beauvoir claimed that fellow panellist Melba Hernández missed the Roskilde session, even though film footage shows the Cuban revolutionary sitting alongside her.[2] The confirmed list was a fascinating one that included members from fifteen countries with diverse expertise. Brave or foolhardy, what they all shared was a determination to hold accountable the most powerful nation on earth.

While Sartre was president of the tribunal, the person appointed to chair its proceedings was Vladimir Dedijer.[3] Born in 1914, the Serb Yugoslavian had led a storied but unsettled life. During the Second World War, he served as a lieutenant colonel in the partisan resistance to Nazi occupation of Yugoslavia, but the war took a deep personal toll. He lost his surgeon wife Olga during the Battle of the Sutjeska River Valley in May 1943. Surviving his own gunshot wound, he suffered further injuries including being blinded in one eye by shrapnel.

After the war, Dedijer represented his country at both the Paris Peace Conference and the United Nations General Assembly. Appointed to a history professorship at the University of Belgrade, he wrote an official biography of Yugoslavian President Josep Tito, translated after its first publication in 1953 into thirty-six languages. He fell from grace two years later, however, after supporting political dissident Milovan Djilas in his criticisms of Tito's regime. Charged with disseminating 'hostile propaganda', Dedijer lost his academic chair and membership of the Central Committee of the League of Communists of Yugoslavia. He left his home country, taking up teaching positions at a number of prestigious universities including Harvard, Yale and the Sorbonne. A tall and imposing figure, Dedijer was an unusual choice as chairperson. Swift to anger and slow to forgive, he would come to blows with tribunal organisers, not only baring his teeth but in one incident actually biting one of them.

The other members of the tribunal were an eclectic group of authors, intellectuals, scientists and lawyers. Some were little known outside their home countries, others were international celebrities. Many drew a distinction between the American people and the government that acted in their name. Others were open enemies of the United States.

'I am happy that you have asked me to be a member of the tribunal,' African American author James Baldwin wrote to Bertrand Russell on receiving his invitation, 'and I will be very honored to serve.'[4] The de facto poet laureate of the Black freedom struggle, Baldwin was born in Harlem on 2 August 1924. His mother Emma was a domestic worker who had left her son's father because of his substance abuse and married Baptist preacher David Baldwin. Baldwin not only had a son from his previous marriage; he and Emma became the parents of eight more children. As Baldwin later recalled, his stepfather was 'righteous in the pulpit' but 'a monster in the house'.[5] Jimmy found solace in religion, preaching from the pulpit of a small Pentecostal church. His faltering faith, however, led him away from the church and into a dispiriting succession of manual jobs that offered little money but a lot of racism on the factory floor.

Baldwin found another form of salvation, in literature. He had started writing while still a child, publishing his first piece in a high school magazine. In pursuit of his ambition to become an author, the teenage Baldwin migrated to Greenwich Village in New York, where for a time he shared an apartment with an up-and-coming actor named Marlon Brando. Baldwin worked odd jobs by day while honing his literary talent at night. His homosexuality, as much as the colour of his skin, sharpened Baldwin's understanding of social injustice. The sense that he could never be free in the United States to embrace fully his identity as a gay Black man motivated him to move to France in November 1948.[6]

Baldwin arrived in Paris with only forty dollars in his pocket but hopes for a new start. The city had a reputation as a place of sanctuary and opportunity for African Americans restricted by the segregation and discrimination of their own country. The success of his autobiographical first novel, *Go Tell It on the Mountain*, in 1953 gave him an invitation into the inner circle of the artists and intellectuals that convened in the bustling bars and cafés of the Left Bank. Here Baldwin became acquainted with the uncrowned royalty of Parisian high culture, Jean-Paul Sartre and Simone de Beauvoir. The friendship between the three of them was strong, if occasionally strained by Baldwin's view that the French couple's existentialist philosophy had nothing to teach him about the plight of African Americans.

Baldwin was at the pinnacle of his fame when the US escalated the war in Vietnam. Further works of fiction such as *Giovanni's Room* (1956) and *Another Country* (1962) strengthened his literary reputation. But it was for his factual writing on the issue of race that he arguably achieved his status as one of the most important, and controversial, authors in post-war America. *Notes of a Native Son* (1955), *Nobody Knows My Name* (1961) and *The Fire Next Time* (1963) all demonstrate his determination to depict the frustrated hopes and smouldering anger of African Americans. His pen spilled rage against white racism across every page he wrote. In his words, he would 'die and go to Hell before I let any white man spit on me'.[7] Yet in person Baldwin was a seductive figure, his language enraged at social injustice while his mesmeric eyes and mellifluous voice wooed audiences, including those who tuned in to watch his many appearances on television chat shows.

That fame reached across the Atlantic. Baldwin and Bertrand Russell had become mutual admirers when they met at the philosopher's London home in February 1965. News footage of the event shows Baldwin stepping out of a chauffeur-driven car looking the epitome of cool in turned-up coat collar and sunglasses that served little practical purpose in the dull grey of a late English winter. Walking through the front door, he seems to have been stepping back in time, greeted as he was by the elderly English gentleman who then sat opposite him over an elaborately filled tea tray. The film is silent, but the warmth of their expressions conveys the rapport between these two very different men. Baldwin later sent Russell a copy of *The Fire Next Time*, which the philosopher praised for its 'precision and intensity of feeling'.[8]

The two men were also united in their opposition to the Vietnam War. Biographers have tended to concentrate on Baldwin's crusading role in domestic racial politics to the virtual exclusion of his involvement in the anti-war movement. For him, however, the two issues were inseparably interwoven. The war, he argued, drained resources from the unfinished fight for civil rights and worsened institutional racism because of the disproportionate number of young Black men drafted into the military. Baldwin first publicly supported the anti-war movement when he participated in a torch-lit parade through the streets of Rome in November 1965. He was also one of the artists and authors who added their names to a full-page advertisement in *The New York Times*, calling on the American people to 'End Your Silence!' about the 'nakedly inhuman' policy being pursued in Southeast Asia.[9] 'I am against United States intervention in Vietnam on moral grounds because it is wrong;' Baldwin later commented, 'on political grounds because we are deluded in supposing that we have the right or the power to dictate the principles under which another people should live.'[10]

Russell shared Baldwin's conviction that the war was inherently racist. But he also invited the Black author to serve on the tribunal in the belief that his friendship with Sartre and de Beauvoir would strengthen its personal and political cohesion. In this, however, he would prove mistaken.

That acrimony, however, would not become apparent for months. In the meantime, Baldwin made a constructive contribution to the organisation of the tribunal, putting Russell in touch with another radical proponent of racial change. Russell was thrilled when Stokely Carmichael accepted his invitation to participate in the tribunal, singling out his recruitment as the 'most important'. Yet Carmichael's involvement also set off a series of memos within and between US intelligence agencies. FBI director J. Edgar Hoover received immediate notification, and in turn responded to a request from CIA chief of counter-intelligence James Angleton for biographical information on the Black militant. News that Carmichael had accepted the invitation from Russell was also included in a daily briefing to President Johnson.[11]

Still only twenty-six years old, Carmichael was, depending

on the political opinion of contemporary commentators, either a courageous champion of civil rights or a dangerous threat to national security. Born in Port of Spain, Trinidad, he had moved while still a child to the United States, settling in Harlem. As a student at Howard University, Carmichael became actively involved in the African American freedom struggle. Arrested during the Freedom Rides campaign to desegregate interstate buses in 1961, he served forty-nine days in Mississippi's Parchman State Penitentiary, a prison that provided the source of many a lament by Southern bluesmen. As a fieldworker for the Student Nonviolent Coordinating Committee (SNCC), he campaigned for voting rights during the Mississippi Freedom Summer of 1964 and on the march from Selma to Montgomery the following year. His activism brought him into increasing confrontation with police brutality. This was true of his efforts to register Black voters in rural Lowndes County, Alabama, in 1965 and twelve months later during a march through Mississippi organised in protest at the gunshot wounding of civil rights campaigner James Meredith.

It was on this march that Carmichael uttered the words with which he became synonymous. Addressing demonstrators in Greenwood, Mississippi, on 16 June 1966, Carmichael rallied them with a militant call to arms: 'We want Black Power!' The slogan struck a resonant chord with younger African Americans frustrated at the pace of civil rights reform and tired of turning the other cheek. It also provoked panic-stricken editorials in the press. As its principal spokesperson, Carmichael became the target of sharp and sustained media criticism. When racial violence broke out on the streets of Atlanta in September 1966 following the police shooting of a Black suspect, the press had no doubt who was responsible. It was 'Stokely's Spark' that 'fanned the flame' of urban unrest, affirmed *Time* magazine.[12]

Carmichael was at the forefront not only of civil rights activism but also of protest against the Vietnam War. Having assumed the chairmanship of SNCC, he rallied the organisation against the draft with the cry, 'Hell no, we won't go!' In January 1966 SNCC issued a statement encouraging African Americans to dodge the draft because of what it believed was the inherent racism of the war.[13] At a time when most Black leaders were reluctant to address the war for fear of alienating the supposedly liberal Johnson administration and thereby undermine the cause of domestic racial reform, the declaration was a serious provocation.

That Russell approached Carmichael to participate in the tribunal says much about his own spiralling radicalism. For the philosopher, the freedom struggles of African Americans and the North Vietnamese were 'part of the same international resistance to exploitation and aggression – a long, arduous and heroic battle to which all of us must commit ourselves'.[14] As the authorities closed in on Carmichael, however, his role in the tribunal would become more complicated. During his many absences as he toured the world, fellow SNCC activist and fellow veteran of voting rights campaigns in the Deep South Courtland Cox would need to deputise for him.

Russell recruited two other American radicals to the tribunal. In late August 1968, thousands of anti-war activists converged on Chicago for the Democratic Party National Convention. Inside the convention hall, delegates endorsed Lyndon Johnson's vice president Hubert Humphrey as their candidate in the forthcoming race for the White House. On the streets, chaos spiralled as protesters clashed with the Chicago Police Department. On Wednesday 28 August, the police used tear gas to disperse a gathering of more than 10,000 demonstrators gathered in Grant Park, indiscriminately attacking those fleeing for safety. They also arrested leading activists and charged them with criminal conspiracy and inciting a riot. The trial of the Chicago Eight (later Seven, after the judge ruled a mistrial in the prosecution of Bobby Seale) was one of the causes célèbres of the Vietnam War.

Born on 22 August 1915, David Dellinger was a generation older than the other accused men.[15] Educated at Yale and Oxford, Dellinger determined to use his own privilege in support of the poor and dispossessed in America, shaped by a seemingly paradoxical belief in what he called 'Christian communism'. In the autumn of 1940, he enrolled at Union Theological Seminary in New York City. His ambition to become a minister, however, was thwarted by world events. In the early morning of 7 December 1941, Japanese military planes launched a surprise bombing assault of the US naval base at Pearl Harbor. A day later, the US Congress formally declared war on its adversary.

That declaration changed Dellinger's life. Although he needed to register for the draft, his status as a divinity student exempted him from active military service. Troubled by his being exempt while others who conscientiously objected to the war were not, Dellinger agonised about what to do. Then he witnessed schoolchildren marching alongside soldiers in a patriotic parade. 'I had a traumatic vision that these students – and thousands like them – would soon be in the trenches, killing and being killed.' His anguish was all the more acute because most of the children came from the impoverished neighbourhoods in which he had ministered. 'And I thought about how that tragedy would be repeated for generation after generation unless we developed a nonviolent antiwar movement.' Dellinger had made his decision. Along with some of his fellow seminarians, he refused to register and was sentenced to a year in federal prison.[16]

On his release, Dellinger helped found the People's Peace Now Committee. In April 1943 the organisation held its first demonstration in Washington. Arrested, charged and convicted, he received a two-year prison sentence.[17] The experience only strengthened his resistance. Following the war, he became a professional peace activist, founding the radical *Liberation* magazine in 1956. Dellinger also saw with own eyes the impact of US military action on North Vietnam. Much of the evidence presented to the Russell tribunal corroborated what he had witnessed on a visit to Southeast Asia in 1966. Dellinger was a willing recruit to the Russell tribunal because he believed celebrities such as Sartre and de Beauvoir would be able to reach a wider audience than his own testimony. Even with all he had seen, however, he would find himself shocked and disgusted by some of the evidence submitted in Stockholm and Roskilde.

Carl Oglesby was young enough to be a child of most of the tribunal members, but he was old compared to typical student activists.[18] Born on 30 July 1935, he grew up in a working-class household in Akron, Ohio, and studied at Kent State University – later to become infamous when on 4 May 1970 National Guardsmen shot dead four students during an anti-war protest – but dropped out and moved to Greenwich Village. Failing to fulfil his dream of becoming an actor and playwright, he returned to university to complete his degree, before moving to Ann Arbor, Michigan. There he balanced a daytime position working for a company that produced systems for the defence industry with part-time study for a master's degree.

In 1964, Oglesby penned a critical article on US foreign policy for the student newspaper of the University of Michigan. The essay brought him to the attention of the radical activist organisation Students for a Democratic Society (SDS), at the forefront of public opposition to the Vietnam War.[19] Having been recruited to the group, Oglesby swiftly ascended its ranks, becoming president after only a year. Abandoning his incongruent position with a defence contractor, he organised a teach-in protest on the University of Michigan campus – a prelude to the ambitious SDS peace rally attended by around 35,000 activists in Washington on 17 April 1965. Oglesby's speech blamed not only conservative militarists for the war but also the supposedly liberal establishment. Yet the SDS president offered the hand of friendship as well as the fist of rage. The politicians responsible for the war were, he insisted, 'all honorable men' who could 'help us shape the future in the name of plain human hope'. Delivered when some demonstrators had started to disperse, Oglesby's words surged through the crowd like a sharp electric current, raising them on their tired feet to applaud.[20]

Not everyone within SDS, however, was so enthusiastic. At a time when the battle lines between revolutionary youth and reactionary authorities had never been more starkly drawn, Oglesby's attempt to reconcile these warring forces led to accusations of treachery from leftist critics. By the late 1960s, this disparagement of Oglesby as 'being trapped in our early bourgeois stage' would lead to his being forced out of SDS.[21] However, it was his relative moderation that made him an asset to the Russell tribunal. A man of firm convictions, he was less inclined towards the moral absolutism of some of the other members, and more willing to win the hearts and minds of US policymakers than cast crude aspersions about their criminality and political chicanery.

'Every word I put down is political.' Sitting in his Stockholm flat surrounded by filing cabinets bursting with folders of materials on seemingly every aspect of world affairs, Peter Weiss was clear about the purpose of his art.[22]

Weiss was born into a prosperous household in Nowawes near Berlin in November 1916. His father had converted from Judaism to Lutheranism, but his heritage made him vulnerable when the Nazi Party came to power in March 1933. The family fled Germany the following year, travelling for five years to England, Switzerland and Czechoslovakia before settling in Sweden. Weiss initially pursued a career in art, producing a series of surrealist films with titles such as *Hallucinations* and *The Mirage* that convey their oneiric ambience. He also illustrated several books by the novelist Hermann Hesse, with whom he became a close friend.[23]

The tumult of the 1960s had a profound impact on Weiss, leading to his embrace of the rationalism against which surrealism had been a reaction. Having shifted to the stage, his first play became an international sensation. Long queues lined up outside London's Aldwych Theatre during the summer of 1964 in the hope of seeing the sold-out *Persecution and Assassination of Jean-Paul Marat as Performed by the Inmates of the Asylum of Charenton Under the Direction of the Marquis de Sade*, a mouthful that prompted one critic to observe that while he had not seen the play, he had managed to make it all the way through the title.[24] Director Peter Brook was also at the helm for the film version, starring Glenda Jackson and with a screenplay by Adrian Mitchell, whose poem 'To Whom It May Concern' remained a rallying cry for the anti-war movement.

Weiss followed this Brechtian story of struggle with *The Investigation*, first staged in Stockholm in 1965 by Ingmar Bergman. That same year, he wrote an essay titled 'The Necessary Decision', in which he denounced German authors for their failure 'to speak out forcibly against the general will to forget' the horrors of Nazism. *The Investigation* was a response to that collective amnesia, based on Weiss's attendance at the trial of officials at the Auschwitz-Birkenau concentration camp. *The Investigation* used the methods of documentary, drawing on the witness testimony of concentration camp internees, to dramatise a history Weiss believed others wanted to forget.[25]

This forensic eye for detail and determination to record the otherwise silenced voices of victims was precisely what the playwright brought to the Russell tribunal. And Weiss made clear the parallel he saw between his own country's recent past and the present conflict in Southeast Asia, accusing the US military top brass of being 'so close to Fascism that they rank with the statesmen and generals who were tried' for crimes committed during the Second World War. For Weiss, the Vietnam War was also about more than the fate of one nation. North Vietnam was a 'representative of the poor people of the world', the struggle of its citizens against the superior forces of the US war machine symbolic of the global fight for freedom from oppression.[26]

The same could be said of the other European author sitting alongside him. Sara Lidman was one of the most eminent Swedish writers of the twentieth century. When the celebrated American broadcaster Studs Terkel travelled to Sweden in the early 1970s, he discovered the novelist was so well known among her fellow citizens that even taxi drivers told him not to leave the country without interviewing her.[27]

Lidman was born in December 1923 in the remote rural community of Missenträsk, near the Swedish border with Lapland.[28] She grew up on a small farm, where she gained a reverence for nature that was to inform her fiction. The thought of a farmer's daughter like her becoming a novelist first took form when, as a teenager, Lidman contracted tuberculosis. During a long period of convalescence at a local sanatorium, she roamed the stacks of the institution's library, awakening a passion for the written word. Afflicted by recurring symptoms of her illness, Lidman endured several years in and out of the sanatorium but finished high school and enrolled at the University of Uppsala. She achieved instant acclaim with her debut novel, first published in 1953, *The Tar Still*. Her international breakthrough came with the English translation in 1963 of *Rain Bird*, set like much of her fiction in the austere, bucolic environment of northern Sweden.

While British and American readers were gaining their first exposure to the agrarian people and places of Lidman's fiction, she had already moved on – both physically and imaginatively. In August 1960 she travelled to South Africa, an experience that made her as famous in Sweden for her politics as for her fiction. Settling in Johannesburg, she was shocked by the conditions endured by Black people under apartheid. Inspired to support the freedom struggle against the repressive Nationalist government, Lidman befriended fellow novelist and political activist Nadine Gordimer, who introduced her to members of the banned African National Congress including former Youth League Secretary Peter Nthite, one of the ANC leaders arrested for treason along with Nelson Mandela in 1956. Lidman's affair with Nthite attracted the attention of the security police. Late in the evening of 3 February 1961, Special Branch officers muscled into the apartment the couple shared in an inner-city neighbourhood of Johannesburg and arrested them on a charge of violating the country's Immorality Act, introduced four years earlier to outlaw interracial sexual relations. Ruthlessly interrogated and remanded for trial, Lidman was released on bail but reported to be 'in a state of near collapse'. Her conviction was a near certainty and with it a sentence of ten lashes and seven years in the overcrowded and unsanitary prison perched on Constitution Hill as a beacon of brutal government authority. Only the intervention of a fellow Swede, UN Secretary General Dag Hammarskjöld, saved her from that fate, on the explicit

understanding she would never return to South Africa. Returning to Stockholm, Lidman channelled her personal upset and
political rage into the 1961 novel *My Son and I*.[29]

Lidman's exposure to the cruelties of apartheid also sharpened a political concern for the plight of oppressed peoples in the
developing world, which she focused on the peasant population
of Vietnam. In becoming a leader of the Swedish anti-war movement, she had the advantage of living in the country that opinion
polls consistently showed was the most strongly opposed in
Western Europe to US foreign policy, a 1966 survey revealing that
a staggering 88 per cent of Swedes were against the war.[30] Sweden
had an official policy of neutrality in international politics, but
public opposition to the Vietnam War pushed that policy to the
point of collapse. In 1965, 2.7 million Swedes – one third of the
population – signed a petition sent to the US Embassy in Stockholm appealing for an immediate end to the bombing of North
Vietnam. Students took to the streets of the Swedish capital in
their thousands that August, bearing placards declaring 'Yankee
Scram from Vietnam' and 'Viva Vietcong'. These protests grew
as the war escalated. In May 1966, anti-war activists burned US
flags outside the embassy building.[31] Nor was it only rebellious
youth who opposed the war. Swedish Minister for Foreign
Affairs Torsten Nilsson read a twenty-two-page statement in
the Riksdag in which he called on the United States to de-esca-
late.[32] The Swedish government made its position plainer still by
imposing a ban on the export of arms to the United States. Diplomatic tensions between Stockholm and Washington became
so acute that the US recalled its ambassador.[33]

If Lidman did not set the course of public opinion on the
war, she stood on the bridge commanding its speed. As a leader
of the Swedish Vietnam Committee, founded in the spring of
1965, she reappeared on front pages. Lidman travelled to North

Vietnam in October 1965, an experience she recounted in her book *Conversations in Hanoi* published the following year. The portrait of the North Vietnamese people she painted was deeply romanticised. As a university student, she had become a convert to Marxism, and that influence was evident in her idealised image of a poor but spirited population striving for the collective good. In contrast to the ruthless competitiveness of Western capitalism, Lidman saw the social and economic order of North Vietnam as being based on mutual respect and cooperation. That solidarity, she believed, had only become stronger in the face of American imperialist aggression. 'The whole population was united in a common cause,' she reflected. 'Even in the factories or the fields the atmosphere was very human: everybody worked with zeal and self-confidence. They were truly happy.'[34]

This starry-eyed conception of the North Vietnamese caused Lidman to support their cause uncritically; she saw the war in terms of a simple moral binary between an evil and overbearing giant and a heroic underdog. Her reasoning was not entirely sentimental; she saw with her own eyes the impact of American bombing, hospitals turned to rubble and bridges into twisted metal, parents mourning maimed and dead children, orphans crying for missing parents.[35] Such horrors sharpened the cutting edge of her rhetoric. During one anti-war demonstration, she came to the support of student protesters bearing a placard with the words 'Hang Johnson' by proclaiming to police officers who wanted it lowered that the president 'should be boiled alive in napalm'.[36] Yet Lidman did more than offer moral and political support for the North Vietnamese; she also helped shape her own government's policy. She was one of the Swedish Vietnam Committee representatives who successfully lobbied the government to grant political asylum to US draft resisters, the only country to do so.[37]

With her toothy smile and hair styled similarly to the pixie look of actress Jean Seberg, Lidman was a distinctive presence among the dour and predominantly male members of the tribunal. Fierce yet empathetic, her interventions would do much to emphasise the human tragedy of the war.

While the prominence of these different personalities make them the main players in the story of the tribunal, the other members provided a formidable supporting cast. Drawn from around the world, they brought varied legal, scientific and philosophical expertise to the sessions.

Bespectacled and with a goatee beard, Isaac Deutscher bore more than a passing resemblance to the subject of his literary masterwork, Leon Trotsky. The Polish author was born in April 1907 in the small town of Chrzanów, thirty miles west of Kraków. Renouncing his Jewish faith as a teenager, he became a leading figure in the Polish Communist Party, but was expelled from its ranks in 1932 for criticising Joseph Stalin's conciliatory policy towards Nazi Germany. Deutscher emigrated to Britain in April 1939, five months before the Nazis invaded his home country. As a specialist on the Soviet Union, he served on the editorial staff of the *Economist* and the *Observer*. He also wrote numerous books, including a biography of Stalin and a three-volume study of Trotsky. Deutscher attracted an enthusiastic following among students on both sides of the Atlantic because of his participation alongside the likes of Norman Mailer and Benjamin Spock in the first teach-in at the University of California, Berkeley in May 1965.[38] Approaching the age of sixty, the heavily accented and formally attired Polish expatriate became a surprising spokesperson for the counterculture erupting across college campuses.

Shoichi Sakata was a Japanese physicist whose theoretical

research advanced international understanding of subatomic particles. Haunted by the atomic bombs that fell on Hiroshima and Nagasaki in 1945, he warned that modern science had the power both to liberate and to annihilate the human race, and publicly campaigned to restrict the use of nuclear power to peaceful purposes.[39]

Although not a scientist, Günther Anders complemented Sakata on the panel. The German philosopher (and former husband of Hannah Arendt) had lived in the United States for many years after being forced into exile by the Nazi regime before resettling in Vienna. Anders was a forceful critic of the role of technology in modern life and in particular the threat posed by the atomic bomb. In the 1950s he befriended Claude Eatherly, the guilt-ridden pilot who flew one of the planes over Hiroshima in August 1945. Their correspondence became the basis of the book *Burning Conscience*, an indictment of nuclear weaponry for which Bertrand Russell wrote the introduction. He and Anders shared a conviction that the Vietnam War had brought the world a step closer to nuclear catastrophe.[40]

The other scientist at the tribunal was the French mathematician Laurent Schwartz. Winner of the Field Medal, the most prestigious international award in his discipline, he too was selected as much for his political opinions as his professional knowledge. A Trotskyist, Schwartz had stood alongside Sartre in opposing the Algerian War. The two men were also among the founding members of Comité France-Vietnam, which staged an anti-war protest in the amphitheatre of Paris's Maison de la Mutualité on 28 November 1966. If Sartre was the commander of the tribunal, Schwartz was a trusted aide-de-camp.[41]

The rest of the tribunal included a diverse range of expertise. There was an international team of lawyers: Mehmet Ali Aybar from Turkey, Mahmud Ali Kasuri from Pakistan, Kinju

Morikawa from Japan, and Lelio Basso, a former member of the Italian Resistance during the Second World War. Other members included Lázaro Cárdenas, the former President of Mexico; Israeli politician Haika Grossman; Filipino author and activist Amado Hernandez; and the Scotsman Lawrence Daly, an executive member of the National Union of Mineworkers in Britain who also travelled to North Vietnam as a member of one of the tribunal's investigative teams. The most controversial appointment, given her country's hostile relationship with the United States, was Melba Hernández, a close confidante of Fidel Castro known in Havana as the 'Heroine of the Cuban Revolution'.[42]

Recruiting so many celebrity intellectuals to the tribunal was a risk. With their enormous egos, the situation was akin to the delicate mixing of combustible materials: add one wrong element and everything could explode. Trouble began brewing before the tribunal had even met, with Deutscher complaining about its format and composition. What was needed, he insisted, was a serious and sober scrutiny of the facts. Sartre, however, with his 'dramatist's instinct', had insisted on 'the stage effect of a Trial'.[43]

Yet the recruitment process was actually the easy part of planning. What Russell and Sartre still needed was a place to convene and the money to pay for it. While the focus of the tribunal was on United States foreign policy, its members would also soon realise they were on a collision course with not one but three governments, each of them determined to end proceedings before they had even begun.

6

SMEARS, SURVEILLANCE
AND SUPPRESSION

When the tribunal convened more than six months after the
public announcement at Caxton Hall in November 1966, it
was neither on the date nor at the location planned by Bertrand
Russell and Jean-Paul Sartre. The intervening period had been
one of intense political controversy and conniving, in which
successive governments prohibited the tribunal. Their reason
for doing so was in part to promote themselves as power brokers
who would negotiate a peaceful settlement to the war, but also
to placate an administration in Washington prepared to use its
prodigious power and influence to stifle criticism of its foreign
policy.

Russell had taken the fight to President Johnson in a letter
calling on him to defend the actions of his government. 'Within
living memory only the Nazis could be said to have exceeded
in brutality the war waged by your administration against the
people of Vietnam,' the philosopher wrote. 'Will you appear
before a wider justice than you recognize and risk a more profound condemnation than you may be able to understand?' It
is hard to imagine that the philosopher expected the president
to accept such a request, but that was his point. Declining the
invitation would further reveal Johnson's reluctance to answer
criticism of the American war effort. Sartre though was sincere

in wanting Johnson or another senior Washington official to attend, cabling politer messages to the White House right up to the point when the tribunal was already in session. Neither he nor Russell ever received a reply.[1]

While the public strategy was to say little or nothing that would bestow any legitimacy on the tribunal, behind the scenes the US government conspired to disable or destroy it. The decision of numerous governments to refuse to allow the tribunal to meet in their countries revealed the brittleness of relations within the Atlantic Alliance. Britain did not trust France, France resented the United States, and the United States was willing to bully both to get what it wanted.

The timing was too coordinated for it to be coincidence. To lose one head of state might be regarded as unfortunate, to lose four looked like conspiracy. In November 1966 the leaders of four African nations announced that they were withdrawing their sponsorship of the Bertrand Russell Peace Foundation, in protest against its formation of the war crimes tribunal. The signatories were some of the most eminent politicians on the African continent: Kenneth Kaunda of Zambia, Julius Nyerere of Tanzania, Haile Selassie of Ethiopia and Léopold Senghor of Senegal. Their renunciation of the foundation was less a financial than a reputational blow, stripping the tribunal of power and prestige. Russell and Sartre had hoped to mobilise as much support as possible in the developing world. The US government was determined to contain communist influence in the politically non-aligned nations of Africa and Asia. Rallying the opposition of those countries to the Vietnam War could therefore provide powerful political leverage over Washington, forcing a change of foreign policy to appease them.[2]

Russell was suspicious, sensing the hand of the US

government in the statement issued by the African leaders. He accused Washington of having placed 'intolerable pressure' on them, presumably by threatening to cut off foreign aid.[3]

Was Russell being paranoid? Had he succumbed to an increasing tendency in his infirmity to see conspiracies that were not there? Or was the US government really working to undermine the tribunal?

In December 1966, White House aide D. W. Ropa sent a secret memo to US National Security Advisor Walt Rostow. Less than a week earlier, Rostow had conceded to a colleague that Lyndon Johnson's government was taking 'a beating' over the Vietnam War. Russell's announcement of an international war crimes tribunal represented the most serious threat so far faced by a US government struggling to safeguard its global reputation. Action was needed to suppress or stop it. The memo from Ropa confirmed that the matter was in hand. According to its author, the CIA 'is monitoring preparations for the tribunal and otherwise attempting to discredit it'.[4]

Nor was it only the CIA. When Russell first announced the war crimes tribunal, US Secretary of State Dean Rusk instructed his departmental adviser Richard Kearney to determine 'what legal remedies' there were in domestic and international law to impede or prosecute the philosopher and his associates, only for Kearney to advise that it would not be wise for the government to pursue measures 'that would be so plainly unconstitutional'.[5]

Since the law offered no recourse, the government determined it must resort to more covert means. Undersecretary of State George Ball coordinated a team that included representatives of numerous governmental departments as well as the CIA, FBI, US Army and United States Information Agency (USIA). Its mission was to minimise the impact of the tribunal by whatever means necessary. From the autumn of 1966 to

the spring of 1967, the inter-agency group conducted surveillance, spread disinformation and pressured other governments
not to permit the tribunal meeting on their countries' soil. They
also enticed potential sponsors, most notably the four African
heads of state, to withdraw their support. Russell realised what
was happening when one of those politicians – he discreetly
refrained from mentioning who – clumsily sent him a copy
of the letter he had written to Lyndon Johnson requesting his
attendance at the tribunal.[6] Washington officials also nobbled
other prominent sponsors of the Russell Foundation, including the renowned cellist Pablo Casals, using the influence of his
friend US Supreme Court Justice Abe Fortas.[7]

The US government's first counteroffensive tactic was to
brief diplomatic officials so they were able to rebut the criticisms
of the tribunal and thereby control the public narrative on what
American military forces were and were not doing to win the
Vietnam War. The State Department and USIA issued a memo
to US embassies around the world with instructions on how to
respond to approaches about the conflict from representatives
of foreign governments. The best scenario was to say nothing at
all, but if that was not possible officials should follow a carefully
prepared script.

Some of the statements were nuanced. Yes, American
bombers were dropping napalm, a highly incendiary device
capable of causing destructive fires over a wide area of the
Vietnamese countryside, but 'only sparingly'. And, yes, the
US military did use anti-personnel weapons, although only in
defence against Viet Cong gun attacks on their aircraft. For the
most part, however, the instruction to embassy officials was to
deny emphatically accusations that Washington sanctioned the
use of controversial and, indeed, illegal tactics against the enemy.
No, the United States was not using any weapons in violation of

international law, and that specifically included poison gas. The only chemical compounds used against the Viet Cong were the same as those police forces around the world routinely deployed to contain civil unrest. No, the defoliants that reduced enemy cover in dense jungles had no harmful effect on people, only plants. And no, air strikes had not been launched against anything other than military targets. To the contrary, 'U.S. pilots exercise care and caution to avoid damage to civilian facilities, and injury to non-military personnel.' Nor was it true that prisoners of war suffered any mistreatment. If either side was guilty of ignoring the conventions of war it was the Viet Cong: 'Communist forces regularly use torture, murder, and terror tactics as part of a systematic campaign against [the] civilian population of SVN.' And emphatically no, the US was not pursuing a campaign of genocide in Southeast Asia. This was a war to save Vietnam, not to lay waste to it.[8]

A second approach to winning the propaganda war was for the federal government to try to turn the tribunal to its advantage. One suggestion was for Washington to insist that the tribunal hear the evidence of South Vietnamese witnesses who would be carefully selected for their support of US war aims. Walt Rostow was convinced this was a means to outmanoeuvre Russell and Sartre. Should the philosophers agree, the testimony of these hand-picked participants would counterbalance other evidence presented to the tribunal; should they say no, it would compromise any claim of their impartiality. The US government would emphasise that point by having the South Vietnamese witnesses occupy the corridors near the room where the tribunal convened, in order that they could talk to reporters coming in and out of sessions. Alternatively, US officials could convene a concurrent event close by headlined by 'prominent Vietnamese and others who support our Vietnam objectives.'[9]

These proposals to steer the flow of information on the war were defensive measures on the part of the federal government, but its tactics against the tribunal were also aggressive. Washington secondly aimed to smear the character of its accusers. US government agencies gathered and shared intelligence on tribunal organisers and members, with the intention of besmirching their reputations. In October 1966, the CIA provided FBI chief J. Edgar Hoover with a list of American citizens who were potential participants. 'We would appreciate receiving biographic profiles,' read the cover note, 'including derogatory material.' Only one of the names submitted to Hoover appeared on the eventual press release from the Russell Foundation. Stokely Carmichael was already familiar to the federal government, having been a surveillance target since becoming a prominent civil rights activist in the early 1960s. But the FBI intensified its investigation to find out more about his relationship with Russell and Sartre. That included tapping a source who attended a party in New York where a drunken Carmichael let slip details of his intended involvement in the tribunal.[10]

The surest means for the US government to undermine the tribunal was to weaken it from within. It is unclear from heavily redacted CIA files who its source was within the Russell Foundation, but what is certain is that a continuous flow of information allowed the federal government to get at least one step ahead of the tribunal. The source provided summaries and, in some instances, hard copies of the confidential minutes of planning sessions, within days and even hours of their taking place. This intelligence ensured that US authorities knew precisely what would be discussed at the tribunal, the timing of sessions and the names of witnesses scheduled to testify, before such details were shared with the public. It also pleased federal officials to learn that the tribunal was afflicted with internal troubles that threatened its future. Months before the tribunal met, the opening skirmishes in what would become a war of egos had already begun. There were tensions between the scientist Laurent Schwartz and the playwright Peter Weiss over politics, and between the chair Vladimir Dedijer and general secretary Ralph Schoenman over planning. Above all, with Sartre as president of the tribunal, the Paris administrative team assumed increasing control of the planning process. This was the cause of resentment among the London organisers, a situation compounded by Sartre arriving late to and leaving early from meetings because of his relentless speaking schedule.[11]

Ultimately, though, the US government aspired not to impair the impact of the tribunal but to prevent it from taking place. White House officials contacted their foreign counterparts with the purpose of persuading them not to permit Russell and Sartre to stage the event in their countries. Their conversations made clear who held the power in the relationship between the United States and even its closest allies. The tone was pleasant but persistent, the embrace warm but firm. Washington was in communication with numerous governments, but its diplomatic efforts focused on the countries where the tribunal would most almost certainly try to convene, Britain and France.

For many, Paris in the spring meant cherry blossoms on the trees and chatter in pavement cafés. But for Bertrand Russell and Jean-Paul Sartre it was their chosen location to convene the international war crimes tribunal.

The City of Lights would have been an ideal host for the event. As home to Sartre and de Beauvoir it afforded access to logistical support from local activist networks, sympathetic media contacts and high-end hospitality. There was also a hostile mood in much of France towards US policy in Southeast Asia. In Paris, it was already possible to smell the fumes of anti-war rebellion that were to catch fire in May 1968.

On the evening of 28 November 1966, Sartre and de Beauvoir participated in 'Six Hours of the World for Vietnam', an event intended to create public momentum for the forthcoming tribunal. Publicity posters featured an abstract painting contributed by the artist Max Ernst, chaotic lines dripping red across the canvas to convey the carnage of war. Five thousand people lined the pavement outside the art deco Maison de la Mutualité, waiting to take their seats inside the amphitheatre. The audience ready, singer Pia Colombo and peace activist Jacques Martin took to the stage with a performance of protest anthems. There was also the premiere of a documentary about the war by Australian film-maker Wilfred Burchett, but what most people had turned out in the winter weather for was the array of international activists and intellectuals, including not only Sartre and de Beauvoir but also many of those appointed to the war crimes tribunal. 'Their fight is ours,' Sartre proclaimed of the Vietnamese people, the audience rapturously applauding. 'It is the fight against American hegemony, against American imperialism.'[12]

As plans for the tribunal progressed, the organisers were confident they had the implicit support of the French government. Relations between the Élysée Palace and the White House during the 1960s were troubled. Following the humiliations of Nazi occupation during the Second World War and the Algerian independence struggle, French President Charles de Gaulle was determined to restore his country as a world leader. Resentful of US domination of the Western alliance, he sought in partnership with West Germany to promote a more powerful and independent Western Europe. 'From NATO to the U.N., Latin America to Red China,' exclaimed *Time* magazine, 'there is hardly an issue or an area in world politics on which France has not taken a stand at variance with U.S. policy.'[13]

This was none more so than with regard to the Americanisation of the Vietnam War. In the words of French Foreign Minister Maurice Couve de Murville, France and the United States 'had totally different views on the war in Vietnam'.[14]

De Gaulle was one of the first and most forthright foreign critics of US policy in Vietnam. As early as 1963, the French statesman called for a negotiated settlement to neutralise the Indochinese region as a source of conflict between East and West. On a tour of Cambodia three years later, he addressed an audience of thousands at Olympic Stadium in Phnom Penh, endorsing the determination of their leader Prince Norodom Sihanouk to keep his country out of the war raging across its eastern border and calling on the United States to withdraw its forces. The longer Washington delayed, the less likely was a lasting peace. It was time to end the fighting; time, he implied, for the French president himself to show his prowess as an international statesman by helping to negotiate a settlement between the warring factions. The United States, de Gaulle concluded, must abandon 'a far-flung expedition when it becomes clear that it is without benefit and without justification'.[15]

The tribunal organisers therefore had good reason to trust that the French government would be sympathetic towards their efforts to expose US war crimes. March 1967 was announced as the date of the tribunal. With the month fast approaching, the Russell Foundation informed the press of a delay to the starting session, now scheduled for 10 April. As that day approached the schedule changed again, this time with the tribunal beginning on 29 April. The location also kept changing. First it was a return to the Maison de la Mutualité, where 'Six Hours of the World for Vietnam' has been such a success. Then it was the

Théâtre Municipal in Issy-les-Moulineaux, to the southwest of the capital. Subsequently, the organisers confirmed the tribunal would convene closer to the heart of the city, at the Hôtel Continental.[16]

Ultimately, though, the tribunal met neither on any of these dates nor at one of these locations. The press had speculated for months that the French government might prohibit the event because it risked infringing an 1881 law forbidding defamation of a foreign head of state. There was even speculation that Sartre and his associates could provoke rioting in the streets of Paris. The first indication of trouble came when the director of the Hôtel Continental abruptly announced that he was cancelling the booking for the event 'because I am pro-American', a statement that had as much to do with wealthy tourists as the war in Vietnam.[17] Confirmation of the media rumours came only five days before the tribunal was due to convene. On 24 April, newspapers around the world ran the story that the government had imposed a ban on the members meeting in public and averted the possibility of a private assembly by denying a visa to Vladimir Dedijer, the chairman.

De Gaulle had made his decision. Less clear was his reason why. That was especially so given what British government officials believed was a last-minute change of mind. According to their sources, the French president had overturned a decision to prohibit the tribunal only to reverse his position.

Sartre, for one, sensed a conspiracy. The French press had already reported 'discreet diplomatic overtures by American officials' to prevent the tribunal taking place in Paris.[18] In a furious letter, the philosopher now accused de Gaulle of having succumbed to 'economic blackmail' from the US government following a recent visit from Vice President Hubert Humphrey.[19] In fact, it was this very pressure that at first persuaded de Gaulle to overrule his own government officials and approve permission for the tribunal. According to a source who divulged the situation to the British Embassy, an indignant president 'apparently felt that the Americans needed to be exposed to criticism and taught a lesson'. The tribunal would therefore be a means to bloody the noses of the bullies in Washington, showing them that France would not tolerate being treated as anything other than an equal partner. Or, as British diplomats less empathetically put it, saying yes to Sartre was 'another step in the anti-U.S. escalade, taken deliberately by the General'.[20]

In the end, it was precisely because his relationship with the United States was so dismal that de Gaulle decided not to give the tribunal the go-ahead. The French president might resent the controlling behaviour of his transatlantic partner, but his country was too dependent to countenance a divorce. De Gaulle replied to Sartre that he had no wish to silence criticism of the Vietnam War, especially when the opinions of the tribunal members were 'close to the official position of the French Republic on the subject'. But he could not allow the already fraying ties between Paris and Washington to snap altogether because of 'proceedings that are beyond the bounds of justice and international practices'. Sartre might have been more sanguine about the decision had de Gaulle not also reminded the philosopher who had the real power to stand up to American hegemony. 'Without questioning Lord Russell and his friends, I am obliged to note that they have been invested with no special powers, they possess no international mandate, and they therefore cannot carry out any act of justice.' Power emanated from the president, not a self-appointed assembly of authors and intellectuals, even those who acted otherwise 'by assuming robes for the occasion'. The tribunal would not take place in France.[21]

Sartre was not alone in perceiving international power politics behind the decision to prohibit the tribunal from Paris. As the information leaking from inside the Élysée Palace demonstrates, the British government also sensed skulduggery behind de Gaulle's decision. In this case, however, France was the conspirator and Britain the intended victim. The level of paranoia within Whitehall reveals much about the temperamental relationship between two partners competing for power and status in the broader Western alliance.

London was the obvious alternative venue for the tribunal. The Russell Foundation was located there, within a larger peacenik network of activist groups, student organisations, trade unionists and leftist politicians – all of which made Washington uneasy. Meeting with British Home Secretary Roy Jenkins in September 1966, George Ball made clear that allowing the tribunal to convene in London would incur the 'displeasure' of President Johnson. During the following months, US officials wasted no opportunity to repeat the message to their British counterparts. A Foreign Office memo of February 1967 conveyed a message from Sir Patrick Dean, the British ambassador in Washington, in which he 'warned of the importance to our future relations with President Johnson that, if it meets at all, it should not do so here'. Two months later, and Washington was still leaning hard on London. According to another secret memo, 'The Americans are exerting as much pressure as they can.'[22]

The British government was unworried about the tribunal being held in Paris. If anyone was going to infuriate the Americans, let it be the French. De Gaulle was as much the bane of Britain as the United States, vetoing its request to become a member of the European Economic Community in 1963 and three years later threatening Western security with his announcement that France would withdraw from NATO. British officials believed that the tribunal taking place in Paris would demonstrate to Washington that they, not their French counterparts, were more loyal diplomatic and military partners. It was an enticing prospect. Here, with unintended irony, was de Gaulle presenting his adversaries Harold Wilson and Lyndon Johnson with an opportunity to ease their strained relationship.

Yet as the winter of 1966 turned into the spring of 1967, British officials started to worry that the French had outwitted them. The French government had no intention of allowing the tribunal, they suspected, but was deliberately refraining from a public decision. Their purpose was to encourage Bertrand Russell to pressure the Wilson administration for permission to hold the event in London. If the government said yes, it would snap the fraying ties with Washington; if it said no, it would bind Britain closer to an unpopular war. 'The French are trying to bounce us,' concluded one Foreign Office memo, 'to put the onus for action that might be claimed as "pro-American" on to us and off their own anti-American shoulders.' Pending a decision from the prime minister, Whitehall officials formulated a contingency plan. Should the tribunal go ahead, the government would try to limit the diplomatic damage by emphasising to Washington that the real 'driving force' behind it was not Russell but disaffected American expatriates who were manipulating the philosopher for their own political ends.[23]

Aware that the decision would upset some of its own backbenchers, the Labour government ultimately deemed it had no choice but to inform Russell there would be no London session of the tribunal. Roy Jenkins wrote to the philosopher that 'it would not be in the national interest to grant the facilities you seek'. Nor would North Vietnamese witnesses invited to give evidence receive travel visas. Harold Wilson insisted in a further letter to Russell that the tribunal 'would make the Government's peacemaking efforts substantially more difficult', presumably by antagonising Washington. The philosopher replied by claiming the prime minister would never be seen as an honest broker by Hanoi if he continued to curry favour with the Johnson administration. In truth, the US government did not thank Wilson either for his efforts to reconvene the Geneva Conference, believing he was no better than de Gaulle in wanting to elevate his own importance as an international statesman.[24]

The prospect of the tribunal meeting in London had shown how volatile the relationships were between Britain, France and the United States. In the end, though, the three countries had thwarted Russell and Sartre. The war in Southeast Asia was spreading while their options narrowed.

Moral certainty impelled Russell to persevere. The philosopher approached other heads of state in the hope their country would host the tribunal. The Swiss government declined on the grounds that it would undermine their nation's tradition of neutrality. Canadian authorities also said no. There was a groundswell of interest from activists in Belgium, but nothing came of it. The situation was becoming so desperate that Russell and Sartre even contemplated holding the tribunal aboard a boat outside territorial waters, in imitation of pirate radio stations.[25]

Salvation came when the Swedish government reluctantly granted permission for the tribunal to take place in Stockholm. The Swedish capital had long been near the top of the list of alternative venues. As the home of tribunal members Sara Lidman and Peter Weiss, there was bound to be much local media interest. Stockholm also promised a welcoming political environment, opposition to the Vietnam War being widespread not only in the city but throughout Sweden.

US officials were at first confident the Swedish government would fall into line by impeding the tribunal from meeting in its country. Prime Minister Tage Erlander rebuffed the first approach from Russell in November 1966. 'The Swedish government,' he sharply informed the philosopher, 'is of the opinion that such a meeting will not a favour a solution of the tragic situation in Vietnam.' Foreign Minister Torsten Nilsson affirmed the standpoint of the prime minister in a statement to the press that the tribunal would be an unnecessary distraction for a US government that wanted only to secure a prompt and permanent peace in Vietnam.[26]

This resolve weakened, however, in the ensuing months. Mounting pressure from the political left persuaded Erlander it would be an electoral liability not to allow the tribunal. On 25 April, the prime minister issued a statement on national television. Personally opposed as he was to the tribunal, he proclaimed, the liberal freedom-of-speech laws that were a defining feature of Swedish democracy meant the government had no power to prevent it from taking place in Stockholm. His sole proviso was a vague warning about the threat of civil unrest. 'The government expects as a matter of course,' Erlander concluded, 'that the participants in the meeting will observe those rules and regulations which are valid in the country they visit.' Russell and Sartre would have their tribunal, but it must be a calm meditation on the facts and not an angry rousing of anti-Americanism.[27]

The Swedish government might have reached its decision reluctantly but there was a rush to condemn what opponents saw as an act of political recklessness. Yngve Holmberg, leader of the centre-right Moderate Party, denounced Erlander for surrendering to 'ruthless leftist forces' and demanded that he reverse the decision and prevent the potentially irreparable damage to Sweden's relationship with the United States.[28]

The furious reaction of American officials appeared to confirm his fears. For the US Embassy in Stockholm, the timing could not have been worse. Ambassador J. Graham Parsons had completed his tenure only a week earlier and his successor had yet to present his credentials to King Gustaf VI. Embassy officials nonetheless busied themselves with an investigation of the motivations behind the Swedish decision. They, too, concluded that fractious domestic politics 'had been given greater weight than Sweden's relations with us'.[29] In particular, they suspected a plot by prominent left-wingers in the cabinet – including Olof Palme, soon to be the new prime minister – who had undermined both Erlander and Nilsson by taking action while the two men were out of the country. Whether there was any substance to this is open to speculation. More important was that the prime minister himself had made the announcement. Embassy officials pressed the Swedish Foreign Ministry on the prime minister's commitment to keep the tribunal in line. In the ominous words of one memo, 'we will be watching closely'.[30]

Erlander might have calculated that the domestic benefit outweighed the international risk, but now he had to wonder whether he had miscalculated the political arithmetic. The newspaper *Dagens Nyheter* claimed that Lyndon Johnson had administered 'the treatment' in a letter to the prime minister. There is no evidence that the correspondence was written or sent, but there can be no doubt that the US president made his disapproval abundantly clear. The two leaders coincidentally had an opportunity to meet that same month at the state funeral of former German Chancellor Konrad Adenauer. An anxious Erlander waited for an opportunity to talk to Johnson over lunch, only to find himself competing with other foreign leaders for the attention of a president who probably chose on purpose to ignore him. The prime minister had to make do later that day with Walt Rostow. 'Honest, sir,' the national security advisor boasted afterwards to his boss. 'I delivered the message loud and clear.'[31] So too did the American press. 'Shame on Sweden' pronounced the *Washington Post*, a sentiment shared on the editorial pages of newspapers from East to West Coast. So worried was Erlander that he wrote to several other heads of government on how to win back the trust of the US administration. Run a parallel event that would put across the American point of view, proposed Harold Wilson, advice straight out of the US government's own playbook.[32]

Erlander was not alone in his anxiety. For all their efforts, US officials had failed to thwart Russell and Sartre. The tribunal had a start date, 2 May 1967, and a location, the Folkets Hus, in the heart of Stockholm.

Washington was absorbing that blow when it was hit with the announcement of a second tribunal. The Japan Committee for Investigation of War Crimes was associated with, but not subordinate to, the Russell Foundation. Its members planned to meet on the anniversary of the atomic bombing of Hiroshima, before deciding there would be too many competing peace demonstrations. Instead, 28 August was set as the first of three days of testimony in Tokyo. Telegraph cables pulsed under the Pacific Ocean as the CIA reported on the opening of a second front in the propaganda fight against international critics of US foreign policy.[33]

Securing a site for the tribunal had involved months of negotiation. No matter how frustrating that process, the momentum of the enterprise had not faltered. Washington might dismiss Russell and Sartre as armchair propagandists more reliant on abstract reasoning than actual understanding of the realities of the war, but the philosophers were determined to win public opinion through a presentation of facts they accused the US government of suppressing, manipulating and supplanting with falsehoods. While they were wrangling with world leaders about where and when to hold the tribunal, investigative teams were sent to North Vietnam to uncover evidence of what was happening on the ground. These investigators were to venture further than much of the Western press in search of the truth about the war.

7

HANOI

Christmas Eve, 1966, and people hurried through the frozen streets of New York City in search of last-minute presents. Inside the warmth of his home, John Gerassi and his daughter Lara were decorating their tree when the phone rang. On the other end of the line was one of the tribunal organisers. Less than forty-eight hours later, Gerassi was en route to a destination more than 9,000 miles away, travelling to Hanoi as a member of an investigative team intended to uncover the truth about the Vietnam War.

Gerassi was a man of the political left, the son of a Republican military commander in the Spanish Civil War. As Latin America editor, first for *Time* and later *Newsweek*, he had befriended the likes of Che Guevara and Fidel Castro. Born in Paris, he was also close to Jean-Paul Sartre. On the night Gerassi was born, the philosopher had abandoned a drunken gathering of artists and intellectuals to witness the arrival of the new baby. The bond between them endured, Gerassi becoming one of Sartre's biographers. Supporting the war crimes tribunal was therefore as personal a matter as it was political.

Accustomed as he was to long flights, Gerassi's itinerary was arduous. From New York he flew to Paris and two days later to the Cambodian capital Phnom Penh. There he boarded a Boeing 307, a Second World War airliner better suited to a museum than the sky, and travelled northwards to the Laotian capital Vientiane. As he waited for his connecting flight, Gerassi looked across the airfields. All around were US military planes, one accelerating along the runway and into the air every three minutes. Gerassi was headed in the same direction. As dusk settled, he started the final stage of his journey, flying 300 miles northeast across the border into North Vietnam. Three hours later, he was in Hanoi.[1]

Gerassi was not travelling alone. He was one member of a team sponsored by the Russell Foundation to discover through direct evidence whether the United States was committing war crimes against the Vietnamese. Where Gerassi and his associates went, others followed. Four teams travelled to North Vietnam between December 1966 and March 1967. Their members came from around the world and brought with them a broad range of professional skills, from engineering to agronomy, medicine to law. Critics would point out that they were all politically on the left and therefore saw only what they wanted to see. But while some team members may have succumbed to corroborative bias, others were uncertain what lay ahead, inquisitiveness hardening to outrage the more they witnessed.[2]

The teams arrived in North Vietnam in search of answers to five questions asked by the tribunal:

1. *Have there been civilian bombings in North Vietnam?*
2. *Did these bombings take place far from military targets?*
3. *What are the civilian targets of US planes?*
4. *Are the weapons used intended to destroy steel and concrete blocks or human life?*
5. *Are there any factors to conclude that the US is committing a crime of genocide in Vietnam?*

Touring thousands of miles from urban centres to remote rural villages, they found their answers.[3]

*

It was a wonder that they ever made it to Hanoi. The tribunal was attempting to immobilise the wheels of the mightiest military machine in the world. What it needed was plenty of money, unity of purpose and sympathetic press coverage. What it had was a mass of problems. Behind the scenes there were problems within the London office, problems between that administrative team and their counterparts in Paris, problems raising funds and problems caused by feuding egos.

Most of the funding for the investigative teams came from Bertrand Russell, but for all his fame and family inheritance, the philosopher was not blessed with bottomless pockets. There were, for a start, too many former wives, whose maintenance he had to pay. It was the need for income that had led him even in old age to pen an endless stream of articles for the popular press, undermining his reputation among snobbier intellectuals. His Peace Foundation boasted an illustrious list of sponsors, from heads of state to Nobel laureates, but even with the occasional illustrious donation such as a painting by the Catalan artist Joan Miró, it was often barely solvent. Its offices were located in the choice real estate area of London's Haymarket, but the furnishing was sparse, the green painted walls in need of a new coat, and other than volunteers the work was carried out by only half a dozen employees.[4] It was a mark of his resolve but also his lack of an alternative that Russell raised the funds for the tribunal through the advance he received for the third volume of his autobiography and the overseas sale of his archive to McMaster University in Canada. Embarrassed about adding to the philosopher's financial burden, one of the factfinders who travelled to North Vietnam, American biochemist Joe Neilands, chose to pay his own way.[5]

Russell also found himself in a difficult dance with North Vietnamese officials, each attempting to lead the other. The philosopher admired Ho Chi Minh for what he saw as his heroic resistance to US military aggression. The two men never met but were on affectionate enough terms to cable one another birthday greetings. Each was an asset to the other in advancing their cause, without wanting for political reasons to be associated too closely.[6]

The investigative teams intended to venture deeper into North Vietnam than any other Westerners since the outbreak of the war, which necessitated close coordination with local and national officials. Russell had sent a Peace Foundation representative to Hanoi as early as 1964. His associate Ralph Schoenman had also prepared the ground for the arrival of the investigative teams through a series of meetings with National Liberation Front officials from the autumn of 1965.[7]

Russell and his associates supported the NLF cause and needed their cooperation for access to North Vietnam. But for the Western world to treat their work seriously, they needed to show that they were working with but not for the Hanoi government. Ho also seemed to understand this. When Russell had written to him in November 1964, inviting him to become a sponsor of the Peace Foundation, the North Vietnamese leader declined. He did, however, offer a small financial contribution.[8]

As plans for the tribunal gathered pace, the relationship between the NLF and the Peace Foundation nonetheless became more complicated. In October 1966, Russell complained to Ho that North Vietnamese representatives in London and Paris were attempting to use his dependence on their cooperation as leverage to control the selection of the investigative teams. Such interference, he warned, would ruin the credibility of the tribunal. 'To have the proper effect on Western opinion,' the philosopher informed Nguyen Van Sao, one of the North Vietnamese representatives in London, 'the procedures of our

Tribunal must be exact and unimpeachable.' For that reason, he also declined to add his name to a letter protesting US war crimes that the North Vietnamese circulated to Western intellectuals.[9]

The wrangling continued. North Vietnamese representatives wanted the tribunal to pass sentences on US government officials who sanctioned war crimes. We can only make moral, not legal, judgement, Russell responded. Hanoi also pushed for hundreds, if not thousands, of witnesses to testify to the tribunal. This would turn a serious enterprise into a circus, retorted Russell. The philosopher got his way, but the back and forth further slowed the momentum of the tribunal.[10]

It was difficult enough for Russell to fend off demanding North Vietnamese officials without also having to worry about feuds between the tribunal organisers themselves. Much of the problem rested with Peace Foundation Co-Director Ralph Schoenman. Hailed by some but hated by others, Schoenman was a divisive figure even among his fellow activists on the political left. Born in 1935, he was the only son of Hungarian Jews who immigrated to New York after the First World War. Graduating from Princeton University, he pursued postgraduate study at the London School of Economics under the supervision of Ralph Miliband. In July 1960, Russell received a letter from the American student that by the philosopher's own admission appealed to his vanity.[11] Within months, Schoenman had become a trusted aide to Russell. Through him the frail, elderly philosopher found a new lease of energy, a surrogate on whose younger legs he could convey his message far better than his own faltering limbs. In October 1960 Schoenman co-founded, together with Russell and others, the Committee of 100, an anti-war group that emulated the non-violent civil disobedience of the US civil rights movement. The following September, he received a two-month prison sentence for defying police orders at a demonstration in London, the first chapter in a long story of his confrontations with the authorities. His student visa having expired while he was serving his term in Stafford Prison, Schoenman applied for a work permit that would allow him to remain in Britain. The Home Office instead ordered his deportation, a decision reversed only through the intervention of several MPs acting at the behest of Russell.[12]

Without Schoenman, much of the hard work recruiting the investigative teams, securing the cooperation of the NLF and liaising between the London and Paris offices would never have been done. But with him, more work was created for others, thanks to of his unerring ability to turn allies into enemies. The 'untouchable self-confidence' that Russell saw as the great virtue of Schoenman also turned out to be his main vice. He had the energy and conviction to get things done; the problem was how he went about it. Angry and abrasive, he tended to dictate rather than delegate. There was tension caused by his necessary absence from the Foundation, and even more on his return. Funds were insufficient, accounting absent, salaries and expenses unpaid. Volunteers were not entitled to a wage but might have been shown they were valued in other ways. But Schoenman could be belligerent and bullying, workers becoming victims of the venomous temperament that earned him the nickname 'Russell's viper'.[13]

Circumstances in London might be fraught, but the relationship between that office and Paris was even worse. The Paris team soured towards Schoenman because of his failure to treat them as equal partners. If failing to consult a fellow administrator was imprudent, paying no heed to the tribunal president was unpardonable. The phone in the London office rang with the insistence of an alarm siren when Paris called once more to complain. Acting as his intermediary, French lawyer Gisèle Halimi protested that Sartre 'feels he is being treated like a flower-pot, some kind of decoration put there only for ornamental reasons'. Schoenman was unwilling to accept the criticism. Not only were the French doing nothing to raise funds, he retorted, but they seldom even showed up for meetings in London. He proved his point with a petty act of spitefulness, scheduling a planning session on a day the French team had informed him they would be unable to attend. He then proceeded to reverse all the decisions agreed between the two offices at their previous meeting.[14]

A charged situation was made even worse by the fact that the Parisians fell out not only with the London office but also themselves, as personalities clashed and political factions feuded for control. From London it looked as though the Paris team was about to implode. Peace Foundation member Ernest Tate travelled aboard an overnight ferry from Dover to Calais in an attempt to resolve the chaos. Seasick from the motion of the Channel, he had barely recovered before being buffeted by the turbulence in Paris. The outcome was the forced resignation of the French administrative team leader Claude Cadart. Time, however, would show that Tate had sutured rather than healed the wounds within and between the administrative teams.[15]

Whatever news stories they had read and whatever photographs they had seen, none of the investigators knew for certain what to expect as they prepared for their flights to North Vietnam. Few Westerners had set foot in the country since the start of the war. It was for many a place of the imagination rather than a political and geographic reality.

Among the first outsiders to set foot in North Vietnam were three Americans who arrived in December 1965. The trio consisted of academics Herbert Aptheker and Staughton Lynd together with Tom Hayden, a leader of the anti-war organisation

Students for a Democratic Society, who would later marry Jane Fonda. Acting in an unofficial role as diplomats, the three men discussed with North Vietnamese officials their conditions for peace negotiations with Washington. Their intervention received little press coverage, as was the case with four female peace activists who ventured to Hanoi a year later.[16]

A more immediate precedent for the investigative teams was the visit to North Vietnam by British reporter James Cameron. Arriving shortly before the American trio, Cameron inspected a country whose infrastructure was scarred and fractured by US bombing. The impact was visible in the rubble of roads and bridges, in the smoking remains of hospitals and houses. Cameron did not believe that the American military had deliberately set out to intimidate and murder civilians, but whether they did was not the point. Whatever the intention of their actions, the impact was horrendous. Bomber pilots might not intend to injure or kill civilians, but nor did they care enough if that was the consequence of their raids on military targets. Too many of them 'are not only rather poor shots, but have no particular reason to care about the secondary effects of their performance', as Cameron wrote in a book about his visit to North Vietnam, which came out in Britain under the dispassionate title *Witness*. That contrasted with the United States, where the publisher renamed it without apparent irony as though it were an instruction manual, *Here Is Your Enemy*. The new title was a measure of what the reading public would and would not be willing to consume about the conflict.[17]

The small number of Western visitors to North Vietnam in the early stage of the war also included one member of the tribunal. Russell recruited Dave Dellinger because he had seen for himself the effect of aerial bombardment, an experience that transformed his perception of what his own country was attempting to achieve through the conflict. When he travelled to North Vietnam in the autumn of 1966, Dellinger had at first refused to believe that the US military was deliberately bombing civilian targets. 'Something, perhaps my own type of Americanism, rose up inside me and I tried to deny that Americans would knowingly bomb and strafe civilians, at least as part of deliberate government policy.'[18] He took heart from the fact that Hanoi was not at that time the focus of air raids, assuming that what little damage he saw must have been caused by accident. What he saw when he ventured outside the city changed his mind. Driving through the countryside, he had his first taste of what lay ahead on the potholed road when overhead aircraft forced him to take cover in a muddy ditch. Above him, the flares from the planes had turned night into day. When it was over, he saw widespread destruction. In Phu Ly, a bustling small town thirty-five miles south of Hanoi, no building was still standing. Further south, in Nam Dinh, residential areas were reduced to debris. Worst of all was Thanh Hoa, where the indiscriminate bombing had destroyed everything from a tuberculosis sanatorium to a Franciscan seminary. Apology for his government turned to shame and apoplexy.[19]

How aware the investigative teams were of these antecedents is unclear. What is certain is that such knowledge would not have prepared them for what they were about to witness as they boarded the first of several flights that took them to their destination.

On board the mood was light, laughter filling the passenger cabin. As the plane prepared for landing, however, repartee turned to tense silence. Through the darkness of night, dots of electric light gave shape to the city below. Wheels touched down on the pockmarked runway of the little-used airfield and slowed to a stop.

This was the experience of each of the investigative teams as they completed the last stage of their long journey. They had travelled on the only plane taking Western passengers into the North Vietnamese capital. Operated by the International Control Commission, the body established to oversee implementation of the Geneva Accords following the end of the First Indochina War, it flew under the cover of night for safety. Anxieties eased as the teams stepped out of the plane and into a reception from North Vietnamese officials. The young women who presented them with bouquets of long-stemmed blossoms were a welcome distraction for many of the predominantly male investigators, although the more perceptive noticed that their hands were calloused from hard labour.[20]

Home during their time in Hanoi was the official government guesthouse, a French colonial-style mansion formerly known as the Métropole but renamed the Reunification Hotel following the First Indochina War. Its rooms were comfortable but cold, the guests complaining that for all the space in their large, canopied beds, their feet were never warm. It was not the cold, however, that kept them awake. Before the guests retired for the night, the reception staff pointed out the recently constructed concrete bomb shelter in the hotel courtyard. Behind the black curtains of their rooms, the investigators wondered how soon they would need to use it.[21]

The team with which John Gerassi travelled did not have to wait long. On the afternoon of their first full day in Hanoi, the air raid sirens sounded. There was a scramble for the cement shelters lining the city streets, men and women cramming into the dark and confined underground spaces. When the skies cleared, Gerassi looked around at the fortified city. On the roofs of one building after another, anti-aircraft batteries stood ready for further assaults. On the streets below, people resumed their daily lives. There was something missing from the scene, though Gerassi could not identify what. Slowly, he realised. There were no children. They had, he learned, been evacuated to small towns and villages for their safety. Hanoi had not become a ghost town, but nor was it entirely living.[22]

'I will only tell what I saw,' John Gerassi reflected of his time in North Vietnam, 'and what I saw convinced me that while the documents may seem at times fantastic, it is in fact the reality which is fantastic.' The papers to which he referred were the work of a North Vietnamese commission that produced a report on alleged war crimes by the US military. Without corroborative evidence, those documents could be dismissed as the misrepresentations and manufactured truths of North Vietnamese propagandists – but the events that Gerassi related in his account of visiting the country were ones that he had witnessed with his own eyes. Through the evidence that he and the other members of the investigative teams accumulated, the places they toured and the people with whom they spoke, there emerged a clear and consistent portrait of human suffering. Between them they travelled 2,000 miles, enduring danger and hardship in search of a truth they believed the Western press and political establishment had either only hinted at or intentionally concealed. Some of those who came to North Vietnam were sceptical that the US Army was intentionally attacking non-military targets; none of them returned home with the same disbelief.[23]

Before embarking from Hanoi, the teams received a briefing from the North Vietnamese government. That included Prime Minister Pham Van Dong and a brief audience at the Presidential Palace with Ho Chi Minh. The chain-smoking septuagenarian was smaller and frailer than they had expected, but no less gracious a host than they had hoped.[24]

The investigators did not need to venture beyond Hanoi to observe the impact of US air raids. They spent their first day in North Vietnam touring the capital, and what they saw was entirely at odds with official statements from Washington that there had been no sustained bombardment of the city. In the downtown district of Hoan Kiem, the team stood amid the scattered and charred remains of a residential block. To John Gerassi, 'it looked like an abandoned cemetery, with the remnants of a chimney or of a huge collective water jug standing crookedly like decaying tombstones'. The team travelled on through other areas of the city. Here a Buddhist pagoda bore the scars from being hit by bombs, there in the arboreal neighbourhood whose colonial villas were home to foreign diplomats were the battered Chinese and Romanian embassy buildings, further beyond the badly damaged University of Pharmacy.[25]

What fell from the skies onto Hanoi was a light shower compared to the deluge that rained upon other areas of the country. The investigative teams made their way by jeep under cover of darkness out of the city and into small towns and rural villages. As the sun rose, they could see what had only been dimly sensed as they drove around deep craters in the road, the brutal destruction caused by saturation bombing. From Hanoi, the second team separated into two smaller groups, Scottish trade unionist Lawrence Daly and Canadian doctor Gustavo Tolentino travelling north, American author Carol Brightman, French nuclear physicist Abraham Behar and British activist Tariq Ali heading south.

Ali was one of the most conspicuous public faces of the anti-war movement in Britain. The Oxford graduate had led demonstrations outside the US Embassy and made himself one of the sharpest thorns in the side of the British establishment. Russell recruited Ali after reading a letter that he had written to the *Observer* criticising press coverage of the war. In his own words, the conflict was his 'obsession'. What he had imagined of the situation in North Vietnam still could not compare with what he witnessed, an experience that further ignited his moral outrage.[26]

Driving in darkness was slow, the roads uneven and the bridges hastily erected over rivers less sturdy than had been the bombed structures they replaced. Night was cold and sleepless. By day, the beauty of the natural landscape stood in stark contrast with the human carnage. Amid the rivers and limestone mountains of Ninh Binh province, the team who travelled south beheld bombed houses, churches and schools. In the southerly bordering province of Thanh Hoa, US planes had only hours earlier hit a hospital, with a local Red Cross administrator among the dead. En route from the interior of the country to its coast, the investigators travelled from one village targeted by US bombers to another. In some communities there were no homes still standing. In one coastal village, Ali talked through his translator to Nguyen Thi Tuyen, a twelve-year-old schoolgirl. She had lost not only a leg but also her brother in the air raid. 'Will you please tell me why they are bombing us?' she asked. The team had no answer. Sadness, bewilderment and despair were common among those who had lost homes and loved ones, but there was also anger. Before she burst into uncontrollable tears, one bereaved woman vowed that when her surviving child reached adulthood, she would send him to avenge his father and brother.[27]

Having spent a week inspecting different parts of the country, the two halves of the second investigative team reconvened, heading from Hanoi to the city of Haiphong and from there to what remained of a number of coastal mining communities. For a man who devoted his life to the mining industry, it was a moving experience for Daly to see pit families forced to live in caves. The Scotsman gave an emotional speech to an audience gathered in torch-lit gloom.[28]

A week later, the second team had returned home. The third and fourth sets of researchers who succeeded them had little intimation of what the others had seen, not that it would have prepared them for what they were about to witness. Their visits conformed to the pattern of the previous investigators: the night-time arrival in Hanoi, the audience with North Vietnamese officials, the troubled sleep in anticipation of air raid sirens, the perilous motoring along cratered roads, and the death and destruction en route. American civil rights lawyer Hugh Manes was a member of the third team. His camera captured images of buildings with collapsed roofs and plaster peeling like skin from their scarred facades. The camera lens was impassive but not the human eye that peered through it. 'Seeing old people crying and weeping, seeing children dead and the like,' Manes later reflected. 'It was very, very difficult to see these sights and not be terribly moved.' A collapsed bridge, an imploded building; these could be repaired. But what could be said to the child who asked him whether his amputated arm would grow back?[29]

There were moments that lightened the darkness of what they saw and heard. Ali and Daly bonded during sleepless nights over bottles of single malt whisky the Scotsman had brought with him, with Daly succeeding in drinking a bottle intended as a present to Ho Chi Minh and having to have another one sent by courier. Before returning home, they and the other members of the second investigation team recovered from their tour on the long sandy beach lapped by gentle waves at the coastal resort of Sam Son.[30] Julius Lester and Charles Cobb were SNCC colleagues of Stokely Carmichael who were among the members of the fourth investigative team. Lester found solace from the ugliness of war in the beauty of North Vietnamese women. Far from the only man among the investigative teams to welcome the interruption, he was alone in actively pursuing romance, even composing a poem about how it helped him briefly lose sight of the war:

> I sent her a rose
> From the bush at
> The bombed pagoda
> But the birds still sing
> In Vietnam.
> By the third day,
> I hardly noticed the bombing.[31]

Would that it were so easy for the others, haunted by the horrors they witnessed – and not just in their dreams. All were moved by memories of the survivors of bombing raids whose eyes were as hollow as the burnt-out buildings they once occupied.[32]

What the investigative teams witnessed was not only the misery of war but also the resolve of ordinary men and women to recover from their losses and ultimately to win the war. Japanese economist Setsure Tsurushima, travelling with the first team, was horrified by the devastation but heartened by the determination of its victims. 'We could see the Vietnamese working day and night,' he later wrote, 'harvesting sweet potatoes, planting rice paddies, repairing the roads and dikes which American planes had bombed.'[33] Gerassi was also pleasantly surprised how people retained a sense of humour about their predicament. That included the bombed-out educational building on which one wag had written in chalk, 'Hooray, no more school'.[34]

For SNCC activists Charlie Cobb and Julius Lester, there

was an especially strong sense of affinity with the North Vietnamese. Their organisation was in solidarity with people of
colour around the world resisting what they saw as the cruelty
and coercion of white Western imperialism. That sense of
common struggle was made all the more acute by the physical
landscape of Vietnam reminding the civil rights campaigners of
the Mississippi Delta region, where they had fought to improve
the lives of Black farm labourers. The time Cobb and Lester
spent in the country instilled a deep personal feeling of kinship
towards its people that led them to record a broadcast for Radio
Hanoi. In a message directed towards African American troops,
they declared that a white racist government in Washington was
sending young Black men to fight and die in a war against fellow
people of colour. It was time, uttered the two men, to lay down
arms, to tear off uniforms and to desert the US Army.[35]

Their tours through ravaged towns and villages had caused
the investigative teams to identify closely with the struggle of
the indigenous population, to become as strongly pro-Viet-
namese as they were anti-American. Lawrence Daly had been
an opponent of the war before he came to the country, but was
undecided whether the US military was intentionally assault-
ing civilian homes and institutions; by the time he left he had
no doubt. Daly was shocked and saddened but also inspired by
the determination of the North Vietnamese to restore houses,
rebuild bridges and repair places of learning and worship. In a
media interview, he affirmed he had 'no words' that could 'ade-
quately convey the courage displayed by the people in their
struggle'.[36]

The tribunal had posed five questions to the investigative
teams before they flew to North Vietnam. By the time the
researchers returned home they had accumulated bulging dos-
siers of evidence to corroborate their answers. Individually and

collectively, the investigative team members concluded that what they saw in North Vietnam was not the unintended consequence of air strikes against military targets but the deliberate and systematic bombing of civilian population centres. Some of the investigators went on record about what they had seen before they testified to the tribunal, including at press conferences at which they made clear their conviction that the US military was endeavouring to win the war by undermining the morale of enemy civilians.[37] But it was not only the impact of bombs that they had witnessed. Of all the scenes to which they were observers, some of the most shocking involved the use of other weapons. The tribunal had asked whether the purpose of the US military was to destroy the steel and concrete infrastructure of North Vietnam or to harm civilian life. What the investigators would disclose in Stockholm addressed not only that issue but also the most disturbing matter raised by the tribunal, the war crime of genocide. It was time for the tribunal to begin.[38]

8

THE STOCKHOLM SESSION

The arrival of May in Sweden marks the first promise of spring following the long winter. The hours of sunlight lengthen, the cold morning air warms slightly during the day and the skeletal branches of trees start to bear buds.

It is at this time of year that Swedes gather for the annual celebrations of Walpurgis Night and May Day. For some, the latter is little more than an opportunity to recover from the excesses of the former. Yet to others it is a means to demonstrate solidarity, traditionally with the labour movement, but also other political causes. That was certainly true of the May Day parade that passed through Stockholm in 1967. Accompanied by the pomp of a brass band, people walked through streets glossed by light rain bearing placards promoting political causes from apartheid to Zionism. As a bemused British broadcaster observed, however, for every sign proclaiming support for a particular cause, there were a hundred more denouncing the Vietnam War. The parade therefore acted as a curtain up on the international war crimes tribunal that convened in the city the following day. Among the marchers were several members of its cast, including Sara Lidman, who clutched Viet Cong flags.

A day later, focus turned to the Folkets Hus, the nine-storey steel and concrete conference centre a short distance to the east of the Klara Sjö, the canal that winds its way through central

Stockholm. Outside, flags fluttered in a cool wind. Inside, across the white tiled floors of the reception area and upstairs was the facility reserved for the tribunal. Here in this semicircular space, television camera crews and newspaper photographers occupied the sloping wooden seats immediately in front of a crowded dais. At the left of that small stage stood a lectern from where witnesses would testify. Towards the centre were tables arranged in a horseshoe shape. On those tables and around the room were the headsets that afforded simultaneous translation of proceedings in five languages. And at the centre of the horseshoe, tapping yet another cigarette into an overflowing ashtray, sat tribunal president Jean-Paul Sartre. To his left, chairman Vladimir Dedijer. On either side, the other members of the panel. It was time for the opening session to begin.

Over the course of eight days, they would testify to the tribunal. Drawn from around the world, the witnesses included biochemists and ballistic specialists, professors and reporters, physicists and physicians. Collectively they constructed a narrative of the Vietnam War completely contrary to what the US government and much of the Western media were telling the world. This was a conflict in breach of international laws on war and human rights, larger and deadlier than the public understood. With no power to pass sentence, Sartre would announce that the American people in particular should look to their conscience about the crimes being committed in their name.

There was one last-minute impediment to proceedings, when one of the tribunal members contacted the organisers to inform them that he would not be attending. The reasons why James Baldwin chose to remain in Turkey rather than travel to Sweden were intricate, and his own account provided only a partial explanation. 'There may be something suspect in the spectacle of Europeans condemning America for a war which America inherited from Europe,' he wrote in an article published that summer, 'inherited, in fact, directly from France.' His implication was that the tribunal members were in no position to claim the moral high ground when their own countries were far from innocent of committing crimes against humanity. Sartre, Baldwin continued, would be better to convene an investigation of the excesses of French colonial rule. There was merit to this argument, but Baldwin was mistaken to claim that the tribunal consisted entirely of Europeans. Its members included representatives not only of Asia and Latin America, but also, crucially, his own country. It was therefore dishonest of him to accuse the panellists of being motivated by 'envy and fury' towards the United States. Casting these aspersions would also have made more sense had Baldwin dissociated himself from the tribunal, which he did not; his name continued to appear on official documents including the published proceedings and he retained a role in administrative decisions.[1]

Baldwin's criticisms would also have carried more weight had he made any effort to follow through on his recommendation to convene an alternative tribunal in Harlem, to investigate the disproportionate numbers of African Americans being drafted into the US Army and dying in Vietnam. 'I challenge anyone alive,' Baldwin declared, 'to convince me that a people who have not achieved anything resembling freedom in their own country are empowered, with bombs, to free another people whom they do not know at all.'[2] It was a powerful assertion, but not one that Baldwin was prepared to pursue through a public investigation. Had he done so, it would have strengthened the cause of the SNCC members who attended the tribunal. Courtland Cox recalls how frustrated he and his fellow African American activists became with white panellists who they failed to interest in the institutional racism of the US war machine. 'I trust, gentlemen,' Isaac Deutscher proclaimed after pausing to lower the stem of his perpetually smouldering pipe, 'that we will not inject race into the discussion.' Cox was lost for words, a condition from which Baldwin never suffered – but he was not there to intervene.[3]

So for what reason other than belated concerns about its moral and political shortcomings did Baldwin not take his seat around the table in Stockholm? A statement from Ralph Schoenman accused him of being lazy, but that was little more than malice.[4] 'In spite of my somewhat difficult reputation,' Baldwin wrote, 'I have never had any interest in attacking America from abroad.'[5] This was perverse from someone who had made a career out of doing precisely that, but his continued ability to do so was another matter. At almost the same time as Baldwin decided not to travel to Stockholm, Martin Luther King declined an invitation to discuss his possible involvement in peace negotiations with North Vietnamese representatives in Paris. His reason for doing so was apprehension that the US government would revoke his passport, a favourite tactic of the State Department, which had used it to restrict the freedom of movement and speech of many political dissidents, including the African American activist Paul Robeson.[6] The American activists who travelled to Stockholm ran the risk that they would be forced to surrender their passports on returning home but Baldwin appears to have been less willing than the others to take his chances. His caution proved well placed, when two months later the British Home Office ordered his detention at London Heathrow Airport. Officials used much of the two hours they kept him in custody to interrogate him about his association with the war crimes tribunal. Only when they were convinced he had not been in Stockholm did they allow him entry. US authorities would nonetheless use his connection with the tribunal as a pretext to keep him under surveillance for years to come.[7]

Tuesday, 2 May 1967. Outside the Folkets Hus, police interceded in a street fight between rival demonstrators, on one side those protesting US foreign policy, on the other supporters of military intervention furious that their home city was host to the war crimes tribunal. Tempers and fists rose, officers bundled members of both groups into the back of Volvo station wagons, and order resumed before violence was renewed the following day. As the streets cleared, a television camera focused on a foot trampling on a torn US flag, a potent symbol of the diplomatic tensions caused by the war and the tribunal investigating its conduct.[8]

Inside the Folkets Hus, another camera panned across the table around which the panellists sat. With the first session about to start, some reached for their headphones, others shuffled through their papers, a few shared words. All around, the room filled with tobacco smoke that only partially concealed the No Smoking signs.

Peter Weiss stood and walked to the lectern. The lights throwing his long shadow on the wall behind him, he read his welcoming statement with slow deliberation. Through the evidence about to be presented, the panellists would have the opportunity 'to analyse the character and the mechanisms of war which increasingly destroys the crops, destroys the villages and cities, and exterminates the people of Vietnam'. The sombre tone endured through a written statement by Russell, who was not well enough to attend in person, read on his behalf by Ralph Schoenman. For the philosopher, the tribunal promised not only to expose the atrocities committed in Vietnam but also to establish a precedent for holding other governments to account for future crimes.[9]

Now it was the turn of Sartre. Leaning towards a microphone, he read his remarks in a bold and deliberate baritone. The philosopher began by anticipating criticism of the tribunal for its lack of formal legitimacy. In 1945, he observed, the Allies had implemented the Nuremberg Trials to prosecute Nazi leaders accused of war crimes. Nuremberg should have established the model for a permanent institution empowered to try those who, like the colonial powers that brutally suppressed nationalist revolts, continued to perpetrate militaristic atrocities. The Russell tribunal filled the void created by the failure of governments to found such a body. Critics claimed that the tribunal had no authority, that its members represented no one other than themselves. That, according to Sartre, was a strength rather than a weakness. Some had claimed of Nuremberg that it was a case of victors' justice, the Allies prosecuting Nazis for war crimes while remaining unaccountable for the atrocities they had committed. That accusation could not be levelled against the Russell tribunal. 'Representing no government and no party,' stressed Sartre, 'nobody can give us orders: we will examine the facts "in our hearts and consciences" one might say or, if you prefer, openly and independently.' The fact that the tribunal had no power to pass sentence further liberated it from punitive acts of retribution. Its duty was to lay out the evidence and allow the rest of humanity to decide whether they agreed with the decisions of the panellists. As Sartre concluded, 'the judges are everywhere: they are the peoples of the world, and in particular the American people. It is for them that we are working.'[10]

With that, it was time for French lawyer Léo Matarasso to read out the questions to which the tribunal intended to provide answers:

1. *Has the United States Government (and the
    Governments of Australia, New Zealand and South
    Korea) committed acts of aggression according to
    international law?*
2. *Has the American army made use of or experimented
    with new weapons or weapons forbidden by the laws of
    war?*
3. *Has there been bombardment of targets of a purely
    civilian character?*[11]

When the tribunal reconvened the following morning, the
conference centre had the atmosphere less of a court than a classroom. A succession of academics accounted for how, when and
why the United States became embroiled in Vietnam. The tribunal sat attentively through tutorials by the French scholars Jean
Chesneaux and Charles Fourniau, but allocated much of its first
full day to discussion of a report by University of Pennsylvania
historian Gabriel Kolko. In appearance a conservatively attired
campus intellectual, the thirty-four-year-old professor was
intellectually cut from a more radical cloth. A member of the
National Mobilization Committee to End the War in Vietnam,
he would soon thereafter resign his position over covert research
at his university of chemical and biological weapons used by the
US military.

The tribunal cross-examined Kolko. How much public con-
sultation had there been about the decision to go to war, asked
David Dellinger. Almost none, affirmed the academic, suggest-
ing that the White House had manufactured the Gulf of Tonkin
incident as a means to manipulate opinion, especially in a war-
wary Congress. Deutscher asked whether Washington therefore
had a clear strategic objective. They did, determined Kolko. US
policy planners adhered to the domino theory, the notion that

the fall of democracy to communist dictatorship in one country would lead to a toppling of regimes throughout the neighbouring region. The US government might understand why it had intervened in Vietnam, but it was far less certain about how to achieve victory. Was there a risk, wondered Weiss, that Washington would resort to the use of the atomic bomb to resolve the military stalemate? Kolko did not consider that probable; the infrastructure of North Vietnam was too decentralised to allow for a decisive strike against a single target. 'In the last analysis,' affirmed Kolko, 'wars against popular revolutionary movements can only be won on the ground by the foot soldier' – not that the use of conventional forces meant the US was any more likely to avert catastrophe. When Cox wanted to know whether there was anything new about the military tactics being used in Vietnam, Kolko drew an analogy with the Philippine–American War of 1899 to 1902. Then, as now, he warned, the US had occupied a country that wanted its independence and ended up slaughtering the people they claimed to be liberating. The lesson of history was that Washington had not learned the lesson of history.[12]

The tribunal turned from historical to legal matters. Eminent lawyer Samuel Rosenwein made the case that US intervention in Vietnam violated international law. This was true both of its prevention of a national election and its unilateral military action.[13] A report produced by the legal team of the Tokyo war crimes tribunal supported this position, concluding that the US had contrived a situation in which it used the pretext of protecting another country from outside threat to impose its own control over that same nation. The democratic rhetoric from Washington was a gloss for a colonialist land grab. 'To hide the nature of its aggression,' read the report, 'the U.S. has used various methods of camouflage, such as establishing the puppet regime in South Vietnam and then ostensibly answering a request for assistance from that very regime.'[14]

Some of the witness statements to the tribunal during the course of the week were open to criticism. The speakers were politically biased, leftist opponents of the war, intent on proving that the United States had committed crimes against humanity. Sceptical of whatever Washington said about the war, they were all too credulous of claims made by Hanoi. Their own accounts of North Vietnam were also selective in their use of evidence; among the investigative teams, even the more impartial members had not travelled far enough to form more than an impressionistic sense of how the war affected civilian life. The tribunal dismissed some testimonies, especially those of Cuban activists who had travelled to North Vietnam, because of their blatant rhetorical excess.[15] Yet for all these fallibilities, many of the witnesses had been far more methodical than critics later allowed. That became clearer with the appearance of the French nuclear physicist Abraham Behar.

Behar was a member of the second investigative team. His report spelled out the precision with which he and the other researchers had approached their roles. They had begun, he explained, by comparing US and North Vietnamese reports of bombing raids. Each of the warring sides spun these stories in a way that served their own political interest. According to the US, civilian buildings had rarely been bombed and then only by accident. In the estimation of the North Vietnamese, the destruction was both larger and deliberate. The investigative teams had attempted to determine the truth by travelling to a representative sample of the places affected by air strikes. Behar gave as an example the ninety-five hospitals and medical centres that the North Vietnamese claimed US planes had bombed. Between them the researchers had toured thirty-four of these

locations across eight of the twelve provinces where the incidents were said to have happened; in every case, what they saw
corroborated the claims made by the North Vietnamese. Behar
looked up from his notes. 'We state furthermore that the attacks
on health institutions are not due to large errors or to impreci-
sion on the part of the American planes. Rather, it seems to the
contrary, that the hospitals themselves have been the principal
objects of attacks.' The Frenchman offered one example after
another. Among them was his account of an attack on a hospital in Bac Thai province on 22 June 1966, in which nine patients
died. Located on a remote hillside far from any civilian centre –
let alone military installation – it was difficult to conclude that
US forces had simply made a mistake.[16]

The same was true of schools. In communities constructed
mostly from bamboo and straw, it was not difficult to distinguish modern school buildings – but the air raids had happened
all the same, and often in classroom hours. Behar told many
stories of schools struck by US planes. One of the most startling
was how air-to-ground missiles had hit an institution in Ninh
Binh province four months earlier, killing seventeen children
and two teachers.[17]

Behar then turned to places of worship, where the situation,
he told the tribunal, was no different. American pilots should
be able to see that they were not military targets. 'The numerous churches which we have visited had been usually built in
western style, perfectly visible, with the bell towers very high,
standing out clearly from the neighbouring houses.'[18]

The Frenchman might have conceded that these incidents
were accidental, had he not witnessed US air raids with his own
eyes. At noon on 20 January 1967, bombs fell on a densely populated neighbourhood in the city of Thanh Hoa, demolishing the
local district hospital. Rescue teams moved in, but the planes

fired at them as they attempted to evacuate the burning building. The nearest strategic target was a river crossing five miles away; Behar could only conclude that Thanh Hoa and other civilian areas were premeditated targets.[19]

First to cross-examine Behar was Laurent Schwartz. Behar had said it should be obvious to US pilots when they were flying above civilian targets. Unless, that was, conditions obscured what they could see on the ground. 'Were those bombings carried out from a low or a high altitude, and during any kind of weather conditions, both cloudy and clear weather?' Schwartz asked.

Behar conceded that some of the planes had flown through clouds at high altitude. 'At certain times, however – those which we were able to observe for ourselves from our shelter – I can confirm that the sky was clear and that the planes bombed from a very low altitude.' There were also other occasions when they could have done more to identify targets, including using illumination flares when flying at night.[20]

David Dellinger then raised the issue of whether some of the buildings bombed by the US could be considered strictly civilian targets. 'The usual explanation given for these attacks in America,' he said, 'is that those buildings, the churches for example, are used for military purposes as well as for religious services. Have you investigated this?'

'That explanation does not strike me as being very serious,' Behar responded.

Lelio Basso pushed the witness on the issue of whether the raids on civilian establishments were planned. 'In the bombing raids which you have witnessed,' he wondered, 'were particular targets being attacked and others avoided?'

Behar referred to what he had witnessed in Thanh Hoa. 'The fact that the bombs had been concentrated on this area,' he reminded the tribunal, 'leads one to believe that it was a special target.'

The French scientist had done more than enough to convince his interlocutors that it was less a matter of belief than of fact.[21]

Dates. Locations. Names. During the next several days, the testimony of one witness after another documented in precise detail the American destruction of Vietnamese civilian lives and infrastructure. That this was deliberate there was no doubt for those who gave evidence. The witnesses enumerated the places and properties they had seen laid to ruin: from hospitals to houses, paper mills to power generators. Then there were the people. The reports all emphasised the disfigurement and death to civilians caused by napalm, cluster bombs and other weapons.

While the statements to the tribunal were consistent in content, they could be sharply contrasting in tone. Lawrence Daly presented a substantial but sober account of his time in North Vietnam, as did Professor Saburo Kugai who had travelled to the country as a member of the Japanese investigative team. Others showed less restraint. Anticipating what would become a contentious matter later in the tribunal, their testimony trod a delicate line between the unsettling and the sensationalist. Ralph Schoenman balanced between the two by telling stories of mutilated and dismembered bodies through the words of North Vietnamese witnesses. SNCC activists Charles Cobb and Julius Lester went further with their own explicit descriptions of Vietnamese civilian injuries, including those of napalm victim Hoang Tan Hung. Cobb and Lester had met the middle-aged rice farmer and merchant in his Hanoi hospital bed. 'His ears and one side of his face had literally been melted out of shape. The burns covered his whole body with the most severe on his back and neck and left arm. He had to look straight ahead because he couldn't move his neck, and his left arm seemed to be welded from his armpit to his elbow to the upper part of his torso.' If this were a cause of discomfort for anyone in Folkets Hus, what soon followed would be almost insufferable.[22]

The tribunal continued with a succession of witnesses, their spoken and photographic evidence delineating finer points of detail to the landscape of civilian death and injury mapped out by previous speakers. This included a series of reports focused on the bombing of the drainage and irrigation system that sustained Vietnamese agriculture. It was only possible for Vietnamese peasants to cultivate rice crops on the low-lying plains of their country because of the dykes that regulated the flow of water. Destroying them was a deliberate act of aggression intended to flood the land, the loss of their sole agricultural staple causing deprivation and ruin. A malnourished and demoralised Vietnamese people would be starved into surrender. In the words of returning witness Gabriel Kolko, it was 'a war crime of the first magnitude'.[23]

The testimony of many witnesses, including the detailed report by Abraham Behar, centred on the bombing of civilian buildings, but Behar had briefly alluded to another military tactic that became the focus of attention. What the tribunal was about to hear would be some of the most sensational evidence shared during the seven days of the Stockholm session.

Jean-Pierre Vigier had outstanding credentials. A renowned weapons expert, he was the former officer in charge of armaments inspection in the French army – and the current director of his country's national centre for scientific research. The tone of his words was dry and technical, but the content was distressing. Vigier presented a scientific report on anti-personnel weapons salvaged by the inspection teams. By the time he was done, the tribunal had a detailed understanding of one of the newer innovations in the US arsenal, from the chemical formula of the explosive to the velocity and angle of projection. What really mattered was their capability and purpose. There were two types of bomb, named pineapple and guava because of their resemblance to the fruits. On impact, the casing of the weapons opened to release hundreds of steel pellets that indiscriminately sprayed whatever – or whoever – was close by. The shrapnel was too small for it to affect steel or concrete structures. Its intended target was people, and it could tear through flesh and bone.

The following morning, the tribunal recalled Vigier for further discussion of his report. David Dellinger leaned in. Press statements from the US government repeatedly emphasised the precision of bombing raids on North Vietnam. How, he wanted to know, did the fragmentation bombs fit into that narrative?

Not at all, answered Vigier. Their purpose was not to hit a specific target. 'As I said yesterday, they are used after a conventional bombing. The high-explosive bomb destroys factories and sets houses on fire, and then the fragmentation bombs hit people who have been flushed out of the houses, or who try to dig out the victims.' The weapons, he continued, were also a means to prevent civilians from attempting to repair bombed buildings.

Courtland Cox pursued another line of questioning. Vigier had observed that fragmentation bombs would have little impact on modern structures, but the mud and straw dwellings of North Vietnam had no such immunity. Had the US, asked Cox, specifically developed such weapons for use in poorer countries without a modern infrastructure?

Vigier believed that was so. Cox pushed harder. Would it be possible to conclude that the purpose of targeting civilians was genocide?

Vladimir Dedijer interjected, firmly reminding the civil

rights activist that genocide was not on the agenda for the first session in Stockholm. For now, it was sufficient to demonstrate the impact of US military tactics rather than their purpose; summer would long since have turned to autumn by the time they turned to this most contentious issue at their second session in Roskilde.[24]

Some of the most compelling testimony heard by the tribunal brought to light a shadow war being fought by the US. Witnesses focused less on Vietnam than the nation with which it shared 720 miles of its western border.

Cambodia was ostensibly a neutral country, but incursions by the US and South Vietnamese military had nonetheless incited its leader Prince Norodom Sihanouk to sever diplomatic relations with Washington in May 1965. He also consented to Hanoi establishing bases that allowed soldiers to cross the border into South Vietnam. That included the Parrot's Beak, a protuberance of land that hooked around the neighbouring country little more than thirty miles northwest of Saigon. The decision by US President Richard Nixon to order the bombardment of Cambodia in March 1969 remains a matter of controversy, not least because it was four years before the public became aware. But later archival discoveries have shown that these air strikes started as far back as October 1965, under the authorisation of Nixon's predecessor Lyndon Johnson. Between then and the end of the war, US planes dropped 2,756,941 tons of explosives on Cambodia. Much of the bombing was of military installations, but more than 10 per cent of it indiscriminately hit unknown targets, killing high numbers of civilians. The evidence submitted to the tribunal about the situation in Cambodia exposed this unknown story of a war that had illegally expanded beyond the territorial boundaries of Vietnam.[25]

The tribunal heard the first-person testimonies of several

witnesses on how the war had overrun the border between Vietnam and Cambodia. French journalist Bernard Couret submitted statistics that showed the increasing infringement of Cambodian territory: from 621 incidents in 1965 to 1,332 in 1966 to 1,395 in the ongoing year. Some of his claims were contentious. His report did not identify the source of the data, presumably the Cambodian government, and his dismissal of US accusations that the Viet Cong were running troops and supplies through Cambodia pointed to the possibly intentional limitations of his investigations. His eyewitness account included credible evidence, however, that US and South Vietnamese forces had repeatedly crossed the border into Cambodia, with deadly consequences. According to Washington, any bomb raids on the country were accidental. Absurd, retorted Couret. From his own experience flying over the region, it should be obvious to any pilot that a natural frontier formed by sugar palm trees differentiated Cambodia from the rice paddies of Vietnam. If that was insufficient for a foreign aviator, the people below offered further help by painting the roofs of their dwellings with the blue and red stripes of the Cambodian flag. Still the bombs fell from the skies; the result was a refugee crisis caused by civilians being forced to relocate from their rural borderland communities. Couret recalled his encounter with one of the tented facilities that provided temporary shelter: the absence of proper sanitation, the crowded bamboo trestles that provided a place to sleep, the bodies disfigured by burns from napalm or the cigarettes of South Vietnamese torturers.[26]

Other witnesses corroborated the claim that the US intentionally violated the territorial sovereignty of Cambodia. Wilfred Burchett was a veteran war reporter who had been the first Western journalist to witness the devastating impact caused by the atomic bomb dropped on Hiroshima. Partisan in his support of the North Vietnamese, he was still a highly respected member of the press who as a resident of Cambodia for the previous two years had seen at close hand the consequences of US bombing raids. If those incidents were caused by 'mistakes in map-reading', he informed the tribunal, then the US showed little capacity to learn from its errors. Burchett narrated numerous episodes, the most powerful of which was the US assault on the village of Chrak Kranh in February 1967. The reporter related how 'Every house was destroyed before they pulled out; every buffalo, pig and chicken that had remained were killed, fruit trees cut down. Incendiary grenades had been thrown into every building as they left, including the little school, the public health clinic and pagoda. Not a single building spared.'[27]

Tariq Ali told similar stories. As a member of the second investigative team, he had devoted several days to inspecting sites in Cambodia before travelling on to North Vietnam. All around the conference centre, eyes focused on him as he held the stage with a searing account of what he and his team members had witnessed. As they toured along the border, one village after another revealed its tragic tale: the inhabitants of Soc Noc tortured by US and South Vietnamese troops, the child in Ba Thuoc mutilated by napalm, the list of casualties at Ba Thou so long it would have taken hours to include every name. As with Couret and Burchett, Ali could not conceive how so many incidents might be inadvertent. 'There was no doubt in our minds,' he declared, 'that this was an absolutely deliberate attack.'[28]

Saturday 6 May. The centrepiece of the entire Stockholm session was the testimony of Vietnamese civilian victims of US bombing brought to the tribunal by representatives of the Hanoi regime. Some of these individuals had already appeared indirectly, through the reports of the investigators who visited them in hospital. Now the panellists had the opportunity to see how closely the real people aligned with the characters they had constructed in their imaginations.

Chairman Dedijer invited Léo Matarasso to introduce each witness in turn. In a flutter of bright light from flashing camera bulbs, they walked with some deliberation towards the stage where their names were chalked on blackboard for the benefit of Western reporters unfamiliar with Vietnamese spelling. The reason for their slowness of step soon became apparent.

The first witness to address the tribunal was Thai Binh Dun, the eighteen-year-old son of peasant farmers. Thai told of the events of fourteen months earlier, when his preparations for the evening meal had been interrupted by the sound of planes over-head. He ran immediately towards the nearest shelter but was too late to avoid the detonation of a napalm bomb. Thirteen days later, he awoke from a coma. The incendiary had burned his face, arms and legs, which were covered in keloids that restricted his movement including his ability to chew and swallow food. 'When the weather is cold,' said Thai through a translator, 'my scars harden and become purple and numb. When it is hot, the scars keep me from perspiring, pus collects, and my skin itches terribly when I'm asleep.' Despite his pain, he considered himself one of the luckier victims of the attack, since he was still alive.[29]

Next to speak was Nguyen Hong Phuong, a peasant farmer from Quang Nam province. He still bore the blisters from a US air raid that had left him hospitalised for two months. His hearing was also still impaired, as were the fingers on both his hands.[30]

Unsettling as these stories were, the testimony of the third witness was truly shocking. Hoang Tan Hung, the merchant farmer whose napalm injuries Charles Cobb and Julius Lester had so explicitly described, punctuated his story with dramatic pauses to allow its translation. Like the other witnesses, his life had been transformed in a moment. In his case, the planes had appeared while he was at the local market. There was the sound of an explosion followed by screaming and running as he realised his body was on fire. Then there was silence. The doctors could not heal Hoang's wounds that, cumbersomely removing his jacket and shirt, he now showed the tribunal. A phosphorous bomb had burned his body from the crown of the head to the shoulder blades. As he turned to face the tribunal members, the scale of mutilation became clearer, raw skin where there had once been hair, the left ear a mockery of the human form. Hoang also disclosed that his left arm was partially fused to his torso. The measured tone with which he had given his testimony surrendered to emotion. 'Today,' he said, 'I denounce before the Tribunal the barbaric crimes of the American imperialist aggressors, who have brought so much suffering to me and to my country.'[31]

There was more testimony to come. Next to the lectern was Ngo Thi Nga, a primary school teacher in her early twenties. Doctors had been unable to remove the steel pellet from a fragmentation bomb that had become lodged near her brain. Summoned towards the tribunal members by Dedijer, she leaned down to allow inspection of her surgical scars.[32]

In her testimony, Ngo recalled the screaming of the children under her care, children like Do Van Ngoc. The appearance of the nine-year-old son of peasants from Quang Ninh province was the single most unsettling moment of the tribunal. Standing centre stage, Do was instructed to remove his clothing. With his trousers tangled around his ankles, his small body was raised in the air and shown one by one to the panellists around the table. Cameras caught only moments of their grim faces as they gazed at the wounds that blighted Do's body. On the typewritten notes of his appearance someone later added a handwritten note that summed up the mood: the testimony of this horribly scarred child 'was the most moving I have heard'.[33]

Following their testimony, the Vietnamese witnesses posed for group photographs. Ngo Thi Nga placed a protective arm around Do Van Ngoc, the young boy gazing at the cameras with the same disconcertingly blank stare he had throughout his appearance at the tribunal.

The involvement of the Vietnamese civilians in proceedings raised important ethical issues for the intellectuals and philosophers on the panel. The world media was forced to confront the humanity of ordinary people caught up in the conflict; men, women and children wounded by weapons the US insisted it was not using in attacks it denied had taken place. The experience did as much, however, to undermine as to emphasise the witnesses' personalities. Parading them on a stage objectified them as specimens of human suffering both pitiable and inspirational for their endurance of pain. The tension may not have been possible to resolve. As important was that none of the panellists wrestled publicly with whether they should try. It was left for them to ponder privately whether they had crossed the line between documenting the war in all its detail and exploiting the suffering of others for their own political purpose.

The next two days of testimony focused on medical reports about the human suffering caused by the conflict. Jean-Pierre Vigier had documented at length the use of fragmentation bombs against North Vietnamese civilians, but said little about the nature of the injuries they caused. Joe Neilands from the third investigative team filled in the details. The biochemist had consulted the hospital records of many victims. His testimony listed a succession of cases, from the farmer with a pellet lodged in the left side of his skull who could no longer walk to the housewife paralysed by a wound to the base of her brain.[34]

Swedish physicians John Takman and Axel Höjer recounted their tour only weeks before, through the ruins of villages laid to waste by bombing. Their narrative contained what was by now a familiar abundance of detail: the flattened and cratered landscape, the charred rubble that had once been buildings, the bereaved adults and orphaned children. What set apart the story was the professional expertise with which the two doctors examined civilian victims, most of them suffering injuries from fragmentation bombs. While full of praise for the efforts made by North Vietnamese medical teams to treat the wounded, their account was unsparing in its description of the afflictions that caused their hospitalisation. Men, women and children, they told the tribunal, were being admitted with 'chronic disabilities', typically 'in a state of shock with many pellet holes in their intestines, bones shattered, soft tissue pierced'.[35]

French surgeon Jean-Michel Krivine had travelled to many of the same locations as the Swedish doctors, and his narrative mapped closely onto theirs. Precise in detail and dispassionate in tone, his words were all the more powerful for eschewing the occasional rhetorical excess of the previous speakers.[36]

The last of the medical reports was also the most unsettling. Where the other doctors had provided a panoramic picture of North Vietnam, French physician Marcel-Francis Kahn produced an intimate portrait of a single institution, the leper colony in the province of Nghe An. When the first bombs fell in the early morning of 12 June 1965, officials reassured themselves that it must be a mistake. Reconnaissance planes had flown over the colony many times and could not have failed to observe the red cross painted on the roof of the hospital. The error, however, was theirs. A day later, more planes appeared in the sky. Their deadly cargo took the lives of 139 people and wounded many more. Administrators ordered the evacuation of patients to nearby caves, but the planes infiltrated that refuge, too. Further attacks on the colony occurred during the following days. By the time they had finished, none of its buildings remained undamaged. Kahn had travelled to the remote valley that was supposed to provide a safe place for the colony and made his way across hollowed earth to the remains of the hospital. 'The fragments of walls still intact were riddled with shell holes and round holes which we thought to be caused by machine-guns and 20mm cannons. Here and there, we found the twisted debris of medical implements, some old bottles which had contained antibiotics, plus a bed frame of hospital design.' At the nearby cemetery, bombs had fallen with such force as to raise the dead from the ground.[37]

The tribunal had called the last witness. For almost a week the members had watched, read and listened to a succession of eyewitness accounts, photographs, films and written reports. It would be another twenty-four hours before the members reconvened to announce their decision.

Wednesday 10 May. Even though the denouement had never been in doubt, there was more than a touch of drama to the occasion. The tribunal members had spent the previous day in private deliberation. Now the conference centre hummed with activity as they took their seats. Lights beamed, camera lenses focused, microphone tests sounded one last time before the room settled into expectant silence. Jean-Paul Sartre leaned forward in his seat, his eyes on the script in front of him. Speaking slowly and emphatically, he read aloud the decisions of the tribunal.

'Has the government of the United States committed acts of aggression against Vietnam under international law?' Sartre paused. 'The answer is yes.' 'Has there been bombardment of targets of a purely civilian character?' 'Yes.' The United States had committed these war crimes, he continued, not only in Vietnam but also Cambodia. 'Have the governments of Australia, New Zealand and South Korea been accomplices of the United States in the aggression against Vietnam in violation of international law?' Once more, 'Yes.' The conclusions of the tribunal were, in all three instances, other than one unidentified dissenter on the issue of Cambodia, unanimous. Sartre and the other tribunal members looked solemnly around the room. Dedijer beat a gavel on the table in front of them. There was a brief lull before the conference centre burst into applause.

What remained to be seen was whether the world was not only listening but also agreed with what it heard.[38]

Sartre and his fellow panellists had presented a united front in their condemnation of US war crimes. Behind the scenes, however, the tribunal had faltered close to collapse. That it had endured long enough to deliver its verdict was a victory in itself, given what was going on away from the cameras.

The large personalities of some of the tribunal members caused problems. A harmonious mood prevailed most of the time; many of the panellists were friends or admired one another by reputation, all shared a sense of common purpose. Seating so many large egos around one table, however, was almost an act of incitement.

In front of the cameras, the tribunal members comported themselves with a calm sense of deliberation compelled by the occasion. There were exceptions. Rising to his feet during formal introductions, a nervous Carl Oglesby became tangled in his microphone wires. Announcing himself by name and nationality, he sat down and assisted Simone de Beauvoir, who was also ensnared in electric cable. 'I object!' bellowed the chairman Vladimir Dedijer, to silence around the table. His issue was that Oglesby had called himself an American rather than a citizen of the United States. 'People from Cuba are Americans!' he proclaimed. 'People from Canada are Americans! People from Brazil, from Ecuador, from Peru, from Mexico, they are all Americans!' Oglesby met the glare of the chairman but said nothing, inching his chair away in tactical retreat. The introductions continued. 'David Dellinger,' announced the next American around the table, 'from the United States.'[39]

After this less than auspicious start, proceedings ran relatively smoothly. The one serious interruption came from Amado Hernandez. Overcome by emotion, he attempted on three separate occasions to denounce the US government as murderers. Each time, Dedijer and Sartre interceded, but US reporters seized on the outbursts as evidence of the crude anti-Americanism behind the impartial demeanour of the tribunal members.[40]

That incident revealed the crucial rule of conduct respected by the tribunal members. Whatever their opinions about the order of proceedings and what was said, Sartre was indisputably in charge. Courtland Cox, who stood outside the hierarchy of European intellectual culture, found the deference towards the philosopher unnerving if entertaining. The least pronouncement from the tribunal president would, he recalled, prompt de Beauvoir to lead a refrain of '*D'accord! D'accord!*'[41]

Regardless of their role or reputation, everyone at the tribunal understood that they were supporting players to one star performer. Everyone, that was, other than Ralph Schoenman. The tension caused by his tactless treatment of others became all the more acute now that he stood in front of the camera. In the estimation of one broadcaster, Schoenman saw himself as 'impresario, stage manager and star rolled into one', an impression emphasised by his puffing imperiously on a cigar while Sartre read his opening statement. That overbearing behaviour caused a commotion even before the start of the tribunal, when he scolded Swedish Prime Minister Tage Erlander for not formally welcoming the tribunal to his country. Given that Erlander had not wanted the event held in Stockholm, this should have been no surprise – but it was in any case not even true. The premier might have been frustrated with the liberalism of Swedish free-dom-of-speech laws, but he had not forgotten his manners.[42]

Determined that Schoenman should cause no further embarrassment, Dedijer appointed four tribunal members – Mehmet Ali Aybar, David Dellinger, Isaac Deutscher and Laurent Schwartz – as official spokespersons. The move did not silence him, and nor did Schoenman show any more deference when he tried to take a seat among his fellow panellists at the start of proceedings. By this time, many of those around the table were becoming infuriated with his lack of courtesy. Even his face became a source of irritation. According to de Beauvoir, 'he was the only man I have ever met who hid his chin under a beard not to mask the weakness of his features but on the con-trary to hide their stubborn arrogance.'[43]

The peremptory tone with which Schoenman issued instruc-tions purportedly from Russell pushed the panellists beyond the limits of their patience. Grabbing Schoenman by the lapels, Dedijer pushed him against a wall and pressed his hands into his neck. Depending on the source, he either bared his teeth at the suffocating American or took a bite out of him.[44]

When Schoenman contacted Russell with his version of events, the philosopher went on the offensive. 'I know of your physical attack on Ralph Schoenman,' he informed Dedijer, 'during which you tried to strangle him and bite his head.' Russell also accused the tribunal chairman of other incidents of 'uncontrollable temper, screaming fits and threats of physical violence' towards Peace Foundation staff. In the circumstances, he had no choice but to demand Dedijer resign. 'I appreciate that you are an ill man,' Russell wrote. 'This seems to make mandatory your withdrawal.' The philosopher contacted other tribunal members in the hope of persuading them to pressure Dedijer into stepping down. 'In the event that he does not do so,' he insisted to Lawrence Daly, 'I urge that he must be unseated.' Confined to his home in the remote Welsh countryside, however, Russell found to his frustration that he no longer commanded the same influence. One after another, the tribunal members made clear that they took the opposing side in the schism. Sartre and Laurent Schwartz wrote a letter to Russell in which they claimed that Dedijer had been badly misrepresented. Isaac Deutscher also rebuffed Russell. Privately he considered Dedijer 'tactless and inept', but publicly his removal from the chairmanship would 'provoke too much gleeful hostile comment' from an already antagonistic press.[45] The power struggle between Russell and the rest of the tribunal was torturously slow, being handled almost entirely by letters that sometimes crossed in the mail or were lost altogether. Deutscher regretted that Sartre did not lead a deputation to Russell's Plas Penrhyn home to resolve the dispute, allowing tensions to linger in the months between the tribunal sessions in Stockholm and Roskilde. That Sartre did not deem it necessary revealed much about the shifting balance of power within the tribunal.[46]

Disputes over money also threatened the future of the tribunal. Russell had raised most of the finances, but on the understanding that the money was a loan and not a donation. He therefore took exception when members wrote to him for reimbursement of their expenses. In a letter of 4 May, the philosopher informed them that the tribunal was supposed to be financially independent of the Peace Foundation – yet here they were, having made no effort to raise the necessary capital and looking to him to reach once more into his now empty pockets. That accusation was not entirely accurate. According to the CIA, one of the local organisers, academic Joachim Israel, had remortgaged his home to cover the deficit between what Russell had paid and the cost of the tribunal. The situation became even more strained when Schoenman handed administrative staff an invoice. According to this document, the cost of the event was £25,000. The problem, as tribunal members pointed out, was the absence of any itemised list of expenses, without which there was no way to determine the accuracy of the demand. The confrontation soured the taste of the refreshments served at a closing reception for the tribunal members and fuelled an exchange of angry letters between Russell and Laurent Schwartz, in which the Frenchman protested the failure to comply with repeated requests for proper accounting. There had, he wrote, never been any intention not to reimburse Russell. How much of the loan was repaid remains unclear, but it was sufficient for the philosopher to offer support for the second meeting of the tribunal in Denmark.[47]

Russell had written not only in anger but in despair. The resentment of the tribunal members towards Schoenman had also led them to decide that their main administrative office should be relocated from London to Paris. In an act of more than symbolic importance, they agreed to drop the philosopher's name from the official title of what was now referred to as the International War Crimes Tribunal. Only Amado Hernandez and Mahmud Ali Kasuri had dissented, although a despairing Isaac Deutscher walked out of the meeting without casting a vote. Without a word having been spoken between them, Russell had ceded control of the tribunal to Sartre. Russell was far from giving up his fight against the war, but Plas Penrhyn had never seemed so far from the rest of the world.[48]

9

SECOND SESSION: ROSKILDE

For the restless couple, it was a rare moment to reflect on their life together. They had first come here twenty years earlier, in the fullest flush of their fame. The building had lost a little of its elegance, having been used as regional headquarters of the German High Command during the war, but Simone de Beauvoir and Jean-Paul Sartre had happy memories of the Hotel d'Angleterre from their first visit to Copenhagen. The stroll through the city to Kongens Nytorv where the splendidly restored neoclassical building stood was therefore a sentimental journey.

Sartre and de Beauvoir had not returned to the Danish capital merely to retrace the steps of their former lives. The nostalgic saunter along the canal and the pedestrianised shopping precinct was a welcome relief from their responsibilities at the second session of the international war crimes tribunal. It was not only the harrowing testimony from which they sought escape but also the stifling atmosphere of the place that hosted them. The tribunal met not in Copenhagen but twenty miles west, in the smaller city of Roskilde. That location had its attractions, but its provincialism nonetheless made the short distance to the cosmopolitan capital seem much greater. As de Beauvoir admitted, 'the idea of being shut up day and night in a place the size of Roskilde had very little charm for me'. Choosing to stay in Copenhagen did not entirely solve her discomfort. Other than the tediousness of the daily commute to and from Roskilde, she was taken aback by the high cost of living in a city where the coffee cost twice the price in Paris but tasted half as good.[1]

That was of some concern to Sartre and de Beauvoir, since caffeine (rather than the 'indigestible sandwiches') was what sustained them through the long sessions.[2] The start of the tribunal was no less stodgy with the reappearance of familiar faces repeating similar information about the war. But over the course of eleven days it built momentum, culminating in a contentious discussion of whether the US was committing genocide in Vietnam. Sartre's indictment of US foreign policy was to prove one of the most powerful but divisive public statements ever made about the war.

The Roskilde meeting of the international war crimes tribunal took place in a trade union building between 20 November and 1 December 1967.[3] Much had happened in the six months since the Stockholm session. The war had continued to escalate, bombing raids proliferating in number and intensity, the number of ground troops exceeding half a million. Opposition to the war had also increased, with demonstrations not only in the United States but around the world. The tribunal had contributed to that cause by sending two more investigative teams to collect evidence in North Vietnam. In August, the Tokyo tribunal running on parallel lines to the London and Paris teams reached its own unanimous decision that the US had committed war crimes.[4]

The US government was, as ever, watching these events closely. While the Japanese tribunal had little impact in the West, the CIA conceded that it had been a domestic propaganda success.[5] The agency also monitored the planning of a sequel to the Stockholm event. Having intercepted a communication that disclosed Denmark as the host country, it liaised with the US Embassy in Copenhagen for on-the-ground information, while the State Department continued to observe the overseas movements of US citizens involved in the tribunal.[6]

Roskilde was far from the first choice of location. The Cuban government had offered to host the event in Havana, but that had been declined as unnecessarily antagonistic towards the United States.[7] That was also true of the permission given by the Polish government to meet at Auschwitz, a symbolic choice that would have appealed to Bertrand Russell who likened the current administration in Washington with the Nazis, while offending almost everyone else. Denmark was a shrewder political option. As a founding member of NATO in 1949, the country was a close ally of the United States and its hosting of the tribunal was harder to dismiss as a propaganda stunt by a hostile nation. The Social Democratic administration of Jens Otto Krag shared the Swedish Prime Minister Tage Erlander's reservations about the event but had similarly succumbed to political pressure from grassroots supporters. Keeping the tribunal away from the capital was a careful balancing of competing domestic and foreign needs, respecting freedom-of-speech laws on one hand while maintaining distance to appease Washington on the other.

With the location and date of the second session secured, the tribunal organisers faced another familiar problem. Raising the funds to cover an estimated budget of over £40,000 was no easy matter; thankfully, the tribunal members were able to look to their wealthy friends in the world of art and culture.

Those who answered the call included Pablo Picasso. The artist, who had long been associated with the international peace movement, had made clear his specific opposition to US military intervention in the 1951 painting *Massacre in Korea* and more recently by allowing anti-war activists to appropriate his Spanish

Civil War masterpiece *Guernica* as a symbol of opposition to the Vietnam conflict. Picasso would have made an illustrious addition to the tribunal, but at the age of eighty-six he would probably have declined had Russell or Sartre invited him. What he did, however, was to raise the needed revenue through the auction of some of his artwork. Without this financial support, the first session of the tribunal might have been the last.[8]

When the tribunal members once more took up their seats around the table, there were some conspicuous absences. Courtland Cox once more stood in on behalf of Stokely Carmichael, although the Black Power leader would make a belated and much contested appearance. Japanese lawyer Kinju Morikawa also substituted for the unavailable Shoichi Sakata. The other changes to the composition of the panel aroused the most public attention. First of these was Isaac Deutscher, who had died of a heart attack after travelling to Rome for a television broadcast in August. The other loss was less lamented; to the relief of almost everyone, Ralph Schoenman did not attend the Roskilde meeting, the US State Department having used an unauthorised visit to North Vietnam as reason to revoke his passport. Schoenman did not let this stop him twice attempting to enter Denmark, but immigration officials put him on the first flight out of their country. Tellingly, when Russell's secretary tried to contact the tribunal organisers, there was no reply. According to the CIA, the reaction of Sartre and his associates to news of Schoenman's deportation 'ranged from outright pleasure to unconcern'. So strong was the animosity towards him that the agency even suspected some of the tribunal members of colluding with Danish authorities to deny him entry.[9] The mood in Roskilde was seldom light-hearted, but at least the tension was not between the tribunal members. Simone de Beauvoir spoke for them all that it was 'so much the better' to focus on the evidence without fighting among one another.[10]

The Roskilde session coincided with the start of winter in Denmark, the temperature tolerably above freezing but chilled by southerly winds blowing from the Baltic Sea. Anyone who had attended the first session of the tribunal could be forgiven for thinking as they stepped inside the Roskilde venue that they were back in Stockholm. The wooden folding chairs for the audience were less comfortable than the seats at the Folkets Hus, but otherwise the room looked much the same. Cigarette and pipe smoke once more filled the space, billowing above the members of the international news media in the balcony. Other than a pensive Vladimir Dedijer, the mood of the tribunal members also seemed a little lighter, each of them now familiar with the others and without the threat of another outburst from Ralph Schoenman.[11]

In Stockholm, the tribunal determined that the United States had committed an illegal act of aggression against North Vietnam and that its military forces were deliberately targeting civilians, often with the use of prohibited weapons. The Roskilde session sought answers to three further questions. First, had US armed forces' treatment of Vietnamese prisoners of war breached international law? Second, had they similarly contravened the rights of the civilian population? The third line of inquiry was the most momentous. Based on all the evidence heard at both sessions of the tribunal, did the crimes attributed to the US constitute genocide?

The days leading towards that dramatic summation were at times frustratingly slow. Sartre and de Beauvoir worried that the tribunal was treading in its own footsteps rather than pioneering into new territory. There were numerous reports documenting the devastating impact of biological and chemical weapons, each of them delivered by persons with impeccable professional credentials and scientifically precise, but none adding much that was conceptually new. By the time Japanese scientists discussed their testing of chemicals on every kind of vegetable, the law of diminishing returns had long since set in.[12] The same was true of eyewitness accounts. While the escalation of bombing had increased the scale of human suffering, there was little other than the level of detail to be learned from stories of one more town or village reduced to ruins.

De Beauvoir used the time between sessions to rouse herself from compassion fatigue. She had done much the same in Stockholm, strolling around the cobbled streets of its historical centre, her libertarian sensibilities tested to the limit by the 'staggeringly specific' pornography in display windows. If she assumed sleepier Roskilde would afford fewer surprises, she was wrong. Stepping inside a local newsagents, she was startled by 'a display of more remarkable books than those which had astonished me in Stockholm'. When the elderly lady who ran the establishment offered to ask her granddaughter for advice on specific titles, de Beauvoir scurried back to the tribunal.[13] She found more comfort in the social activities that filled the evenings following another intensive day of evidence. Carl Oglesby recalled a hectic round of parties, one at a mansion where guests sipped champagne while listening to a string trio perform Mozart and another more raucous affair on a houseboat, this time with live music from a rock band. It was here that de Beauvoir found a diversion from the burden of the tribunal by dancing the twist with Peter Weiss. Sartre stood to one side. Not only did he have no reason to be jealous but he was himself surrounded by an entourage of young female anti-war activists more enamoured with the content of his speech than the style of his dance step.[14]

Even amid the revelries there were worrying reminders of

the controversy and danger in which the tribunal members had placed themselves. Sitting in a restaurant one afternoon, de Beauvoir was startled by sudden bangs. Someone had detonated two small explosives in the passageway outside. De Beauvoir was stoical about the matter. She and Sartre had been sent similar warnings in their home city because of their outspoken support of Algerian independence. The moral urgency to end the war meant the tribunal must go on.[15]

The tribunal not only continued but also assumed a new momentum, due to the presence on the witness stand of three Vietnam vets. Former servicemen would later become a core element of the anti-war movement, but the organisation Vietnam Veterans Against the War had been founded only five months earlier in New York; this was therefore a coup for the tribunal. The testimonies made were among the first public appearances by military veterans who wanted not only to condemn the war but also to atone for their personal complicity.[16]

The first former American serviceman to testify was David Kenneth Tuck, a twenty-five-year-old postal worker from Cleveland, Ohio, who had served in the 35th Infantry Regiment between January 1966 and February 1967.[17]

Gisèle Halimi, a lawyer and an additional member of the panel, led his examination. Halimi had become a longtime associate of de Beauvoir since collaborating in defence of torture victims during the Algerian War. Her first line of questioning focused on the abuse of prisoners. Tuck provided a series of episodes, including the pushing of one captive out of a helicopter after he had laughed at the dead body of a US soldier. Halimi asked whether the soldier responsible had to account for the missing prisoner. Yes, replied Tuck, but it was a simple matter to report that he had taken his own life.

Halimi pursued her examination. In all the cases discussed by the witness, were he and his fellow soldiers acting on orders to shoot prisoners rather than capture them alive?

'We were ordered to shoot,' insisted Tuck, 'to take no prisoners just as a matter of standard operating policy.' Many soldiers abided by the mantra that 'the only good Vietnamese was a dead Vietnamese'.

Halimi turned to a particularly macabre practice, the cutting off of ears as souvenirs of military victory. It was a fleeting craze, responded Tuck, but yes, it had happened. 'The person who had the most ears was considered the number one V.C. killer, and also when we would get back to base camp, the one who had the most ears would get all the free beer and whiskey that they could drink.'

Halimi moved on to other matters including the conditions in refugee camps and the indiscriminate shooting of civilians. The course of her inquiries advanced determinedly towards the issue of genocide. 'Can you say, if, before battle, your officers' words indicated that they wished you to fight a purely defensive war, or that they wished you to exterminate the Vietnamese people?'

Tuck replied that his instructions in training were clear. The US was sending troops overseas to liberate the people of Vietnam from the tyranny of communism. Soldiers should at all times respect the rights of the indigenous population. When he reached the war front, however, the attitude of officers was entirely different. Soldier or civilian, man or woman, adult or child, the Vietnamese were 'gooks'. The army had no interest in winning their hearts and minds, only imposing military control. It was a shocking moment of revelation for the young soldier: 'all at once it came to me that perhaps these people were going to practice genocide after all.'

There followed a torrent of questions from the tribunal members. Peter Weiss pushed Tuck on the incidents he had described of US soldiers disposing of wounded prisoners. How representative were they of what was going on across the country?

'This happened all the time in Vietnam,' avowed the witness.

'Is it a rule?' Weiss pressed him.

'Yes.'

Günther Anders wanted to know whether soldiers acted on direct orders to shoot prisoners. The command was only spoken, responded Tuck, and there were exceptions made, especially of enemy officers. But, yes, troops were acting on instructions. Anders also elicited laughter around the table by teasing Tuck about the anatomical trophies taken from dead prisoners. Did soldiers ever send the ears home to their families? Not that Tuck had ever heard. 'He just showed the ear to get his free beer?' Anders concluded, to the amusement of the other tribunal members.

There had been considerable tension in Stockholm over whether the tribunal should address the issue of racism within the US Army. Courtland Cox had felt frustrated with the indifference of some of the white panellists around the table. Sartre saw an opportunity to make amends by asking Tuck, who was Black, about the disproportionate deployment of African American troops to front-line combat duties. Not all Black soldiers were conscious of discrimination, answered Tuck, but some of them shared an affinity with the Vietnamese for their victimhood.

The tribunal members pressed on with their interrogation but with little purpose other than to refine points of detail. The appearance of Peter Martinsen transformed the witness stand into a confessional stall. Now in his early twenties, he

had enlisted in the army while still a teenager. Trained as a prisoner-of-war interrogator, he travelled with the 541st Military
Intelligence Detachment to Vietnam in September 1966, and
his service over the following ten months earned him numerous
decorations while coming at a cost to his conscience. On his
return home, Martinsen had enrolled as a psychology student at
the University of California, Berkeley, where he was researching
a paper on 'guilt manifestations caused by war crimes'. His testimony to the tribunal was not only an indictment of the US war
machine but an act of atonement. It came at personal sacrifice
too, his family having threatened to cut off his inheritance.[18]

Under examination by Halimi, Martinsen recounted a series
of incidents in which he witnessed or was actively involved in
the torture of prisoners. The first had occurred within weeks of
his arrival in Vietnam. Frustrated with a prisoner who refused
to admit being a member of the Viet Cong, Martinsen had hit
him. When that failed to force a confession, a lieutenant had
administered an electric shock to the detainee's genitals using
the wires of a field telephone. Martinsen told more stories: of
the application of bamboo splinters under fingernails, of his
holding a prisoner at gunpoint and ordering him to dig his own
grave, of another captive who died of heart failure after being
electrocuted. No method for extracting information was out of
bounds, Martinsen told the tribunal, so long as the interrogator left no lasting physical marks on the person in their custody.
'We had absolute power over our prisoners – absolute power, we
were the judge, jury and the god.'

The tribunal had many questions for Martinsen, and there
was nuance to his answers. While female prisoners were not
immune from torture, there were limits to their interrogation.
Asked by Sara Lidman to elaborate on the cross-examination of
a mother while she breastfed her baby, Martinsen replied that

there had been no attempt at physical intimidation. 'Did the woman talk?' asked Lidman. Not to their satisfaction, Martinsen responded, but the soldiers had allowed her to leave. Nor was he aware of any child being tortured. His answers to most queries all the same created an impression of a US military acting with little legal or ethical restraint. Were interrogators aware of the legal rights of their prisoners? No. Did any of them refuse an order to use physical force? No. Was the use of torture common practice? Yes. Were senior officers aware of what was going on? Yes. Was it easier to cause harm because the Vietnamese were seen as less than human? Yes. His most telling replies were in answer to Carl Oglesby and David Dellinger, who asked whether torture actually worked. No, he said.

The tribunal saved until last the most publicly prominent of the three erstwhile servicemen. In January 1966, RCA Victor released a single by Staff Sergeant Barry Sadler that became a surprise number one on the Billboard Hot 100. To the beat of a military drum, 'Ballad of the Green Berets' sang of the selfless heroism of the United States Army Special Forces. When Sadler performed the song on television, studio audiences applauded almost every line as his baritone voice intoned the 'Fighting soldiers from the sky/ Fearless men who jump and die'. It was a comfort for the American people to know these elite troops protected the interests of their country around the world. According to the next witness, Donald Duncan, it was also an illusion.[19]

Within weeks of Sadler scaling the pop charts, Duncan appeared on the front cover of *Ramparts* magazine dressed in military uniform, arms folded tight across his chest and troubled eyes looking deep into the camera lens. Above him, two words translated his expression: 'I quit!' On the inside pages, Duncan told a tale about his time in the Special Forces that bluntly contrasted with the 'Ballad of the Green Berets'. It was that experience to which he testified at the tribunal.[20]

Duncan became a member of the Special Forces in 1961. A master sergeant in the field of operations and intelligence, he served in Vietnam between March 1964 and September 1965, receiving numerous decorations. He had also been commended for his briefings to civilian and military leaders, including Secretary of Defense Robert McNamara and General William Westmoreland, the commander of military forces in Vietnam. But the war had caused him to become completely disillusioned. Approached to write an official history of the Special Forces, he had pored through daily intelligence reports only to discover that they were 'pure fabrication'. Resigning from the army, he had written an altogether different book, a tell-all account of his time in Vietnam. His crusade to reveal what he believed was the truth about the US war effort had brought him to testify in Roskilde.[21]

Gisèle Halimi once more led the examination of the witness. Much of what Duncan said in response corroborated the testimony of the other American servicemen. In mastering the techniques of interrogation, 'we were encouraged to use our imagination'. According to Duncan the methods for forcing information from prisoners included beating buckets placed over their heads, spinning bodies suspended in the air by chains tied to the ceiling and numerous forms of genital torture, including the use of telephone wires mentioned by Peter Martinsen. Duncan also agreed with his fellow former soldier that the army sanctioned any procedure provided the prisoner sustained no permanently identifiable wound.

While American soldiers were more than able to inflict pain on prisoners, Duncan asserted that few of them possessed the linguistic skills to conduct interrogations; it was far more routine for them to observe while a South Vietnamese soldier tried to force confessions. In those cases, Americans implicitly sanctioned torture by choosing to 'turn their backs, light a cigarette, you know, until the nastiness was over'. Duncan also recalled times when prisoners had suffered more than flesh wounds. He admitted that in combat situations, detainees could be an encumbrance – and in such instances a bullet could ease the burden.

The tribunal was as interested in why Duncan had decided to testify as what he had to say. The common criticism of the investigative teams sent to Vietnam was they only searched for evidence that validated their conviction the US was committing war crimes, but Duncan and the other servicemen were different; they had gone to Vietnam in the belief that they would be welcomed by an indigenous population who wanted to be liberated from the threat of communist rule, but they had returned home disillusioned. Decorated veterans, their testimony had far more potential to influence public opinion in the United States than any foreign peaceniks, and the tribunal wanted those words spelled out as boldly and plainly as possible.

'Mr Duncan,' asked de Beauvoir, 'could you explain to the Tribunal what has brought you here today?'

Duncan replied that his perception of the war had been transformed by his role in the planning and implementation of Project DELTA. That mission had taken him into some of the most remote rural areas of South Vietnam in search of operational intelligence. What he had learned was that the Vietnamese people perceived Americans not as protectors but oppressors.

Vladimir Dedijer encouraged him to elaborate. The more he had learned about the war, answered Duncan, the less he believed what was said about it in Washington. President Johnson wanted the American people to support military action without providing the facts to allow for an informed decision. He had told the electorate that troops were 'getting ready to come home' while new military bases were under construction. The president had also misrepresented the nature of the actions taken by US forces. 'He was talking about infiltration from North Vietnam, and here in fact I was very closely involved with an operation where we were infiltrating North Vietnam.'

Further to the appearances of the three former servicemen, the tribunal also heard the recorded depositions made by other American soldiers who Halimi had met on a fact-finding mission to the United States. Their stories revealed more detail of the macabre creativity of interrogation practices. One told of a prisoner forced to lie under the wheels of a truck that was then driven over him, another of a detainee lowered repeatedly into a canal until he nearly drowned. Other narratives emphasised a practice of shooting first and asking questions later. As with the other veterans' testimonies, the power of these narratives rested in the tellers of these terrible stories also being the protagonists.[22]

The testimony of the US servicemen was compelling, but there remained the matter of how representative their stories were of the broader soldier experience in Vietnam. In their questions, the tribunal had tried hard to determine whether the witnesses' stories were typical of a conflict that had spiralled beyond any notion of a just war. Had US forces abandoned the basic principle that military action must be necessary and proportionate? Did they bother to distinguish between enemy combatants and civilians, or had the line been blurred as they battled an unwinnable war? If the Vietnamese had become indiscriminate targets, was the US stumbling towards genocide?

One of the main witnesses who addressed these issues was

Dr Erich Wulff.[23] The West German physician had worked in a medical mission at the hospital in the South Vietnamese city of Hue for six years. His opening statements to the tribunal presented another perspective on a country ruined by war through the use of medical metaphor. So scarred was its terrain with bomb craters that 'the landscape resembles a human skin that suffers from smallpox'. Chemical weapons had stripped the countryside of flora and fauna to the point that it resembled a 'blanket of death'. Wulff turned to the search-and-destroy missions in which helicopters transported US troops into remote rural communities suspected of harbouring Viet Cong. The appalling impact of these raids would not become clear for another two years, when the media broke the story of the My Lai massacre. That incident was beyond the scale of anything described by Wulff. His account of examining men and women arrested during an assault on their village was nonetheless an early warning of the arbitrary arrest and abuse of non-combatants. The doctor had assessed an imprisoned farmer from the rural district of Quang Dien who falsely confessed to collaborating with the Viet Cong after torture by his captors. He also appraised a young woman arrested in another raid who suffered similar treatment – and she too signed a pre-written statement. There were around fifty other people who Wulff saw; no more than two or three were involved in the warfare. Most 'were simple peasants who lived quietly at home, and whose only wrong was of not having fled in time'.

Wulff also observed that the limited success of search-and-destroy missions had led to the forced resettlement of entire communities in an attempt to pacify the countryside. The doctor placed the number of displaced persons at around two million, but he suggested it could be double that figure. Other witnesses had described physical conditions in refugee centres. Relocation caused a loss of not only income to farming families, stressed Wulff, but also their way of life. Removing villagers from their homes was entirely counterproductive, sacrificing what the war was intended to save.

The most pointed observation made by Wulff came at the end of his testimony. American military intervention in Vietnam was descending in a downward spiral. US forces had come to the country believing that they were there to protect the indigenous population from communist takeover, but their arrival had been unwelcome. The peasant farmers of South Vietnam regarded them – rather than the National Liberation Front – as the intruders. For many US soldiers, this had induced a sense of alienation and betrayal that soured into 'a kind of aggressive racism' towards the entire Vietnamese people. US troops took out their anger on the Vietnamese, who in turn became more hostile, fuelling crueller acts of recrimination. The effect was disastrous.

'There are many other things that I might tell you,' Wulff closed. 'But I think that this perhaps would not bring much that is new to the Tribunal.' His earlier words, though, had left the tribunal with much to muse on.

Simone de Beauvoir and Melba Hernández wanted to know more about the relocation of civilians. Wulff reiterated that the policy had the opposite impact to what was intended, in some instances converting a peasant population that wanted to stay out of the conflict into supporters of the National Liberation Front.

Some of the other questions returned to points that Wulff had not thought worth repeating, particularly concerning the use of chemical and biological weapons that the tribunal had heard so much about in Stockholm. But then Carl Oglesby steered the line of inquiry back towards the last observation that the doctor had made in his statement about the coarsening of American attitudes towards the Vietnamese.

'I wonder if you could comment – it may be a difficult question – on the strategic change, if any, that you've seen over the period in the conduct of the war by the Americans.'

Wulff reiterated what he had said about a loosening of restraint in the treatment of the civilian population, with a seemingly limitless increase in armed raids and aerial bombardments.

Oglesby pushed harder. 'The question has been put to the Tribunal whether the American troops, perhaps, might have committed acts which would be called genocide in Vietnam.' Was it the doctor's conviction 'that the Americans, because of the techniques of their war and in order to attain military success, might fight against everything which lives, everything which moves? And if this could not be called a war against an entire population rather than a war against a military enemy.'

'Well,' responded Wulff, 'I think I would affirm this, but in a certain form.' He returned to the point that this may not have been the intention but was certainly the effect of the increasingly desperate tactics used by the US military to expel the National Liberation Front from the countryside. 'Most Americans in Vietnam do not realise conceptually, that this is what they are doing; in fact they are.'

The tribunal had time to mull that response during a much-needed recess.

Wulff had seen the fallout from search-and-destroy missions, but not been there when the helicopters had landed and the soldiers stormed a village. The subsequent witness, Jean Bertolino, was an esteemed war correspondent whose reports from the front lines of Vietnam had earlier that year won him the Albert Londres Prize, the highest accolade in French journalism. He had travelled with American troops on a raid in the Mekong Delta region during December 1966. The helicopters fired rockets on the straw huts and opened fire on anyone who ran from the flaming homes, while soldiers on the ground searched for suspects. Fires burned in hearths, water boiled on stoves, but most of the huts were empty, the peasant families having fled through a series of tunnels. Without checking whether any villagers were inside these escape routes, one of the soldiers systematically threw hand grenades into the entrances. Bertolino reassured himself that he heard no human cry from inside the tunnels. 'Later I had proof to the contrary.' Other than the smoking ruins of a small community, US troops had little to show from the assault, except for the arrest of four elderly and unarmed men they had found hiding in a haystack.[24]

Bertolino was also more broadly scathing of Operation Cedar Falls. This was a massive ground operation launched by the US military in January 1967, with the aim of expelling the National Liberation Front from its stronghold in the Iron Triangle region northwest of Saigon. The American top brass boasted of the success of the action, which resulted in the deaths of 720 enemy soldiers and capture or defection of hundreds more, as well as the seizure of arms and the destruction of the tunnel system used to manoeuvre troops without detection. What Bertolino saw instead was irreparable harm to US efforts to win the hearts and minds of the Vietnamese. The campaign had caused the destruction of entire villages, the deportation of their inhabitants to strategic hamlets and the defoliation of swathes of forest. 'All was shattered, burned, and crushed under the tons of bombs, under the caterpillars of tanks and the giant shovels of the bulldozers.' Bertolino had reached the same conclusion as Wulff. In their determination to root out an elusive enemy, the US Army had lost sight of its larger objective to secure South Vietnam as a strategic ally against the global spread of communism.

The tribunal had the opportunity to see what Wulff and Bertolino had described with the screening of an extract from a forthcoming documentary by film-makers Joris Ivens and Marceline Loridon. *17th Parallel: Vietnam in War* documented the destructive impact of US military action both on the physical landscape and also, through first-person testimonies, on the psyche of the populace. Its polemical point was the same as what the previous two witnesses had said. Even if one accepted the dubious claim that US forces were winning the military fight, they had already lost any prospect of securing the loyalty of ordinary civilians.[25]

Other witnesses made similar observations. Some of the most arresting testimony still to be heard by the tribunal came from French writer and war correspondent Madeleine Riffaud, an associate of Sartre and de Beauvoir who as a teenager had worked for the French Resistance and as a journalist reported on the Algerian War before taking up the cause of Vietnamese nationalism.[26] One of the most partisan sources to testify to the tribunal, her seven years embedded with the National Liberation Front had led to the documentary *Dans le maquis du Sud-Vietnam* in 1965 and the book *Au Nord-Vietnam* in 1967. What set her testimony apart was less her account of what the US military was doing to Vietnamese civilians than the reason why. The likes of Wulff and Bertolino had been circumspect about the motivations that underpinned US policy. American military commanders were suffering from a strategic myopia that focused their attention on the immediate need to repel the enemy while blurring the more distant aim of winning the civilian population over to their cause. Riffaud rejected these claims about unintended consequences. The detention and torture of civilians, the bombing of their homes and institutions, the forced internment in strategic hamlets, was all 'part of a deliberate plan'. She did not need to use the word for the tribunal to understand her meaning. The United States was committing genocide.

Riffaud had set in motion a train of thought that gathered an unstoppable head of steam. Among the closing witnesses were several who were even more explicit about US intentions. The ground had been laid for Sartre to make his important pronouncement on the war.[27]

Sartre was absent from some of the proceedings in Roskilde. That the president of the tribunal could remove himself to compose a personal speech about an issue some of the panellists did not believe should even be on their agenda points to the dominance of his personality. Behind the scenes, some of the members had wanted to focus on specific violations of the laws of armed conflict. A broader moral pronouncement on US military action would risk alienating a public on the other side of the Atlantic who the tribunal most hoped to win over to its cause.[28] But Sartre had got his way. Whether he had already reached a decision before he travelled to Denmark is a matter for debate. Carl Oglesby recalled how in Stockholm, Ralph Schoenman had pushed the line that 'Lord Russell says he expects the tribunal to find the United States guilty of genocide.' Sartre had been furious. The outcome of the tribunal would only be determined on the basis of the evidence. 'Our findings will only be significant if they are supported by the facts!' – which had led him to conclude that 'what the United States was doing in Vietnam was just fighting an ugly war in an ugly way'.[29]

In Roskilde, Sartre could reconsider his position while not being seen to agree with anything said by Russell's loathed secretary. His direction of thought was clear from the inclusion of the possibility of genocide as one of the central questions to which the tribunal's second session sought answers. While the statement was his own, it is more or less certain that he would have shared it with de Beauvoir for her opinion.

'On Genocide' started by setting out the challenge to the tribunal in reaching a decision about the ultimate aim of the war. Article 2 of the Geneva Convention defines genocide as a crime committed with intent to destroy a population. Since the US government had never made a public statement to that effect, was it possible to infer intent from the actions of military forces in Vietnam? Sartre prefaced his answer with a disquisition on modern warfare. The concept of total war, he claimed, emanated from the Western imperialism of the nineteenth and twentieth centuries. Conquering nations had used their superior power to impose mastery on militarily and economically weaker countries including 'the extinction of their national character, culture, customs, sometimes even language'.

The Vietnam War was a further manifestation of that policy, an attempt to impose renewed control over a people who had won the right to independence. American intervention had two related aims. Imposing control on Vietnam not only contained communist influence in one region; it also served as a demonstration of power to leftist insurgents who threatened US interests around the world. The only means by which the US military could demonstrate to other nations that guerrilla warfare does not pay, maintained the philosopher, was through the massacre of the Vietnamese people. In the south, that had led to the decimation of a peasant population and the land that sustained them, 'villages burned, the populace subjected to massive bombing, livestock shot, vegetation destroyed by defoliants, crops ruined by toxic aerosols, and everywhere indiscriminate shooting, murder, rape and looting'. The strategic hamlets that were supposed to provide sanctuary to people forcibly displaced from their farming communities only tore the country further apart. 'Husbands are separated from their wives, mothers from their children; family life, so important to the Vietnamese, no longer exists.' The impact of US military action on the North was no less destructive. Bombing raids were leading to 'the systematic destruction of the economic base of the country'.

Washington, observed Sartre, might have persuaded the American public that military escalation was a means to pressure Hanoi into a peace settlement. There could even be government officials who had convinced themselves that was the purpose, he said, but if that was the case, they were deluded. The civilian population had turned out to be in cahoots with the enemy military that US forces were supposedly protecting them from. Confronted by this hostility, US troops had turned on the people they were sent to protect. 'Now we can recognise in those dark and misled souls the truth,' concluded Sartre. 'Hitler killed the Jews because they were Jews. The armed forces of the United States torture and kill men, women and children in Vietnam merely because they are Vietnamese. Whatever lies or euphemisms the government may think up, the spirit of genocide is in the minds of the soldiers.'

Sartre also won out over some of the other tribunal members on whether to give the floor at the last minute to Stokely Carmichael. Courtland Cox had continued to deputise for the SNCC leader in Roskilde. But among the many international commitments that had seen him travel in recent months to Havana, London and Paris, Carmichael finally found time to attend the tribunal. Certain members would rather he had not. The issue of racial discrimination within the ranks of the US Army that he wanted to address was, to them, a distraction from the war crimes committed against the Vietnamese. Isaac Deutscher had been dismissive of the matter when Courtland Cox raised it in Stockholm. Deutscher was now dead, but there were others around the table who retained a blinkered attitude towards the relevance of race. It was this lack of awareness of their white privilege that had helped persuade James Baldwin not to participate in the tribunal.[30] But Sartre and de Beauvoir had been supporters of the civil rights struggle for many years, and the same was true of Russell. All three of them had condemned the US government for sending African Americans overseas to fight and die for the cause of freedom while failing to bestow them with the full rights of citizenship at home. Russell had, for instance, publicly supported Muhammad Ali when he refused his enlistment to serve in Vietnam. That included an offer to draw on the evidence of the tribunal in his legal defence.[31]

Sartre insisted Carmichael address the tribunal. The detractors around the table considered this 'uncalled for'. Technically they were right that the issue of racism within the ranks of the US Army was outside the remit of a tribunal investigating war crimes. The tribunal president, however, saw it as strengthening his moral indictment of the war. Ultimately it was Sartre who prevailed because he was Sartre.[32] Carmichael was an intellectual force in his own right, but his position on the war was consistent with Sartre to the point that he acted as a mouthpiece for the philosopher. Both men shared a sense of solidarity with peoples struggling to secure their independence from Western colonialism. For Carmichael, that situation was compounded by the fact that African Americans were being used to fight a war on behalf of a white government against another people of colour. As did Baldwin, he denounced the disproportionate drafting of young Black men into the US Army. African Americans made up barely 10 per cent of the population, but nearly 20 per cent of conscripts. Assigned in even more disproportionate numbers to combat units, they were as much the victims of the war as the Vietnamese. Some of the tribunal members remained unmoved, yet the address had nonetheless ensured they spoke with a more inclusive voice on the ethical issues raised by the conflict.[33]

There was never any doubt that the tribunal would conclude that the US had violated the rights of both prisoners of war and the civilian population. Those decisions were unanimous, but there was less agreement on the complicity of other countries in supporting the US war effort. Members agreed that Thailand and the Philippines were guilty of the charge, but there were three dissenters when it came to the role of Japan although all accepted its role as a US ally.[34]

What had been uncertain was how the tribunal would vote on the issue of genocide. Some needed little convincing, others were sceptical. Ultimately, though, Sartre imposed his will on proceedings; the decision was unanimous. The news soon travelled across the North Sea to Bertrand Russell, intimately attached to the tribunal despite being far away. The decision gave him deep satisfaction. So different in how they saw the world, on the matter of the Vietnam War he and Sartre were of one mind.

Raising funds. Recruiting witnesses. Supervising investigative teams. Liaising with foreign governments. Listening and deliberating. The tribunal had invested considerable time, effort and resources in reaching its decisions, but still had to convince the rest of the world to accept its verdict. It would become all too evident that for much of the media it was the tribunal members who were the ones on trial.

10

VANQUISHED

'Tell me lies about Vietnam,' wrote Adrian Mitchell – and the US government had long been willing to oblige. Washington officials routinely invented mendacious narratives about the war: from the supposed threat to international security posed by a communist takeover of Vietnam to the role of purportedly civilian advisers sent to support the regime in Saigon, from the Gulf of Tonkin resolution to the escalation of military action into neutral Laos and Cambodia, from the scale of casualties to the supposed closeness of US forces to final victory.

Another of those falsehoods came while the war crimes tribunal was in session at Stockholm. The Johnson administration had resolved from the moment that Bertrand Russell first announced the enterprise not to respond publicly; to do so would bestow legitimacy on the accusations being made by the philosopher and his associates. Better to work behind the scenes to bring down the tribunal. And so Washington had set about applying pressure on other governments, conducting surveillance on those involved and planting press stories intended to besmirch their reputations. The public silence had been interrupted only once. When asked for a statement on the tribunal, Secretary of State Dean Rusk responded, 'I do not intend to play games with a ninety-four-year-old English philosopher.'[1] What finally forced the hand of US officials were the stories told in Stockholm of civilian fatalities of fragmentation bombs. Here was a compromising truth about the deliberate targeting of civilians that Washington determined must be denied for the protection of public support in the war.

'I smell something burning, hope it's just my brains,' continued Adrian Mitchell. 'They're only dropping peppermints and daisy-chains.' The Pentagon issued a statement while the tribunal was still in session that disputed the testimonies of witnesses. First, fragmentation bombs were rarely used. Second, the only reason they caused civilian casualties was because the North Vietnamese positioned the anti-aircraft batteries and missile launching sites that were their intended target inside densely populated areas. The focus of fragmentation bomb assaults was 'appropriate', the infliction of injury or death 'accidental', the number of casualties claimed by Hanoi 'not accepted'. Contemptuous of the political bias of the tribunal, the press showed far less critical discernment in accepting these claims. *The New York Times* ran a story that was more or less a verbatim transcript of the Pentagon statement. Nor was the *Washington Post* any more willing to scrutinise what officials told reporters, dismissing out of hand the 'alleged fragmentation bombs' dropped by American warplanes.[2]

The tribunal was incredulous. 'Our evidence is irrefutable,' asserted chairman Vladimir Dedijer. He and the other members were willing to present it to a US congressional committee; their invitation went unaccepted.[3]

This episode captured the essence of the response to the tribunal. Sartre had said from the outset that its primary purpose was to persuade the American people that crimes were being committed in their name. Instead, the newspapers and television networks treated events in Stockholm and Roskilde with anger and derision – when they could be bothered to report on them at all. The tribunal had made a decision that the United States was committing war crimes, but the American media in turn reached its verdict on Sartre and his accomplices. The tribunal was 'grotesque', 'a travesty', but also 'a total failure'. The only thing its members had exposed was their blatant hostility towards the United States and blind capitulation to the propaganda of North Vietnam.[4]

Russell and Sartre had succeeded not in opening but shutting down public debate about the war. Yet while much of the press and the political establishment believed it had laid the tribunal to waste, something had been sown amid the ruins that would in time start to grow.

The humiliation of defeat in Vietnam has led to much soul-searching among Americans over the last half-century. How did the mightiest military power in the world lose to a small and impoverished nation of peasant farmers? Should Washington have done more to define the aims of the war? Was their military strategy misguided? Could US forces have flattened the enemy with fuller use of their massive firepower? Or was this in reality an unwinnable war?

One of the more enduring narratives is that the US could have achieved victory were it not for an adversarial media that corroded public support for the war. Without the backing of people back home, soldiers on the front lost conviction in their cause. This explanation for the failure of US foreign policy gained currency during the war and in the years since has never been entirely devalued. 'For the first time in modern history,' writes one author, 'the outcome of a war was determined not on the battlefield but on the printed page and, above all, on the television screen.'[5]

No matter how much the tale of media doves defeating

military hawks may be told, that does not mean it is true. The press was free to report without interference on the war, and in time that did have an impact. Stories about spiralling costs, military stalemates and soldier deaths exposed the emptiness of official statements about imminent US victory in Vietnam. But when the tribunal met, that was still in the future. The pivotal moment when CBS anchorman Walter Cronkite, 'the most trusted man in America', announced that the war could only end through negotiation came in late February 1968, months after the tribunal had finished its deliberations.[6]

It was a very different situation when Sartre and his associates were still in session. The story that the media told about the war was broadly the one that Washington wanted it to tell. When Lyndon Johnson lied about the supposed assault that led to the Gulf of Tonkin resolution, the media took the president at his word. When his administration escalated the war on the ground and in the air, it did so with press support. And when they insisted that it was North Vietnamese soldiers who were the cause of civilian casualties, that was chorused on front pages and in editorial columns. There are any number of reasons for the uncritical reporting of war correspondents. Some were sold on the mission and the courage of the men who carried it out, others were aware that their press accreditation and possibly their lives depended on the soldiers they followed into the field of combat. Whatever the rationale, the reports they sent home contrasted the restraint of American soldiers with the ruthlessness of an enemy that showed no mercy towards non-combatants. The US military willingly escorted the small cluster of correspondents stationed in Saigon to the scenes of NLF attacks. But those same reporters had less means to assess the impact of American forces in remoter regions of South Vietnam – and none at all in North Vietnam.[7]

There were exceptions. CBS broadcast a report in August 1965 from the South Vietnamese village of Cam Ne that showed footage of Marines torching thatched homes with cigarette lighters, but these reports seldom broadened the focus to determine whether this and other incidents were part of a wider pattern. 'These are calamities commonly incident to such warfare,' the *Washington Post* conceded, while reassuring readers 'these tragedies differ from the wilful and deliberate destruction of homes in reprisal'. While some newspapers challenged US bombing raids, this too was more about the effectiveness of military tactics than the underlying rationale of the war.[8]

Russell and Sartre were victims of a press unwilling to comprehend that what Washington told them about the war might not be the truth. But the philosophers also brought trouble on themselves, confusing the public by insisting the tribunal had no pretensions to act as a trial court while sometimes speaking in the formal language of the law. They alienated Americans in particular by refusing to countenance that the North Vietnamese could also be responsible for war crimes. And they were credulous to believe that reason could win over those who supported the war with their hearts as much as their heads.

The hostility of the press was made all the worse by the behaviour of Ralph Schoenman. His truculent attitude towards reporters had led the tribunal members to remove him as an official spokesperson at the start of the Stockholm session, but that had not stopped him from battling with the media. Even members of the press sympathetic towards the tribunal found him 'obnoxious and insolent'.[9] Critics turned to their advantage his abrasive outbursts, labelling him 'the world's leading anti-American', a man with a chip on his shoulder 'the size of the Empire State Building', motivated less by moral commitment than personal vindictiveness towards his own countrymen.

Claiming as these commentators did that the real mastermind behind the tribunal was not the eminent philosopher Bertrand Russell but his embittered former protégé was a means to undermine its moral and intellectual legitimacy. The assertion was harder to sustain during the Roskilde session, since Schoenman had been banned from entering Denmark – but by then the damage was done.[10]

In truth, none of the mistakes made by the tribunal mattered. Russell and Sartre could have been clearer about their lack of formal powers, could have considered war crimes committed by both, could somehow have persuaded Schoenman to shut his mouth, but none of it would have made any difference. In claiming that the media had become the unwitting mouthpiece of a government determined to lie about the war, the tribunal had set itself on a collision course with editorial opinion in the United States. On screen, over the airwaves and in print, the media determined that the surest means to defend its record was to go on the offensive.

The fate of the tribunal was foreshadowed by the furious response months before to the first reports on the war written by an American journalist from within North Vietnam: the political and military establishment, a compliant press and a complacent public closed ranks to protect what they told themselves was the truth about the war.

Harrison Salisbury was one of the most renowned reporters in the United States. His dispatches as the Moscow bureau chief of *The New York Times* had won him the Pulitzer Prize in 1955. Whether reporting from the front lines of the civil rights struggle or the scene of the Kennedy assassination, he built a formidable reputation for reaching to the heart of a story. Salisbury was set on travelling to North Vietnam but found it difficult to secure a visa. Hanoi welcomed the prospect of a US journalist providing readers with a more accurate impression of the war than the words of a Washington spokesperson, but sought reassurance about his political impartiality, so turned to Bertrand Russell.[11]

Salisbury and Russell had their differences about the war, the reporter being less polemical and more temperate, sceptical that the political bias of the philosopher allowed him to assess what was happening on the ground with an open mind. But Russell had believed he was serious about seeking the truth and Salisbury was willing to accept his support; in December 1966, he followed the same flight route as the investigative teams sent by the tribunal from Paris to Phnom Penh and finally Hanoi.[12]

Salisbury toured North Vietnam for two weeks, filing twenty-two stories for *The New York Times* later compiled in the book *Behind the Lines*. What he witnessed belied the public statements from Washington – and the news stories written by his fellow reporters – about the war. US aircraft conducted their assaults on North Vietnam with surgical precision, insisted the Pentagon. What Salisbury discovered instead was that bombing raids were less a scalpel than a blunt tool. 'Contrary to the impression given by United States communiqués, on-the-spot inspection indicates that American bombing has been inflicting considerable civilian casualties in Hanoi and its environs for some time past.' Hanoi and Nam Dinh had been hit hard, Phu Ly even harder. Thirty-five miles south of the capital, the entire city was in ruins after being indiscriminately bombed by squadrons of B-52s. Salisbury, who had witnessed the Blitz in London during the Second World War, found himself haunted by the ghosts of his past when the sirens sounded and he huddled with North Vietnamese civilians in a concrete shelter.[13]

What Salisbury encountered in those cramped, dark

conditions also contradicted the line of his own government. Bombing raids on North Vietnam were breaking the will of the hard-line rulers in Hanoi, insisted Washington, bringing them closer to the negotiating table. Not so, discovered Salisbury. All the air assaults had succeeded in was strengthening the resolve of the people and their government to resist US aggression. 'It is my feeling,' wrote the reporter, 'that the bombing has caused the country to acquire a spirit of national purpose or unity which it would not have otherwise.'[14] No sooner had bombs damaged and destroyed the transport routes that moved soldiers and supplies through the country than teams of North Vietnamese bicycled into action. Roads and railway lines were repaired, pontoon bridges erected over rivers.

Salisbury shared none of the sentimentalism of Russell or Sartre towards the North Vietnamese – but as was true of the tribunal, he treated them as individual human beings rather than a faceless enemy horde. While the philosophers were accused of selecting facts to fit their theories, Salisbury had reached similar conclusions only after he had seen the situation for himself. The US was not only in breach of moral and legal constraints on warfare, he concluded, it was also misrepresenting the truth of its military actions. And, for all that, it was failing to win the war. Seen in an iconic photograph before the imploded remains of a building, Salisbury stared into the camera lens, his eyes a blend of sadness and reproach. If anyone had the authority to make the public heed the reality of the war, it was this eminent author – and yet, the public did not pay heed.[15]

On 31 December, President Johnson held a press conference intended to contain any public relations damage caused by Salisbury's reports, making massively inaccurate claims about US forces conducting 'the most careful, self-limited air war in history'. While the White House was content to hold the official line, the Pentagon went on the offensive. According to spokesperson Arthur Sylvester, Salisbury had fallen 'lock, stock and barrel' for enemy propaganda.[16]

Government officials got on the phone to newspaper editors to sway their opinion, but the press had already decided to stand firm with Washington. Salisbury had been a fool to take the civilian casualty figures of Hanoi at face value, asserted editorials across the country. According to the *Washington Post*, he had been used as the 'chosen instrument' of Ho Chi Minh to report only what the North Vietnamese wanted him to see. Sometimes implicitly, other times explicitly, the press claimed Salisbury was a communist.[17] *The New York Times* published a piece by military correspondent Hanson Baldwin who insisted that any civilians wounded or killed in US air raids were collateral damage rather than targets. What was happening in North Vietnam was no worse than any other military conflict – and the bombing was achieving results, forcing an otherwise recalcitrant Hanoi to prepare for peace talks. Nominated for a second Pulitzer Prize, Salisbury lost out on blatantly political grounds. The risks he had taken in searching for the truth about the war had been rewarded with slander and ridicule.[18]

The media also closed ranks against the peace protesters taking to the streets of American cities in increasing numbers. News stories focused more on the drama of activists confronting authorities than what had led them to demonstrate in the first place.[19] Public figures who, like Russell and Sartre, used their celebrity to influence opinion on the war also suffered furious censure. Martin Luther King had long hesitated about a public statement on the war, and when he spoke it was with the predictable outcome. In April 1967, only a month before the tribunal met in Stockholm, King used his status as a Nobel Peace Prize winner to denounce the US government as 'the greatest purveyor of violence in the world today'. There was a furious reaction. Some of it was racist, demanding to know what a Black clergyman understood of foreign affairs; King was accused of being, at best, an unwitting tool of Hanoi, at worst a traitor. In the words of the *Washington Post*, he had 'diminished his use to his cause, his country, and his people'. If Americans were unwilling to heed the words of distinguished fellow countrymen like Salisbury and King, there was little prospect of them responding well to a group of foreign intellectuals who were accusing their military of committing war crimes.[20]

Carl Oglesby had it right. 'To discredit the man,' he wrote in response to coverage of Russell's campaign to expose US war crimes, 'apparently, is to refute the argument.'[21] Rather than consider the merits of the evidence heard at the tribunal, much of the media dismissed proceedings on the basis that the philosopher was a deluded old man. As his one-time associate David Horowitz put it, the press was of the opinion that Russell 'had outlived himself'.[22]

The character assassins were many, but none wielded a sharper weapon than Bernard Levin, a familiar figure on both sides of the Atlantic. A star of the satire boom during the 1960s, his irreverence had won him the accolade of being one of the first people punched on live television during an appearance on the topical programme *That Was the Week That Was*. But Levin was less the anti-establishmentarian than he seemed. A devout adherent of Cold War orthodoxy, he was one of several British authors and intellectuals who wrote a letter published in *The New York Times* championing US policy in Vietnam.[23]

'Bertrand Russell: Prosecutor, Judge and Jury' appeared in *The New York Times*, February 1967, pre-empting the first meeting of the tribunal by three months. Levin stated at the outset that he did not believe the philosopher to be senile, before proceeding to spend the entire article arguing precisely that. 'How has it come about that a man possessed of one of the finest, most acute minds of our time – of any time – has fallen into a state of such gullibility, lack of discrimination, twisted logic and rancorous hatred of the United States that he has turned into a full-time purveyor of political garbage, indistinguishable from the routine products of the Soviet machine?' Levin had spared Russell a diagnosis of dementia, but that did not stop him from concluding that the philosopher suffered from 'insane paranoia'.[24]

While the words were those of Levin, readers were unaware that the US State Department was one of his principal sources. Having read his letter in support of the war, Washington officials sought him out to write the article, supplying him with documentary materials to discredit Russell. There is no reason to assume the editorial team at *The New York Times* knew Levin had colluded with the Johnson administration, but the article was an affront to its proud tradition of journalistic independence.[25]

Not that the *Times* needed to collude with government administrators to proclaim the dimming of Russell's once luminous mind. The paper not only dismissed the philosopher as 'decrepit' but also denigrated the tribunal members, calling them 'mediocrities' with the exception of Sartre.[26] The press spared no one in its spitefulness towards the tribunal, neither the administrative team nor the audience of bell-bottomed hippies and hangers-on described in its reports. Photographs of the audience in Stockholm in reality revealed a diverse assembly of men and women including some who looked as though they might be more acquainted with flower arranging than flower power.

The *Times* set the editorial tone for much of the US media, with newspapers from the western to eastern seaboards insinuating that Russell was as feeble of mind as of body. Long a clarion for US foreign policy, *Time* condemned Sartre as 'a Communist crony', further claiming that his statements in Stockholm were full of 'existentialist flummery'. It too dismissed the other intellectuals and activists sitting around the table, describing their performance as 'a sullen séance of left-wing conjurors'. This and other editorials nonetheless served their purpose; defaming the character of the tribunal members as a motley collection of the has-beens and the never-were meant there was no need to consider the content of what they said about the war.[27]

Trashing the personalities of the participants was only one of the tactics used by the press to discredit the tribunal. Another was to argue that it was irrelevant to wider debate about the war, since it had no formal legal standing. Newspaper reports mocked the pretensions of Russell and Sartre through the ironic use of quotation marks; how dare these egotistical intellectuals make a mockery of justice by staging a 'trial' with the pretence of observing the proper conventions of law; the insolence of these self-appointed 'judges' and the peaceniks and propagandists masquerading as 'witnesses'.[28]

The press also censured the tribunal for focusing solely on the supposed war crimes committed by US forces. Why, the *Washington Post* wanted to know, were Russell and Sartre insisting that President Johnson or one of his senior officials defend the actions of their administration without imposing the same demand on Ho Chi Minh? Without doubt, the tribunal members had a sentimental attitude towards the North Vietnamese, absolving them of blame for their own brutal atrocities. The NLF and the regular military units of the People's Army of Vietnam (PAVN) considered civilians as legitimate targets, intimidating and murdering not only political representatives of the Saigon regime but also any of the peasant folk they suspected of cooperation. At the time when the tribunal convened, the Hue massacre, in which North Vietnamese soldiers tortured and murdered at least 2,800 people and disposed of them in mass graves, was months away. But the NLF and PAVN had by then already carried out countless acts of excessive violence.[29] By their logic, the tribunal nonetheless believed that the North Vietnamese were only committing acts of resistance against an oppressor – and that since their actions were without aggression, they could not be considered war crimes. 'I refuse,' proclaimed Sartre, 'to place in the same category the actions of an organization of poor peasants, hunted, obliged to maintain an iron discipline in their ranks, and those of an immense army backed by a highly industrialized country of 200 million inhabitants.'[30]

It was because of assertions such as this that *Time* accused Sartre of sophistry.[31] If anyone was committing war crimes, claimed White House spokespersons and compliant reporters, it was the North Vietnamese. Yet criticism of the tribunal's bias could also be specious. *Newsweek* ran a story that featured a photograph of a Vietnamese child maimed by an NLF mortar, the surrounding text exhaustively listing the atrocities inflicted by North Vietnamese forces on innocent civilians. There was no attempt in this or any other report on the tribunal published by the magazine to interrogate whether there was any substance to the accusations made against US troops at the tribunal, nor, so far as the editors were concerned, was there any need.[32] How could Americans be committing war crimes when they were heroically defending South Vietnam against a cruel enemy? Here was the simplistic moralising of the press. If one side were war criminals, the other almost by definition were not. This presumption of American innocence showed a press all too ready to condemn the bias of the tribunal but oblivious to its own lack of impartiality.

The press concluded that the tribunal was not only a folly but also an affront to impartial opinion. What seemed the obvious morality of the war was somehow lost on Russell and Sartre. Both men had betrayed the basic tenet of philosophy to search for the truth, either out of mental deterioration or malice. The evidence presented to the tribunal was irrelevant, since its members had reached a verdict before they convened in Stockholm that the US was guilty of war crimes. Thankfully there was no need for those who respected due process to abide by that decision.

It was an irony lost on those who reached this conclusion that they themselves had committed the very transgression of which they accused the tribunal. If Russell and Sartre were not really interested in the evidence heard in Stockholm and Roskilde, nor were they. If the tribunal had already reached a decision about war crimes, they had similarly passed judgement on the tribunal. No matter what was said or shown – not the confession of a former soldier, nor the display of a mutilated civilian body – it would not convince most of the press to reassess the war.[33]

Nor was it only the American press that tore into the tribunal. Across the Atlantic, character assassins also sharpened their pens. Russell had long been targeted by British satirists. The comedy revue *Beyond the Fringe* had most famously lampooned the philosopher's logical analysis, yet the tone even on the part of these young iconoclasts was one of teasing affection.[34] There was little trace of that in an *Observer* article that saw in his outspoken criticism of the war evidence that Russell had become 'Britain's wisest fool'.[35] Russell came in for criticism both for the tribunal and his book *War Crimes in Vietnam*, a compendium of alleged atrocities by the American military. Old age had enfeebled the philosopher, claimed the *Daily Mail*'s Christopher Dobson. Logic and reason had succumbed to absurdity, dispassionate thought to propaganda. 'How sad it is to watch the erosion of a great mind and the shackling of a questing spirit to the aim of an oppressive political creed.'[36] The *Telegraph* went even further, calling for the tribunal to be banned, apparently seeing no contradiction in supporting a war to defend democracy while denying the right to freedom of speech that was one of its core values.[37] Liberal and leftist newspapers were hardly more encouraging. When the tribunal convened in Stockholm, the *Guardian* offered only the non-committal comment that 'there is no reason why it should be either condemned or applauded'. Of the second session in Roskilde, the paper reported that the veterans called as witnesses 'have told a terrible story with an eye for gory detail but they did not disclose anything new about the Vietnamese tragedy and their testimony was one-sided'. Given that the former servicemen were among the first to testify publicly, it was unclear how the paper was already aware of their revelations.[38] Maligned in the mainstream press, it was only on the political margins that the tribunal found favour, among standard bearers of the socialist left such as *Tribune* or in the pages of the nascent countercultural press.[39]

Month after month of raising funds, recruiting team members, researching thousands of pages of documents, reckoning with the testimonies of witnesses, rowing with one another – and all at the sacrifice not only of their own creative enterprises but also of the reputations built on those labours. Had the tribunal been worth the trouble?

Courtland Cox had some reservations. He found contending with the racial and class privilege of many of his fellow panellists frustrating. First there was the lavish social activity surrounding the tribunal; by day the members discussed serious matters about the military oppression of a peasant population but by night they dined in splendour at posh restaurants and went out dancing. It made an uncomfortable contrast for Cox. Here he was, fresh from fighting for the rights of Black people in Alabama, only to find himself sipping drinks from tall-stemmed glasses and sharing small talk with world-famous figures. 'I go to this seven-course dinner,' he recalled, 'you know, with all sorts of liquor and stuff like that. I've just come out of Alabama ...'[40]

Another of the SNCC activists involved in the tribunal took the criticism further. Julius Lester, a member of one of the investigative teams who testified in Stockholm, dismissed the endeavour as 'an intellectual exercise of no political consequence'. It was a talking shop, but nothing more. Lester berated Sartre and his associates for their 'self-satisfaction' in moralising about the war without actually taking any practical measures to change policy. A CIA document suggests that it was the SNCC activist who confided to a federal agent being 'considerably annoyed at the high-brow intellectual politics' of the tribunal members. Such criticism was not entirely without substance, but the aim of the tribunal had always been to mobilise public opinion rather than apply direct pressure on policymakers.[41]

Nor could it be said that the tribunal members had spoken out against the war without personal risk. For all that some of them might have liked the sound of their own voices, those had been lost amid the louder volume of a hostile media. Lester might have gained a tighter grip on the moral high ground had he not by his own admission used much of his time in Stockholm pursuing local women, as he had in North Vietnam.[42]

Even Lester conceded that the tribunal had been revelatory in its exposure of US military tactics, particularly the use of fragmentation bombs so blatantly denied by Washington officials.[43] That, too, was the reason for Tariq Ali deeming the tribunal 'a partial success', an opinion shared by several of the participants in Stockholm and Copenhagen, including David Dellinger and Carl Oglesby. Lawrence Daly and Laurent Schwartz were among the other members who informed Russell of their pride in what they thought the tribunal had accomplished.[44]

The most public faces of the tribunal were the most pilloried by the press. But for Russell, Sartre and de Beauvoir, there was nothing new about the insults. Russell had been slandered, assaulted and sent to prison so many times in his long life as to make him immune from rude editorials. The philosopher was adamant that the tribunal must have succeeded in revealing the darker side of the war for the press and political establishment to come after him with such fury. Newspapers might accuse him of having gone senile, but 'if the charge is true, I fail to see why anyone troubles to remark on my babblings'. Critics naturally would have seen this conviction that the tribunal had scored a victory in the propaganda war with Washington as evidence that Russell really had lost his mind.[45] Sartre and de Beauvoir also cared little about personal abuse, but were frustrated that the revelatory investigative work of the tribunal had been under-reported 'because of the negligence of the press'. The tribunal had presented the truth about the war to a world that chose to avert its gaze. While some of the other tribunal members believed they had partially completed their mission, the fatalism of Sartre and de Beauvoir seemed to be a more realistic assessment. Whatever the situation on the battlefield, the United States had won the propaganda war.[46]

Not only had the tribunal failed to stir the conscience of the American people – it actually caused them to close ranks in support of their military. Most Americans could not conceive that their country was capable of committing war crimes. They were the good guys, the ones who had fought a war to save the world from fascism and were now fighting another to rid it of communism, another existential threat. They would continue to trust what their own democratically elected government told them about the war – not some self-appointed tribunal founded by a politically suspect and probably senile egghead and staffed by turncoats and foreign radicals. If anyone was guilty of a misdemeanour it was surely them – no surprise, then, that National Security Advisor Walt Rostow should crow to Lyndon Johnson that Washington had not needed to pressure newspaper editors too hard. They had reached their own decision that the tribunal was a sham, 'a publicity-seeking "farce" without status as a legitimate forum'. By late 1967, the administration could rest assured that it had prevailed. Opinion polls showed strong support not only for the war but also for the president. The tribunal was over, and with it the reputations of Bertrand Russell and Jean-Paul Sartre.[47]

And yet, what US officials were telling the president about the indifference of world opinion towards the tribunal was not entirely what they confided among themselves. The tribunal won the support of the press in what is now known as the Global South; there was a strong sense of solidarity with the Vietnamese as victims of a war of Western colonial aggression. Newspapers from Africa, Asia and Latin America sent reporters to Stockholm and Roskilde. Editorial opinion regarded Russell and Sartre with reverence rather than ridicule.[48] Did it matter that newspapers from Calcutta to Caracas rooted for the tribunal? To a United States attempting to retain its status as leader of the free world in a global fight against communism, most certainly. True, some of these countries were inherently hostile towards US foreign policy, but the accusations levelled by the tribunal nonetheless made the challenge of winning them over all the harder.

Nor could Washington be entirely confident about the attitude of its Western allies. Reaction to the tribunal in Continental Europe was venomous in some cases, but there was more positive press coverage. In France, Italy and the Netherlands, newspapers treated the event with seriousness and in some instances support. Press reports split along partisan lines. In France, for instance, the conservative *Le Figaro* condemned the tribunal, while the centre-left *Le Monde* gave greater voice to the testimony, publishing Sartre's closing statement in full.[49]

US diplomats privately admitted that they had lost control of the narrative in the countries where the tribunal convened. Sympathetic news stories in Denmark and especially Sweden had lent credence to the testimony of witnesses, swelling the rising tide of opposition to the war. Ironically, the harsher the criticisms levelled at the tribunal by the American media, the more liberal Swedish newspapers believed it had uncovered the truth about the war.[50] The anger of US officials was evident in a State Department memo that condemned the 'fat, smug attitude' of Swedish television and radio stations that bestowed extensive airtime on the tribunal.[51] British representatives in Copenhagen and Stockholm shared the assessment that the event had benefited from a favourable media, and that newspapers on the political left had 'swallowed the whole exercise'. The conservative press was more critical, denouncing the tribunal as a charade that would not only contribute nothing to ending the conflict but would also damage their governments' diplomatic relations with Washington. But even some of their editorials conceded that Sartre and his colleagues had uncovered serious evidence of US excesses in Vietnam. According to the right-of-centre *Svenska Dagbladet*, much of what was said at the tribunal was shameless propaganda. Yet 'some of the testimony has been of such a nature that, quite objectively, it could have stood up before an impartial Court or Committee of Enquiry.'[52]

Contrary to official statements, this correspondence by diplomats from both sides of the Atlantic disclosed that the tribunal had done much to discredit the war among some of the United States' most important Western allies. The US Embassy in Stockholm concluded that for all the adverse press, the tribunal was a success. First, the fact that the countries hosting it were Western democracies had exposed the fault line that the war opened up within the international alliance. Second, through the accumulation of evidence it had compiled a 'basic document for all of the world', a foundational source for further criticism of the war from American allies as well as enemies.[53]

British officials were of the same mind: the tribunal had been a success in their estimate simply by having taken place. 'It is easy to forget,' a confidential memo from the Stockholm embassy reminded the Foreign Office, 'that the Tribunal could have broken up in confusion and disagreement at an early stage.' For all the efforts of governments to forbid it, the tribunal had conducted orderly proceedings that amassed more than two million words of testimony. 'Even among many people who realise that the Tribunal was a biased propaganda effort, the evidence on civilian bombing will have had an effect, and will have helped to confirm the views of many ... that the bombing of North Vietnam is morally wrong.' Distaste for the tribunal did not prevent the embassy from a dispassionate analysis of its impact on public opinion. In being the first international forum to debate the alleged war crimes committed by US forces 'there is little doubt that it was a success, an important feather in the cap of the organisers'. The embassy was prescient in sensing that the full impact of the tribunal could not be measured by its immediate failures; its members had laid the foundation on which anti-war activism would build.[54]

That construction work was in evidence while the tribunal was still in session. Carl Oglesby gave an account in Roskilde of how the tribunal was inspiring peace activism across the United States. According to Oglesby the tribunal was becoming an essential 'clearing-house of information' on what was really going on in Vietnam. American activists also drew strength in their domestic struggle from the international character of the tribunal, he said. They may be a minority in their own country, but they gained courage from a global coalition against US foreign policy.[55]

A disillusioned Julius Lester contended that it would have been better had the tribunal met a year later, by which time the public had grown weary of the war and the grassroots insurgency by peace activists had greater momentum. But that alternative timeline dispenses with the sense of moral urgency that compelled the tribunal to act. It also turns history on its head, proposing that the anti-war movement would have given impetus to the tribunal – when in fact the opposite was true.

While newspaper editors deprecated the tribunal, their readers were sometimes of another opinion. College staff and students, clerical leaders and cultural luminaries mobilised in its support. Joseph Heller, author of the satirical anti-war novel *Catch-22*, defended Russell's reputation from the slanderous assaults. 'Russell's wildest anti-U.S. utterings,' he maintained, 'are no more improbable than the official explanations for our war in Vietnam.'[56] Poet Lawrence Ferlinghetti also defended the philosopher, proclaiming with reference to the Hungarian uprising of 1956, 'We are a people who with complete equanimity judged Khrushchev the Butcher of Budapest, but must now seek to destroy the reputation of a man who passes similar judgment upon us.'[57] The Ferlinghetti article appeared in the radical *Ramparts* magazine, but flattering profiles of the tribunal were not entirely the preserve of publications on the progressive left. *Playboy* ran a feature by the theatre critic Kenneth Tynan that more than an admiring account of events was a call to arms. Don't pretend you're powerless to do something about the war, Tynan told readers. Take inspiration from Russell and Sartre, and set up another tribunal in the United States: 'Arraign your own country in accordance with the international laws it helped to formulate.' How many readers paused to read the opinion piece as they flipped towards the centrefold cannot be known, but the proposal would in time be turned into action.[58]

All the same, Washington officials paid little heed to what *Ramparts* and other radical publications printed about the war, even less editorials in Aarhus or Amritsar. The tribunal would soon be a distant memory, while the US military marched forward to victory. The world did not believe Bertrand Russell and Jean-Paul Sartre – but then, the world had not yet heard about My Lai.

11

VINDICATED

Breakfast rice was still steaming when the artillery battery hit. The impact of exploding shells tore open the ground, setting houses on fire. Minutes later, the sound of helicopters cut through the humid skies. Soldiers started firing the moment they hit the ground, an assault that lasted for four frenzied hours. Hands raised in surrender were ignored. Some locals were shot at random, while others were forced into a drainage ditch where they were mown down by machine gun. The troops encountered women kneeling in prayer, and killed them. There were other women lying in the dirt with their children. They killed them too. The soldiers also raped female villagers, some in their teens, before shooting them and mutilating their bodies. They set fire to the straw and mud homes, slaughtered the livestock and polluted the wells that provided drinking water. By the time it was over on the morning of 16 March 1968, little remained of the South Vietnamese hamlet of My Lai. Between 347 and 504 civilians were dead. The American platoons had suffered one injury, a soldier who accidentally shot himself in the foot. What had started out as a routine search-and-destroy mission ended in one of the worst atrocities in US military history.[1]

The men who committed the massacre were members of infantry platoons collectively known as Charlie Company, their actions part of an operation to root out and destroy the

Viet Cong Local Force 48th Battalion, which was believed to be sheltering in the area. Charlie Company anticipated coming under heavy fire from enemy forces as they reached the landing zone, but the only shots as they stormed the hamlet were from their fellow soldiers. The Viet Cong was not there, but the villagers Charlie Company had been told would be at market were.

The conspiracy to conceal the truth about the massacre commenced the moment it was over. Charlie Company's commanding officer Captain Ernest Medina filed a report falsely claiming that enemy forces were present when his soldiers disembarked from their helicopters and intentionally undercounted the number of civilian victims. The lies continued up the chain of command. Ordered to conduct an investigation, Colonel Oran Henderson lessened the scale of the slaughter, claiming that the small number of non-combatant deaths were inadvertently caused by long-range artillery fire. The military in due course released a fabricated account of the assault that represented it as a victory by American troops over a fearsome enemy.[2]

That would have been how My Lai was memorialised, were it not for a young veteran named Ron Ridenhour. He first heard about the incident during a chance encounter in a Saigon bar with a fellow soldier and wrote a letter to political and military leaders in Washington, leading to the detention of Lieutenant William Calley on a charge of murdering more than 100 civilians. Reports of the arrest appeared in the press, but no editor was curious enough to commission an investigation. It was left to freelance reporter Seymour Hersh to find Calley and from him learn what had happened, but Hersh could not convince an editor to run the story. Only when he turned to a small independent news service did the mainstream press publish his reporting; by this time it was 13 November 1969, twenty months after the massacre.[3]

Now, at last, the story gained momentum. First there were the photographs by Ron Haeberle in *Life* magazine of dead bodies, some of them infants, strewn across a dirt road. Then a CBS radio interview in which Charlie Company soldier Paul Meadlo confessed his crimes to reporter Mike Wallace.

Wallace: 'Men, women and children?'
Meadlo: 'Men, women and children.'
Wallace: 'And babies?'
Meadlo: 'And babies ...'[4]

Under mounting pressure, the army appointed a commission of inquiry led by Lieutenant General William Peers. If the top brass were hoping Peers would facilitate the cover-up, theirs was a serious miscalculation. Four months of investigation and 400 witnesses resulted in a final report running to 225 pages and damning in its conclusions. Peers determined that 'an almost total disregard for the lives and property of the civilian population' had caused carnage on a much larger scale than previously understood. The reason the truth remained unknown was the deliberate withholding of evidence at every level, from the soldiers who had committed the crimes to the senior officers who failed to conduct appropriate investigations.[5]

The story that Peers had uncovered threatened public support for the war in Vietnam. Army officials determined that the less the American people learned of the truth, the better. Much of the report released to the press in March 1970 was censored, Peers forced to replace the word 'massacre' with the euphemistic 'tragedy of major proportions.'[6] Holding anyone to account for what had happened proved no less of a problem. Peers recommended charges against twenty-eight soldiers, only one of whom stood trial by court martial. On 29 March 1971,

William Calley, the man already arrested for his role in the massacre, was found guilty of murdering twenty-two civilians. The court sentenced him to life imprisonment, only for President Richard Nixon to intervene and order him to be placed under house arrest. Little more than three years later, he was a free man.[7]

The excesses of US military action remain a matter of controversy. How the scale of atrocities is measured and whether they were the result of official policy depends on how one assesses the legitimacy of the war. But as to the basic issue, the Russell tribunal had uncovered a story of unwarrantable violence dating long before Charlie Company rampaged through My Lai. For all the official denials, all the lies, the indifference of the media towards the tribunal and the defamation of its members, there is no doubt that US forces committed war crimes in Vietnam. It has taken decades to uncover hidden stories, and even now they cannot be assembled into a complete reconstruction of events. How many soldiers were directly or indirectly involved will never be certain, nor all the crimes buried with the bodies of dead civilians. More certain is that the tribunal proceedings formed a first crucial draft of a revisionist narrative of the war, one that undercut the fictions of the Pentagon and State Department. Fifty years after the tribunal met in Stockholm, *The New York Times* asked 'Did America Commit War Crimes in Vietnam?' Drawing on the documentary evidence deliberated half a century earlier, the paper affirmatively answered its own question.[8]

The tribunal amassed evidence of crimes, which civilian and military leaders either chose to ignore or conspired to cover up. In this they were aided by a media that not only minimised the atrocities committed by US soldiers but also commended them for their supposed restraint. Some of the claims made by the tribunal were overstated but there was more substance to them than Washington officials were willing to admit. Many claims about the criminal misconduct of soldiers were never investigated; others were pursued but the outcomes undisclosed.

Slowly, sporadically, a narrative started to emerge that corroborated the claims of the tribunal. While it took the My Lai massacre for there to be a reassessment of the tribunal, news stories corroborating claims of American war crimes had appeared months earlier. In August 1969, *Esquire* ran a feature by Normand Poirier that used official records to re-enact the story of nine Marines who three years earlier gang-raped a young mother in Xuan Ngoc hamlet in South Vietnam and gunned down her entire family. The truth came out with the discovery of the still-breathing female victim the soldiers had left for dead. No newspapers picked up the story, but other revelations soon followed. Two months after the Poirier exposé, the *New Yorker* published 'Casualties of War', a harrowing account by Daniel Lang of four soldiers who abducted, raped and murdered a female civilian in the Central Highlands of Vietnam.

Political pressure also compelled the military to take appropriate measures, but the results concealed as much as they revealed. In December 1969, the Pentagon established a task force, the Vietnam War Crimes Working Group (VWCWG), to assess the authenticity of war crimes accusations levelled at American soldiers. The 9,000 pages of material documented 320 incidents, seven of them massacres in which at least 137 civilians died. There was sufficient evidence to bring formal charges against 203 soldiers.[9]

The VWCWG revealed a great deal, but more remained hidden. The remit of the task force was to investigate allegations already reported by the press. It did nothing to determine whether more atrocities remained uncovered, and nor were its conclusions made public. The legal process also lessened its impact. Only fifty-seven soldiers faced a court martial, and a mere twenty-three of those cases resulted in convictions. Many of those felons had their sentences reduced on appeal.[10]

The suppression of incriminating evidence in this and many other cases obscured for decades the scale of war crimes committed by American soldiers. The tribunal had exposed cracks in the defensive wall of the Washington establishment, but it would take years in which others persistently chipped away for the light to get through.

Take the story of Tiger Force, the elite military unit that ran amok through the Central Highlands of Vietnam between May and November 1967, torturing, raping and killing hundreds of unarmed civilians. 'We weren't keeping count,' Private Ken Kerney later told a reporter.[11] The army launched an investigation in 1971, after a whistle-blower from another unit came forward. When it appeared four years later, the report led to charges against eighteen soldiers for murder, assault and dereliction of duty. None of them ever stood trial. The case was closed, the report shelved. The public would never have known about the crimes or the official cover-up were it not for the probing of reporters from the *Toledo Blade*, who finally broke the story in a series of articles published in October 2003. It was a belated moment of reckoning about events that uncannily coincided with the first and second session of the war crimes tribunal.[12]

Then there were the incidents that occurred in the months and years following the indifference and disbelief at the accusations made by the tribunal. One of those atrocities that remained hidden occurred in the remote Mekong Delta hamlet Thanh Phong. It was nearly midnight on 25 February 1969 when the team of Navy SEALs reached the location, their mission to capture a Viet Cong military leader. What happened instead was the killing of at least thirteen women and children. Whether it was an accident caused when the soldiers returned fire after being shot at or an intentional act of murder remains a matter of dispute because there has never been an official investigation.[13]

There are still missing pieces that keep from us a full picture of wartime atrocities. We will never know how many civilians died during the war. Hanoi intentionally overcounted; Washington no less intentionally kept no count at all. There were at least 65,000 North Vietnamese civilians killed during the war, many of them victims of the air raids documented in vivid detail by the Russell tribunal.[14] The number of South Vietnamese non-combatant deaths was much higher. Guenter Lewy, who has done as much as any historian to defend the actions of US forces during the war, estimates that there were more than 1.1 million South Vietnamese civilian casualties, 250,000 of them fatal – in a country whose population was around only 19 million.[15]

Death came repeatedly from the skies. The Pentagon insisted that its bombing campaign was proportionate and precise, but the scale of destruction unleashed by American aircraft exposed this as blatant falsehood. US squadrons dropped more than five million tons of bombs on Vietnam, more than twice the amount unloaded in every military theatre of the Second World War. More than two million tons fell on the neutral countries Laos and Cambodia. No area suffered worse than Quang Tri, the north-ernmost province of South Vietnam; by the end of the war, only eleven of its 3,500 villages were unscathed. The rest of the region had been bombed flat, its people dead, wounded or displaced. Ecologist Arthur Westing was witness to the humanitarian crisis caused by the carnage. 'As far as we could determine,' he wrote, 'not a single permanent building, urban or rural, remained intact: no schools, no libraries, no churches or pagodas, and no hospitals.' The carpet-bombing of Quang Tri came in support of US troops engaged in intense ground fighting with the Viet Cong, but that was not true of other areas affected by aerial bombardment. What made much of the destruction so senseless was its lack of strategic importance. A study by the US Department of Defense concluded that only 4 per cent of air sorties were in support of ground troops immersed in heavy fighting.[16]

When mounting public concern compelled a response from the Pentagon, it still would not repent its sins. Officials continued to insist that American forces scrupulously avoided air strikes 'beyond that degree which is necessary for military purposes'. Yes, the Pentagon finally conceded four years after the tribunal first made the accusation that American planes had bombed civilian hospitals in North Vietnam, but explained that the blame rested with an enemy that purposely failed to identify buildings because of the propaganda value when they became accidental targets. So much for the photographs that the tribunal investigative teams had taken of red crosses painted on the roofs of healthcare facilities.[17]

The scarred landscape of Vietnam remains littered with American ordinance. What fell from the skies included the fragmentation bombs that the Pentagon denied using, despite being exposed by the Russell tribunal. The tribunal concluded without hard evidence that the use of these munitions constituted a deliberate assault on civilians, but there are other ways to account for the harm caused to non-combatants. Anti-personnel weapons expert Eric Prokosch has pointed to the carelessness of pilots who attacked 'targets of opportunity' without confirming their military function, the random dispersal of steel pellets beyond an intended bombing location, and even bad weather. He also makes plain that the secrecy surrounding the use of a weapon with the potential to cause death and injury to unarmed civilians precluded public debate that might have led to the imposition of tighter restraints. His conclusion is hardly less damning than the tribunal. 'A major military power, formally committed to upholding the laws of war, introduced a radically new weapon, carrying a high risk of indiscriminate effects on civilians, with no public discussion and little in the way of internal controls.'[18]

That assessment is consistent with the assertion made by the tribunal that the Vietnam War acted as a laboratory for the testing of new military technology. American aircraft were armed with other incendiary weapons including napalm and white phosphorus as well as herbicides and defoliants. Between 1963 and 1973, US forces fired 388,000 tons of napalm on Vietnam.[19] Others had protested its use before the tribunal, but the appearance of civilian victims burned and maimed by the liquid fire provided visceral evidence of its physical effect.

The tribunal did more than document what the US military was doing; it also provided a persuasive explanation. Later attempts to account for the war crimes committed by American troops read much like the narrative that Sartre constructed at the second session of the tribunal. The training some received instilled hostility towards the Vietnamese which drew little or no distinction between Northern soldiers and Southern civilians. Flown into a foreign land, rookie soldiers found themselves surrounded by a dense landscape of mountains, wetlands and forest. Ambushes and booby traps awaited without warning from the peasant population they had been told would welcome them as liberators but in fact scorned and resented them. The rules of engagement for US soldiers were clear on the need for combat operations to minimise civilian casualties, but how words written on paper were interpreted and applied was another matter.[20] American atrocities were therefore a reaction to the extreme nature of the environment. Far from home, frustrated and fearful, soldiers took out their torment in arbitrary military action.[21]

But war crimes were caused by more than the aberrant behaviour of individual units overwhelmed by circumstance; as the tribunal contended, they were the inevitable consequence of policies pursued by military command. The Vietnam War was a conflict without conventional front lines; captured territory might be abandoned as US forces pursued their elusive enemy, and with no clearly defined battlefield, military success came to be measured by the number of kills.[22]

What became an obsession with body counts fuelled the bloodthirstiness of some military operations. The drive against the Viet Cong in the Mekong Delta launched in December 1968 was dubbed Operation Speedy Express. Under the command of 'the Butcher of the Delta', Major General Julian Ewell, the 9th Infantry Division launched an offensive that after four months had a kill ratio of 134:1, double that of any other military unit. That might have made more of a contribution to winning the war if they had killed only enemy soldiers, but most of their victims were civilians. The use of firepower was indiscriminate, a 'spray and splay' policy that made a target of anyone inside the free-fire zone. Bullets, bombs and napalm rained down on the Delta. Not until June 1972 did the truth of what had been proclaimed a military victory threaten to leak out. *Newsweek* published a story much redacted by its own editors, and a subsequent internal military investigation concluded that not only was the claim of 5,000 civilian deaths an underestimate, but that they were the 'constant, accepted and indeed inevitable result' of the operation. Here was evidence that My Lai was no aberration, that the massacre of non-combatants by US forces was the direct consequence of military strategy. It was a truth for which the army would not be held accountable. The report, and with it the revelation of what wanton violence the American military had committed – and more importantly, why – was suppressed.[23]

Also acting under the radar was the CIA. Veteran journalist John Pilger describes as a 'Mafia-style campaign' their kidnapping, torture and assassination of senior NLF cadres. Driven by the same indiscriminate attitude towards all Vietnamese people, the Phoenix Program had 'neutralised' almost 20,000 by 1969, only 150 of whom held high rank within the NLF.[24]

One could go on. When the Russell tribunal had levelled the charge of war crimes against the United States it had been dismissed as a malicious prosecution. But as more evidence of what was happening in Indochina was splashed across television screens and front pages, others renewed the effort to hold the US establishment accountable. While it was dead and buried in the public imagination, the Russell tribunal was about to experience a second life.

As the revelations of US atrocities continued, some commentators started to reconsider their estimation of the tribunal. Some were always willing to defend Russell and Sartre from the blows directed at them. In a necessary corrective to the slanderous article by Bernard Levin published by the same newspaper almost a year earlier, the British journalist Paul Johnson wrote in *The New York Times* that Russell's condemnation of the war was entirely consistent with his moral philosophy. 'To compromise would be to repudiate the workings of his own intellect, and so to betray the moral consistency of a lifetime. He is indifferent to unpopularity or isolation. He has been unpopular and isolated before, and later vindicated by events.' Whatever contemporary critics claimed, cautioned Johnson, the judgement of history could well say otherwise.[25]

There was also sympathy in the press for governmental reprisals against members of the tribunal. In June 1967, de Beauvoir approached the British Council about a holiday in the Lake District she hoped to take with her adopted daughter Sylvie Le Bon, worried about 'any trouble' that her association with the tribunal would cause to the trip. Perhaps concerned about adverse publicity, immigration officials decided to admit the author despite her connection with the tribunal.[26] On the other side of the Atlantic, the US State Department was less accommodating. James Baldwin had not attended the tribunal in part because he feared the revocation of his passport; the treatment of others associated with it proved his fears well founded. First the State Department demanded that investigative team member Conrad Lynn surrender his passport. Then it refused a visa to Vladimir Dedijer, citing immigration rules that allowed the exclusion of foreigners who might 'engage in activities which would be prejudicial to the public interest'. *The New York Times* might have disagreed with Dedijer's opinion about the war, but it still defended his right to say it. It was, the paper said, 'deeply repugnant to this nation's traditions of freedom for the Government to screen and censor the free exchange of ideas', no matter how foolish or offensive.[27]

As the news stories of atrocities committed by American soldiers circulated, some commentators started to reassess their opinion. Might the tribunal have been right all along? Some were still in denial about the stories of American soldiers whose moral compasses were crushed underfoot in the jungles and rice paddies. Others accepted that their side had exceeded the conventions of war, but were unwilling to admit that they had ignored the early warning. But there were also those willing to concede they should have heeded the tribunal. Princeton law professor Richard Falk was among them. In an article for *The*

New York Times, he reconsidered his earlier dismissal of the tribunal, conceding that its proceedings 'provide a generally reliable account of the criminal side of the American war effort in Vietnam'. He was not alone. In the same newspaper, John J. O'Connor noted how Russell had been seen as 'at best a senile fool, at worst a propagandistic tool for Hanoi', before noting that events since then had altered that perspective. A BBC and PBS co-produced programme, screened on both sides of the Atlantic, emulated the tribunal in bringing together a team of international participants to assess whether US forces had committed war crimes and it made for compelling viewing.[28]

Still insisting on some of their earlier criticisms, other commentators conceded that the tribunal had been ahead of the curve in challenging the conventional narrative of the war. *Newsweek* reluctantly concluded that for all its lack of legal authority, the tribunal had 'borne legitimate polemic witness'.[29] The *Guardian* confessed that for all their political bias, Russell, Sartre and their associates had made 'a fair and appealing point' about the excessive use of military force. It was their achievement to 'rivet attention on the contradictions of American behaviour', creating a conviction 'now held by most reasonable people' that 'the United States must get out of Indo-China – and quickly'.[30]

Then there was Neil Sheehan, the soldier turned *New York Times* war correspondent. March 1971 saw the appearance of his essay 'Should We Have War Crime Trials?' Having reported on the accusations made by veterans on their return home and read through the many volumes about the conduct of US forces in Vietnam, Sheehan concluded that the answer was yes. He had once agreed when the conclusions of Russell and his associates were ridiculed as 'a combination of kookery and propaganda'. Now, he wrote, 'They should not have been.'[31]

Sheehan posed a question that others had already positively

answered. The revelation of the My Lai massacre roused activists in the United States to emulate the model established by Russell and Sartre and launch renewed investigation of alleged war crimes. As the optimism of the 1960s soured into the disillusionment of the 1970s, it seemed that the philosophers' struggle to speak truth to power could at last affect public perception of American military action.

The months following the exposure of the My Lai massacre also saw the publication of more than thirty books documenting alleged war crimes by US forces. An earlier volume by the group Clergy and Laymen Concerned About Vietnam had come out with a small independent publisher and made little impact.[32] Now that American atrocities were news, large publishing houses signed up one compendium of real-life horror stories after another – including the republication of the proceedings of the Russell tribunal. First published in the United States by the obscure press O'Hare Books, it found a new readership when Simon & Schuster issued a new edition, alongside translations around the world.

Critics could dismiss many of these publications for being written by the usual suspects of the peace movement, loony clerics and lefty college professors – but not so Telford Taylor. Having reached the rank of brigadier general in the US Army during the Second World War, Taylor then served as lead prosecutor during the Nuremberg trials; in his book *Nuremberg and Vietnam: An American Tragedy*, published in 1970, he applied the criteria used to convict the former leaders of Axis forces to show how the likes of William Westmoreland should stand in the dock for the war crimes perpetrated by their troops. Three years earlier, Russell and Sartre had been scorned for citing Nuremberg as a precedent for investigating American military atrocities; now the lead counsel was making that same argument.[33]

By the time that Taylor's book appeared, anti-war activists had already started to put his words into action. The prime mover was Ralph Schoenman, who had suffered a series of set-backs since his enforced absence from Roskilde. First divorced by his wife, then deported by British authorities back to the United States, he also became distanced from Bertrand Russell after the philosopher finally heeded friends who had long warned of the damage done to his reputation by the relationship. In November 1969 Schoenman suggested to anti-war activists Tod Ensign and Jeremy Rifkin that they establish another tribunal that would show how My Lai was one of many war crimes committed by US forces in Vietnam.[34]

During spring 1970, the National Committee for a Citizens' Commission of Inquiry on U.S. War Crimes (CCI) held press conferences in thirteen cities across the United States. Conservative in attire and calm in demeanour, veterans testified to the many atrocities they had committed or witnessed. Forty travelled to Washington for a National Veterans' Inquiry held at the Dupont Plaza Hotel from 1 to 3 December, the plush red carpet and luminous gold wallpaper of their surroundings contrasting with the brutality of the stories they told. Their narrative of the war was consistent with the Russell tribunal not only in broad terms but also precise details about the dehumanisation of the Vietnamese, from the removal of the ears of dead enemy soldiers to the electric shocks administered during interrogation. As the Russell tribunal had heard in Roskilde, the soldiers who racked up the highest number of kills were rewarded with crates of beer. Medical corps officer Robert Master was representative of the veterans in his assertion that the atrocities were the direct consequence of military strategy. In his words, 'war crimes in Vietnam are not isolated, aberrant acts but the inevitable result of a policy which in direction of waging war against the civilians, Vietnamese civilians, is in itself immoral and criminal.'[35]

The inquiry had been intended as a collaboration between the CCI and Vietnam Veterans Against the War (VVAW), but personnel issues had led to a parting of the ways, with the latter group sponsoring a separate tribunal that came to be known as the Winter Soldier Investigation.[36] Celebrities rallied to its cause, David Crosby and Graham Nash headlining a series of benefit concerts at which they performed a folky protest anthem inspired by Marine turned investigation witness Scott Camil.[37] But among the firmament of stars who turned out in support, none shone brighter than Jane Fonda, her involvement emphasising the enduring impact of the Russell tribunal on American anti-war activism. She read about the Stockholm proceedings and began to take an active interest in the peace movement; the Winter Soldier Investigation was, in her words 'an American version' of the event staged by Russell and Sartre.[38]

They convened in Detroit for three days between 31 January and 2 February 1971, 109 veterans and 16 civilians. Each of them told of their own experience, but the stories collectively amounted to an indictment of US military action. From indiscriminate bombing and chemical warfare to mistreatment of prisoners and slaughtering of civilians, the investigation reiterated the themes first articulated by the Russell tribunal four years earlier. And once more, the emphasis was not on the deviance of individuals but the commands of senior officers who indoctrinated soldiers to see the Vietnamese as less than human. 'It's the policy that's important,' insisted medic Jamie Henry, who had witnessed the killing of women and children by members of Company B, 1st Battalion, 35th Infantry. 'The executions are secondary because the executions are created by the policy that is, I believe, a conscious policy within the military.'[39]

Veterans had found their voice, but few of their fellow citizens were listening. The press paid little attention to either the Washington or Detroit event, more focused as it was on the *Apollo 14* moon landing, and what was printed tended to be hostile or dismissive. For all the evidence that was appearing in their own pages, newspapers persisted in referring to the incidents recounted by veterans as 'so-called' war crimes.[40] The Nixon administration also added the dissident servicemen to its list of enemies of the state, White House officials conducting background checks with a view to smearing the veterans' credentials.[41] Yet the testimonies of former soldiers reached the ears of some influential figures. Senator Mark Hatfield had a transcript of the Winter Soldier Investigation read into the Congressional Record and called on both the State Department and Pentagon to investigate the war crimes accusations. A relatively unknown naval lieutenant also drew on the Winter Soldier testimonies when he appeared before the Senate Committee on Foreign Relations in April 1971. John Kerry would later serve as US Secretary of State.[42]

The congressional investigation of war crimes called for by Senator Hatfield never occurred, but that did not prevent other politicians from pursuing justice. California Congressman Ronald Dellums was a self-styled 'Afro-topped, bell-bottomed radical' who won his seat on an openly anti-war platform. The politician displayed photographs from the Winter Solider Investigation in his office and secured the support of more than twenty representatives in pushing for a congressional probe of war crimes. When that did not succeed, he set up his own commission. Meeting in a congressional committee room during April 1971, it too concluded that war crimes were the direct consequence of military policy.[43]

While there was debate within the United States about war crimes, pressure also continued from without. In June 1971, activists, veterans and intellectuals from twenty countries convened in Oslo for an International Commission of Inquiry into U.S. War Crimes in Indochina. The commission emulated the Russell tribunal in almost every respect, from sending investigative teams to Vietnam to the hearing of testimonies from American soldiers and civilian survivors. So too the commission's conclusion that the US was attempting to destroy enemy morale by intentionally targeting their civilian infrastructure. As had been true of the Russell tribunal, international press reaction was also divided on predictably partisan lines, with plaudits from the left and disapproval from the right.[44] Not that this dissuaded the commission from convening a second time sixteen months later. This time the location was Denmark – and not a trade union hall in a provincial city but the capital, with none other than Prime Minister Anker Joergensen in attendance.[45]

Amid all this activity, it also appeared for a moment that the Russell war crimes tribunal would reassemble for a third session. In the two years between the Roskilde session and the breaking news of My Lai, the members of the war crimes tribunal had been far from inactive. So long as the war raged on, Russell and Sartre saw it as their moral duty to speak out against it. Fuelled by that conviction, both men influenced a younger generation of activists engaged in the global revolt of 1968.

True to his calling as a warrior for peace, Russell continued to wield his pen against the war. Too frail in body, he stood in spirit with the 8,000 demonstrators crowded shoulder to shoulder in Trafalgar Square on the mild spring morning of Sunday 17 March. A shock of colour in the crowd, Vanessa Redgrave stood in white headband and orange cape before the steps of the National Gallery and read a message by the philosopher written with characteristic moral urgency and clarity. Tariq Ali then accompanied the actor as they led a march towards the US Embassy and an ugly confrontation with police.[46] The political situation was still more heated on the other side of the Channel. In May 1968, student protesters launched street demonstrations and staged an occupation of the Sorbonne. Sartre privately wrestled with the meaning of the protests but publicly committed himself to the student cause.[47]

Denounced. Discredited. Defamed. Russell and Sartre had endured the anger and disbelief of the political establishment, the press and the public, before many of their accusations were proven correct. My Lai had occurred three months after the war crimes tribunal had concluded its second session, and it had taken over a year and a half for it to become a news story. Fuelled by an endless reserve of self-conviction, Sartre and Russell had fought on in the face of public indifference and ridicule.

How did the philosophers feel now that the war crimes they had accused the US of committing were front-page news? Pride, perhaps. Anger, certainly. The mea culpas of the media might have given some satisfaction to Russell. Greater still was reconciliation with his own family. The philosopher's daughter Katharine had felt stigmatised by association with her father, embarrassed by the severity of his accusations. But as the slow drip of news stories about civilian massacres swelled to a steady flow, she reassessed what once seemed his deranged tirades. 'We rejected his facts because of his tone of voice,' she wrote, 'but they *were* facts, as we have had to acknowledge since.'[48]

Whatever pleasure Russell took from the easing of family tensions, there was still work to do. 'Now the magnitude of the horror is unfolding,' he wrote, 'and a new duty presents itself.' His hope was for the United Nations to establish an international war crimes commission.[49] Sartre, meanwhile, used a meeting of the International Information Centre for the Denunciation of War Crimes in Paris to publicise the story of a young South Vietnamese woman named Pham Thi Lien. She had survived a US assault on her village that took place in January 1969, but eighteen members of her family had not – and nor had as many as two hundred other inhabitants. Here, Sartre told a press conference, was proof that My Lai was only one of the many crimes committed by American forces.[50]

It was William Calley who faced formal charges for murdering unarmed civilians. But as Russell asserted, 'The entire American people are now on trial.' It was not enough to plead innocence. Only by articulating their 'moral revulsion' would they be acquitted of complicity in the war crimes committed by the likes of Calley. The ailing philosopher would not live to learn the verdict, however. On the evening of 2 February 1970, he retired to bed complaining of a slight touch of flu. For the greatest British philosopher of the twentieth century, it was the beginning of the longest sleep. Six thousand miles away, a war that he had condemned for the senseless slaughter of civilians raged on, three more years passing before the last American troops withdrew. Russell died knowing he had been proven right, but without seeing an end to the wrong. But the friends and associates he had assembled for the war crimes tribunal would continue to cast his light in dark corners.

In May 1972, Sartre and Dedijer approached the other tribunal members about the possibility of a third session. Nothing came of that, but eight months later the tribunal attracted renewed publicity when it invited numerous international statespersons – among them Pope Paul VI, Chilean President Salvador Allende and US Senator Mike Mansfield – to visit Hanoi and experience the impact of bombing raids. None of these notables cancelled their other engagements, but what would once have been dismissed as a publicity stunt attracted admiring comment in the press. The *Guardian* commended the tribunal on being 'the only international group with the reputation and nerve' to encourage greater involvement by world leaders in exposing American military excess.[51]

The tribunal did not reconvene, but the individual members continued to protest the war. Search for photographs of peace demonstrations in Sweden and it won't take you long to find Sara Lidman, as she is often in the centre of the picture. Or scan bookshelves on the war and you'll see the numerous volumes by Peter Weiss, from his travel account of North Vietnam to his study of US air raids to his stage play that draws on the proceedings of the tribunal: *Discourse on the Progress of the Prolonged War of Liberation in Viet Nam and the Events Leading Up to It as Illustration of the Necessity for Armed Resistance Against Oppression and on the Attempts of the United States of America to Destroy the Foundations of Revolution.*[52]

And then there were Sartre and de Beauvoir. Even when the war was over, its impact would be felt around the world for years. Following the fall of Saigon to the PAVN, thousands of ordinary people found themselves in economic hardship, their rights and even their lives at risk from their vengeful new rulers. Thousands died of starvation and disease, many of them after being sent to re-education camps where the inmates were routinely tortured and executed. The result was a mass exodus by more than a million people who boarded ramshackle wooden boats and braved piracy and storms on the South China Sea in search of sanctuary. In 1979, the French government offered to help resolve the humanitarian crisis by accepting 5,000 refugees. Activists, intellectuals and entertainers founded the Boat for Vietnam committee, which lobbied the administration of Valéry Giscard d'Estaing to increase the number to 40,000. One of its most prominent faces was Sartre, the frail and nearly blind figure at the centre of the frame in old newsreels, being escorted through a ruck of reporters into the Élysée Palace. At the press conference afterwards he proclaimed it 'imperative of human rights to save fellow human beings in danger'. The philosopher was less than a year from his death. It had been a struggle for him to lose the sentimental attachment to the North Vietnamese that had blinded him to their crimes, to accept that the people he believed were fighting for freedom should prove to be brutal oppressors. Yet the compassion that had first led him to take up the cause of Vietnamese independence remained undimmed.[53]

By the time Sartre died, the tribunal had been all but forgotten. For a moment it had seemed as though the American public might be on the point of a serious reckoning with the excesses of the war, particularly after the systematic lies of the US government were exposed by Daniel Ellsberg's leaking of the Pentagon Papers to *The New York Times*. Yet shock and anger at news stories about My Lai and other war crimes committed by American soldiers soon abated, succeeded by a sense of numbness for some, forgiveness for others, and resolve for most to move on. It had never been in the interest of the political and military establishment to admit to the pervasiveness of violence against Vietnamese civilians. So too, much of the press and public wanted to forgive or forget without acknowledging what had happened or why. As early as April 1971, Kevin Phillips proclaimed in the *Washington Post* that 'This generation has paid enough for Vietnam.'[54] Whether they saw the war as a national folly or a noble cause, Americans would come to mourn their dead, most solemnly with the 58,000 names of service members carved into the black granite walls of the Vietnam Veterans Memorial in Washington. Memories of the Vietnamese civilian victims of American war crimes would be buried with no marker in the deeper recesses of the public mind.

As histories of the Vietnam War came to be written, the tribunal merited little more than a footnote, if it was mentioned at all. But as the first endeavour of its kind, an attempt by a small group of political idealists to mobilise the power of their celebrity in a challenge to a global superpower, its influence transcends the conflict that brought it into being.

The tribunal's narrative of the war was less than entirely reliable. Its members' enmity towards US military action blinded them to the barbarities of the North Vietnamese. How could they be accused of war crimes, maintained the tribunal, when they were merely defending their nation from invasion by a militarily more powerful aggressor? The North Vietnamese might have been David to the US Goliath, but they did more than sling a well-aimed stone at their enemy. They assassinated political adversaries, launched artillery assaults on residential centres, even occupied villages with the intention of luring attacks from American forces, the propaganda value of which considered to be worth more than the civilian lives lost. The tribunal investigative teams may have toured the locations of US assaults on non-military targets, but Hanoi countenanced no independent inspection of places reported to be the site of atrocities committed by its own forces – and nor did it acknowledge the need to comply with the terms of the Geneva Convention for the treatment of prisoners of war. Contrary to what the tribunal claimed, the vices of the American military did not render virtuous the North Vietnamese.[55]

Nor did the tribunal adhere entirely to the evidence. Rhetorical excess at times distracted from the substance of the documentation it amassed. That was none more the case than with its conclusion that the US was committing genocide. The scale of destruction was immense, the number of deaths innumerable, but among the thousands of documents that have slowly been released to the public, there is no evidence of a deliberate intention to eliminate the Vietnamese people. Before they had first set foot in the field of combat, many army recruits learned to see the Vietnamese as subhuman – but that still fell far short of being drilled to wage a war of extermination. US soldiers committed many atrocities in Vietnam, but that was true neither of all nor even most of them. Some refused orders, others intervened. The My Lai massacre is in part the story of the soldiers who murdered and raped unarmed civilians, but it is in another part the tale of the flight crew led by Warrant Officer Hugh Thompson who landed their helicopter between the women and children cowering in a bunker and the men from Charlie Company advancing towards them. The soldiers who testified at the second session of the tribunal in Roskilde also showed how soldiers could feel horror at what they had witnessed or remorse for what they had done. For the tribunal to demean all American servicemen as the executioners of an entire nation was no less dehumanising than what they claimed the US was doing.[56]

Dismissed at the time as the enterprise of fools and fanatics, the Russell tribunal now occupies a status somewhere between honourable failure and success. It did nothing to bring an end to the war and the excesses of US military action – but neither did a media that for too long compliantly towed the line of official spokespersons, nor international institutions such as the United Nations, not even the thousands of demonstrators around the world. What the tribunal did was to bear witness to the atrocities committed by the most powerful military force in the history of warfare on a small and impoverished nation struggling to step out of the shadow of colonial control. Russell, Sartre and their associates did not get everything right, but for all those who ridiculed them history would uphold their fundamental point that the American military not only exceeded the moral and legal conventions of warfare but also lied about it. The tribunal therefore set an important precedent for private citizens seeking to hold to account those in power.

EPILOGUE

After they shot him, the soldiers threw a grenade on the ground to give the impression that he had been about to ambush them. Their senior officer was suspicious but ordered a staff sergeant to make sure he was dead. The soldier complied, shooting two more bullets into the prostrate corpse. Later, those responsible posed for photographs while standing over their victim, from whom they had severed a finger as a souvenir.

With no investigation of the incident, the soldiers continued their slaughter of civilians for another four months. Individuals who dared to question what was happening suffered threats and intimidation. The Pentagon suppressed images of troops posing with the mutilated bodies of their victims. Eleven soldiers were eventually convicted, either for the abuse and murder of civilians or subsequently attempting to cover up the crimes. 'We will continue to do whatever we need to as an institution to understand how it happened, why it happened, and what we need to do to prevent it from happening again,' read a press release from the US Department of Defense.

This story has all the characteristics of the atrocities committed during the Vietnam War, yet it relates to a much more recent historical moment. The murder of an unarmed civilian, fifteen-year-old Gul Mudin, occurred in the Afghan village of La Mohammad Kalay on 15 January 2010.[1]

'History doesn't repeat itself,' mused Mark Twain, 'but it often rhymes.' US defence officials might be better able to prevent such war crimes if they recognised that they had happened before. Instead, the rhetoric about the misdeeds of a 'rogue unit' prevented a deeper review of institutional failures.

In the late 1960s, the Russell tribunal demonstrated that US forces had committed war crimes in Vietnam, caused not by the aberrant behaviour of individual units but the policies of military command. For all that the later exposure of pervasive violence against civilians proved the accuracy of these claims, there was never a proper public assessment of what had happened. The impact of the war on American servicemen who came home to a country that could be hostile to sacrifice was of more concern than the devastating losses of the foreign civilians they were sent to defend and liberate. When the brutalities inflicted on non-combatants were remembered at all, it was as the actions of a few 'bad apples', and less attention was paid to whether the tree might be infected at the root.

This indisposition to address the systemic causes of human rights violations has been a recurring aspect of the military conflicts fought by the United States and its allies in the half-century since the end of the Vietnam War. Two decades after they were first published, the photographs of American soldiers abusing detainees at the Abu Ghraib prison in Iraq have lost none of their power to shock. Stripped naked, blinded by hoods, leashed like animals, forced to perform one degrading act after another: the scale of prisoner abuse aroused international condemnation. There were, however, resonances of the massacre at My Lai in the response from Washington. President George W. Bush reluctantly acknowledged what had happened, but attributed it to the aberrant behaviour of 'a few American troops who dishonored our country and disregarded our values'. Those soldiers were convicted of various charges, most of them receiving minor sentences. Documents later obtained by the media nonetheless revealed that responsibility for the abuses extended right up the chain of command, the use of 'enhanced interrogation techniques' having been authorised by the US Department of Justice. In the words of these memoranda, the US was engaged in a 'new kind of war' to which the Geneva Convention on the treatment of prisoners did not apply. The soldiers who physically harmed and psychologically humiliated detainees were not disobeying orders; they were doing what they understood as their duty. Referring to the photographs taken inside the prison, Michael Massing wrote in the *Los Angeles Times* how, 'We must recognize that those smirking grins and sadistic leers are not simply expressions of some alien breed – they are the face of America at war.' Yet institutional reform did not follow. As the publication of leaked documents later disclosed, the maltreatment of prisoners persisted even after Abu Ghraib had become the focus of international scandal.

Interviewed in 2006, Mike Sallah, one of the reporters who uncovered the atrocities committed in Vietnam, contended that the US military would be caught in an endless cycle unless it confronted the failures of that war or the more recent conflict in Iraq. 'Airing this stuff could help them become more accountable by creating some kind of institutional memory that helps establish safeguards,' he asserted. 'Without this, they're doomed to repeat the same mistakes.'[2]

Events in La Mohammad Kalay attest to the prophetic nature of Sallah's warning. But much as the killing of Vietnamese civilians by Tiger Force must be seen in the broader context of US military action, so too the incident in La Mohammad Kalay was far from the only instance of unwarrantable violence against Afghan civilians.

Take the use of drone strikes. For all that the Pentagon is adamant about the precision of such tactics, it has an unfortunate record of killing not only suspected militants and terrorists but also innocent civilians. In August 2021, a US bombardment of a densely populated neighbourhood in the Afghan capital Kabul took the lives of aid worker Zamairi Ahmadi and nine of his relatives. General Mark Milley, the chair of the Joint Chiefs of Staff, proclaimed it a 'righteous strike' on Taliban members who were preparing a bomb attack on the city airport only for the explosives being loaded into the boot a car to turn out to be water bottles.[3] US bombs have also hit humanitarian structures, including a Médecins Sans Frontières hospital in Kunduz, and the abuse of civilians during night raids by CIA-backed Afghan forces has also come in for criticism.[4]

It is not difficult to see the parallels between the cruel and careless attitude towards civilians condemned by the Russell tribunal and events in Afghanistan and Iraq many decades later. So, too, the reluctance of the US government and military to take remedial measures. Military officials will reluctantly admit their regret for mistakes made, but without making anyone answerable or assessing the merits of their strategy. According to an analysis of 228 military inquiries into potential civilian casualty incidents in Afghanistan, Iraq and Syria between 2002 and 2015, only 16 per cent led to on-site investigations by the army.[5]

One does not have to dispute the purpose of the War on Terror to accept that military action has led to excessive civilian fatalities. The Watson Institute for International and Public Affairs calculates that, as of September 2021, American wars since the 9/11 terror attacks have caused the violent deaths of an estimated 432,093 civilians. All sides in these conflicts are responsible, but the US could be clearer about its culpability by including these numbers in its official reporting.[6]

Vietdamned

The US has also resisted accountability by not recognising the jurisdiction of the International Criminal Court in The Hague. The American Service-Members' Protection Act of 2002 empowers the president to use 'all means necessary and appropriate to bring about the release of any U.S. or allied personnel' detained by the ICC. When ICC officials have pursued the prosecution of Americans for alleged offences against civilians, Washington has retaliated by cancelling visas and threatening criminal charges.[7] This situation is ironically counterproductive to US global strategy. Defence officials have, for instance, opposed handing over evidence of Russian war crimes in Ukraine, for fear that their cooperation could set a precedent for future prosecution of Americans.[8]

None of this is to contend that the US more than any other nation exceeds the legal and moral constraints of warfare. But accusations that the US has violated the human rights of civilians caught up in military conflict are a concern because of its status as leader of the free world. It has long seen itself as a civilising influence in global affairs, yet its moral force is undermined when American soldiers commit war crimes, with implications for us all.

What can be done to hold world leaders to account? Russell and Sartre may be long dead, but later generations of authors, artists and intellectuals have similarly attempted to use the power of their celebrity to protest military aggression against innocent people.

'The invasion was an arbitrary military action inspired by a series of lies upon lies and gross manipulation of the media and therefore of the public,' he avowed. The world had witnessed 'a formidable assertion of military force responsible for the death and mutilation of thousands and thousands of innocent people.

242

We have brought torture, cluster bombs, depleted uranium, innumerable acts of random murder, misery, degradation and death.' The Nobel Prize laureate was in declining health, yet so long as his voice could still be heard he was determined to speak out against what he considered the criminal aggression of the United States and its allies. Some admired him, others mocked. 'His recent output has consisted almost entirely of rabid anti-war, anti-American' ranting, commented *The Times*.[9]

It might sound like Bertrand Russell and the Vietnam War, but this was playwright Harold Pinter using his speech on winning the Nobel Prize in Literature in December 2005 to denounce the US-led assault on Iraq. Pinter is not the only public figure to have assumed the mantle of Russell and Sartre in braving censure and ridicule to speak out against the excesses of recent military conflicts. The tribunal that met in 1967 had a short and troubled existence, but it has enjoyed a curiously enduring afterlife.

There have been many more Russell tribunals during the last half-century. In 1974, Lelio Basso convened new sessions, this time focused on human rights abuses committed by the dictatorships in Brazil and Chile. Further tribunals have followed, including investigations of alleged criminal transgressions relating to the Iraq War in 2004 and Palestine in 2009. Their panels continue to be filled by famous names, including the likes of activist and author Angela Davis and novelist Alice Walker.

The Russell tribunal in turn inspired the creation of similar bodies that attempt to hold the powers-that-be accountable for their supposed abuses. The Permanent Peoples' Tribunal founded by Lelio Basso met for the first time in Bologna in June 1979, with the purpose of facilitating justice for those frustrated by the bureaucratic slowness of the United Nations.[10] Then there was the World Tribunal on Iraq, which held hearings in twenty cities from 2003 to 2005, with the novelist Arundhati Roy delivering its damning verdict on purported crimes committed by US-led coalition forces.[11] In 2016 a tribunal convened in The Hague to investigate human rights violations by the chemical manufacturer Monsanto.[12] And most recently, there has been the Belmarsh tribunal convened by philosopher Srećko Horvat. Named after the prison where WikiLeaks founder Julian Assange was imprisoned following the release of leaked documents relating to the conflicts in Iraq and Afghanistan, the tribunal is a further attempt to indict Washington informally for alleged war crimes. Its membership encompasses a diverse array of celebrities, from economist Yanis Varoufakis to philosopher Slavoj Žižek.[13]

These tribunals typically fail to solve the imperfections of the model on which they are based. Those involved are no more immune to criticism than Russell and his associates were nearly sixty years ago. The tribunals claim to be acting in the interest of a public who have no say in their purpose, the persons they appoint or the procedures they follow. The accused is usually the United States and its Western allies, the presumption is that they are guilty, and the outcome is entirely predictable. It is bad enough that facts are selected to fit preconceptions rather than to inform opinions, but the tribunals seldom adhere even to select evidence, their decisions embellished by the burning flame of moralistic rhetoric. The tribunals are therefore doomed by the fault of their own design never to have much sway on policymakers or the public.[14]

As was true of the Russell tribunal, some of these criticisms hit the mark but others are more wayward. Condemning such enterprises for their lack of formal authority would carry more weight if they attempted to enforce their decisions; the role of tribunals is not to arrest and sentence but to present evidence of crimes for review by the broader court of international opinion. The tribunals may also be partisan, but it is hardly the case that those accused of human rights violations have no means to put their own point of view. Reflecting on the World Tribunal on Iraq, Arundhati Roy said, 'If there is one thing that has come out clearly in the last few days, it is not that the corporate media supports the global corporate project; it is the global corporate project.' It is not necessary to share that simplification of the mainstream media to appreciate that governments in Washington and elsewhere have enormous access to news outlets.[15]

Whether acting alone like Harold Pinter or in concert with others, do public figures have any real purpose agitating against the possible criminal transgressions of governments? What can they really achieve other than aggrandise already large egos? Can they actually make a difference?

We live in different times to those in which Bertrand Russell and Jean-Paul Sartre sought to prove that the US was committing war crimes in Vietnam. At that time, theirs were rare voices raised against a powerful political establishment. The tribunal anticipated a later era of investigative journalism, human rights activism and whistle-blowing that formed a chorus of dissent on domestic and international politics, an era that seems to have passed its high-water mark. Public figures are still important, and as long as governments suppress or misrepresent the truth about conflicts fought in our name, as long as elements of the press collude through the passive acceptance of official narratives, and as long as international organisations such as the United Nations seem incapable of holding strong countries to account, there will be a place for those who – like Russell and Sartre – attempt to speak truth to power. The two philosophers were never in a position to end the Vietnam War, but they imparted an important lesson: bearing witness to what is happening around us communicates a greater solidarity with the suffering of others.

In documenting the crimes committed in the world's endless wars, those who follow in the footsteps of Russell and Sartre raise awareness of human atrocities in the hope that they will not always be tolerated. The broader legacy of the tribunal can be seen in the continuing efforts of celebrities to use their fame and influence as a means of holding governments accountable. From Live Aid to the dissenting artists at the forefront of opposition to the Iraq War, public personalities have pursued the pioneering path of the Russell tribunal in mobilising moral pressure on politicians for their action or inaction. In this, they honour the words of Bertrand Russell that 'One must care about a world one will not see.'

ACKNOWLEDGEMENTS

On a visit to Stockholm in the summer of 2024, I turned left at the graffitied sign for Peter Weiss Plats and headed towards the Folkets Hus, only to find the building closed for extensive refurbishment. Hopefully this book will preserve something of what seems to be a disappearing history.

I could not have written it without the support of many people. My sincerest thanks go to my agent Sally Holloway and publisher Andrew Franklin for their interest and enthusiasm. I am indebted to William Carrigan and especially Nicholas W. Mason for rescuing me at the last moment with essential overseas research. My editors, Calah Singleton and Nick Humphrey, immeasurably improved the manuscript. Patrick Taylor provided meticulous copyediting and Seán Costello proofreading. Georgina Difford skilfully and patiently oversaw completion of the project. Any errors that remain are my responsibility.

Others who have offered advice and encouragement include Steve Bishop, Anthony Booth, Sam Edwards, Simon Hall, Malcolm Hardy, Wendy Hardy, Al Kendall, Mahon O'Brien, Steve Pearce, Sarah Sawyer, Michael Stagg, Matthew Thames, Nick Turse, Paul Uncles and Hugh Wilford. I am most grateful to my brother Neil Webb for his belief in the book and, above all, to Kathy Kendall for her faith, love and wisdom. Thanks also to Pippin for much-needed outdoor walks.

From conception to completion, I lost three members of my family, my father Brian, my mother Marjorie and my brother Paul. This book is dedicated to their cherished memories.

BIBLIOGRAPHY

Archives
Bertrand Russell Archives, McMaster University Library, Hamilton,
    Ontario, Canada
CIA Historical Collections
FBI Records: The Vault
International War Crimes Tribunal Records, Tamiment Library and Robert
    F. Wagner Labor Archives, New York
Lyndon Baines Johnson Presidential Library, Austin, Texas
Modern Records Centre, University of Warwick
National Archives, Kew, London

Interviews
Tariq Ali, 11 February 2021
Courtland Cox, 1 March 2021
John Pilger (email), 6 March 2021
Vanessa Redgrave (email), 18 February 2021

Audio and visual material
British Pathé
CIA Freedom of Information Act Electronic Reading Room
John F. Kennedy Presidential Library and Museum
US National Archives

Books and pamphlets
Tariq Ali, *Street Fighting Years: An Autobiography of the Sixties* (London:
    Verso, 2018)

William Thomas Allison, *My Lai: An American Atrocity in the Vietnam War* (Baltimore, MD: Johns Hopkins University Press, 2012)

Günther Anders and Claude Eatherly, *Burning Conscience: The Case of the Hiroshima Pilot* (New York: Paragon House, 1989)

Lisa Appignanesi, *Simone de Beauvoir* (London: Haus, 2005)

Herbert Aptheker, *Mission to Hanoi* (New York: International Publishers, 1966)

Harry S. Ashmore and William C. Baggs, *Mission to Hanoi: A Chronicle of Double-Dealing in High Places* (New York: G. P. Putnam's Sons, 1968)

Sarah Bakewell, *At the Existentialist Café: Freedom, Being and Apricot Cocktails* (London: Chatto & Windus, 2016)

James Baldwin, *The Fire Next Time* (New York: Franklin Watts, 1963)

Simone de Beauvoir, *The Long March*, trans. Austryn Wainhouse (Cleveland and New York: World Publishing Company, 1958)

Simone de Beauvoir, *Memoirs of a Dutiful Daughter*, trans. James Kirkup (Cleveland and New York: World Publishing Company, 1959)

Simone de Beauvoir, *All Said and Done*, trans. Patrick O'Brian (London: André Deutsch and Weidenfeld & Nicolson, 1974)

Simone de Beauvoir, *Adieux: A Farewell to Sartre*, trans. Patrick O'Brian (London: Penguin, 1985)

Simone de Beauvoir, *The Second Sex* [1949], trans. H. M. Parshley (New York: Vintage, 1989 edition)

Michal R. Belknap, *The Vietnam War on Trial: The My Lai Massacre and the Court-Martial of Lieutenant Calley* (Lawrence, KS: University Press of Kansas, 2002)

Richard Boyle, *Flower of the Dragon: The Breakdown of the U.S. Army in Vietnam* (San Francisco, CA: Ramparts Press, 1972)

Andrew Byrnes and Gabrielle Simm, eds, *People's Tribunals and International Law* (Cambridge: Cambridge University Press, 2017)

James Cameron, *Here Is Your Enemy: James Cameron's Complete Report from North Vietnam* (New York: Holt, Rinehart & Winston, 1966)

William H. Chafe, *The Unfinished Journey: America Since World War II* (New York: Oxford University Press, 3rd edn, 1995)

The Citizens' Commission of Inquiry, ed., *The Dellums Committee Hearings on War Crimes in Vietnam* (New York: Vintage, 1972)

Ronald W. Clark, *The Life of Bertrand Russell* (New York: Knopf, 1976)

Clergy and Laymen Concerned About Vietnam, *In the Name of America* (Annandale, VA: Turnpike Press, 1968)

James W. Clinton, *The Loyal Opposition: Americans in North Vietnam, 1965–1972* (Niwot, CO: University Press of Colorado, 1995)

James Clotfelter, *The Military in American Politics* (New York: Harper & Row, 1973)

Ken Coates, Peter Limqueco and Peter Weiss, eds, *Prevent the Crime of Silence: Reports from the Sessions of the International War Crimes Tribunal Founded by Bertrand Russell* (London: Allen Lane, 1971)

Annie Cohen-Solal, *Sartre: A Life* (New York: Pantheon, 1987)

Michel Contat and Michel Rybalka, eds, *The Writings of Jean-Paul Sartre, Volume 1: A Bibliographical Life* (Evanston, IL: Northwestern University Press, 1974)

Gary Cox, *Existentialism and Excess: The Life and Times of Jean-Paul Sartre* (London: Bloomsbury, 2016)

Donald E. Davis and Eugene P. Trani, *The Reporter Who Knew Too Much: Harrison Salisbury and the New York Times* (Lanham, MD: Rowman & Littlefield, 2012)

David Dellinger, *From Yale to Jail: The Life Story of a Moral Dissenter* (Eugene, OR: Wipf and Stock, 1993)

Ronald V. Dellums and H. Lee Halterman, *Lying Down with the Lions: A Public Life from the Streets of Oakland to the Halls of Power* (Boston, MA: Beacon Press, 2000)

L. S. Dembo and Cyrena N. Pondrom, eds, *The Contemporary Writer: Interviews with Sixteen Novelists and Poets* (Madison, WI: University of Wisconsin Press, 1972)

James W. Douglass, *Lightning East to West: Jesus, Gandhi, and the Nuclear Age* (Eugene, OR: Wipf & Stock, 2006)

David Drake, *Sartre* (London: Haus, 2005)

John Duffett, ed., *Against the Crime of Silence: Proceedings of the Russell International War Crimes Tribunal* (Flanders, NJ: O'Hare Books, 1968)

Donald Duncan, *The New Legions* (London: Victor Gollancz, 1967)

Sylvia Ellis, *Britain, America, and the Vietnam War* (Westport, CT: Praeger, 2004)

Adam Fairclough, *Martin Luther King, Jr.* (Athens, GA: University of Georgia Press, 1995)

Barry Feinberg and Ronald Kasrils, *Bertrand Russell's America: His Transatlantic Travels and Writing, A Documented Account, Volume Two 1945–1970* (London: Routledge, 1984)

Jonathan Fenby, *The History of Modern France: From the Revolution to the Present Day* (London: Simon & Schuster, 2015)

Andrew Fiala, *The Just War Myth: The Moral Illusions of War* (Lanham, MD: Rowman & Littlefield, 2008)

Helena Forsås-Scott, *Swedish Women's Writing, 1850–1995* (London and Atlantic Highlands, NJ: Athlone, 1997)

Joseph A. Fry, *Debating Vietnam: Fulbright, Stennis, and Their Senate Hearings* (Lanham, MD: Rowman & Littlefield, 2006)

Joseph A. Fry, *The American South and the Vietnam War: Belligerence, Protest, and Agony in Dixie* (Lexington, KY: University Press of Kentucky, 2015)

John Gerassi, *North Vietnam: A Documentary* (Indianapolis and New York: Bobbs-Merrill, 1968)

William Conrad Gibbons, *The U.S. Government and the Vietnam War: Executive and Legislative Roles and Relationships, Part IV: July 1965–January 1968* (Princeton, NJ: Princeton University Press, 1995)

Robert Gildea, *France Since 1945* (Oxford: Oxford University Press, 2nd edn, 2002)

Joseph Goldstein, Burke Marshall and Jack Schwartz, eds, *The My Lai Massacre and Its Cover-Up: Beyond the Reach of Law? The Peers Commission Report with a Supplement and Introductory Essay on the Limits of Law* (New York: Free Press, 1976)

Doris Kearns Goodwin, *Lyndon Johnson and the American Dream* (New York: Signet, 1976)

Bernd Greiner, *War Without Fronts: The USA in Vietnam* (London: Vintage, 2010)

Nicholas Griffin, ed., *The Selected Letters of Bertrand Russell, Volume 2: The Public Years, 1914–1970* (London and New York: Routledge, 2001)

David Halberstam, *The Best and the Brightest* (New York: Random House, 1972)

Daniel C. Hallin, *The 'Uncensored War': The Media and Vietnam* (Berkeley and Los Angeles: University of California Press, 1986)

Ronald Hayman, *Writing Against: A Biography of Sartre* (London: Weidenfeld & Nicolson, 1986)

George C. Herring, *America's Longest War: The United States and Vietnam, 1950–1975* (New York: Wiley, 1979)

George C. Herring, *LBJ and Vietnam: A Different Kind of War* (Austin, TX: University of Texas Press, 1994)

Seymour Hersh, *My Lai 4: A Report on the Massacre and Its Aftermath* (New York: Random House, 1970)

Mary Hershberger, *Traveling to Vietnam: American Peace Activists and the War* (Syracuse, NY: Syracuse University Press, 1998)

William I. Hitchcock, *The Age of Eisenhower: America and the World in the 1950s* (New York: Simon & Schuster, 2018)

David Horowitz, *Radical Son: A Generational Odyssey* (New York: Touchstone, 1997)

Andrew E. Hunt, *The Turning: A History of Vietnam Veterans Against the War* (New York: New York University Press, 1999)

Andrew E. Hunt, *David Dellinger: The Life and Times of a Nonviolent Revolutionary* (New York: New York University Press, 2006)

Richard H. Immerman, ed., *John Foster Dulles and the Diplomacy of the Cold War* (Princeton, NJ: Princeton University Press, 1990)

Andrew L. Johns, *Vietnam's Second Front: Domestic Politics, the Republican Party, and the War* (Lexington, KY: University Press of Kentucky, 2010)

Howard Jones, *My Lai: Vietnam, 1968, and the Descent into Darkness* (New York: Oxford University Press, 2017)

Edward Kanterian, *Ludwig Wittgenstein* (London: Reaktion Books, 2007)

Kate Kirkpatrick, *Becoming Beauvoir: A Life* (New York: Bloomsbury, 2019)

James Simon Kunen, *Standard Operating Procedure: Notes of a Draft-Age American* (New York: Avon, 1971)

A. J. Langguth, *Our Vietnam: The War, 1954–1975* (New York: Simon & Schuster, 2000)

Mark Atwood Lawrence, *The Vietnam War: A Concise International History* (New York: Oxford University Press, 2008)

Julius Lester, *Revolutionary Notes* (New York: Richard W. Baron, 1969)

Julius Lester, *All Is Well* (New York: William Morrow, 1976)

Guenter Lewy, *America in Vietnam* (Oxford: Oxford University Press, 1978)

Sara Lidman, *Samtal i Hanoi* [Conversations in Hanoi] (Stockholm: Bonniers, 1966)

Fredrik Logevall, *Choosing War: The Lost Chance for Peace and the Escalation of War in Vietnam* (Berkeley, CA: University of California Press, 1999)

Fredrik Logevall, *The Origins of the Vietnam War* (London and New York: Routledge, 2001)

Mark Hamilton Lytle, *America's Uncivil Wars: The Sixties Era from Elvis to the Fall of Richard Nixon* (New York: Oxford University Press, 2006)

John Marciano, *The American War in Vietnam: Crime or Commemoration?* (New York: Monthly Review Press, 2016)

Douglas T. Miller, *On Our Own: Americans in the Sixties* (Lexington, MA: D. C. Heath, 1996)

Ray Monk, *Bertrand Russell: The Spirit of Solitude, 1872–1921* (London: Jonathan Cape, 1996)

Ray Monk, *Bertrand Russell: The Ghost of Madness, 1921–1970* (London: Jonathan Cape, 2000)

Paul Muldoon, ed., *Paul McCartney: The Lyrics, 1956 to the Present* (London: Allen Lane, 2021)

N. S. Nash, *Logistics in the Vietnam Wars, 1945–1975* (Barnsley: Pen & Sword, 2020)

Robert M. Neer, *Napalm: An American Biography* (Cambridge, MA: Belknap Press, 2013)

Michael J. Nojeim and David P. Kilroy, *Days of Decision: Turning Points in U.S. Foreign Policy* (Washington, DC: Potomac Books, 2011)

Carl Oglesby, *Ravens in the Storm: A Personal History of the 1960s Antiwar Movement* (New York: Scribner, 2008)

Kendrick Oliver, *The My Lai Massacre in American History and Memory* (Manchester: Manchester University Press, 2006)

Eric Prokosch, *The Technology of Killing: A Military and Political History of Antipersonnel Weapons* (London and Atlantic Highlands, NJ: Zed Books, 1995)

Chalmers M. Roberts, *First Rough Draft: A Journalist's Journal of Our Times* (New York: Praeger, 1973)

Bertrand Russell, *The Practice and Theory of Bolshevism* (London: George Allen & Unwin, 1920)

Bertrand Russell, *16 Questions on the Assassination* (Richmond, VA: Minority of One, 1964)

Bertrand Russell, *The Autobiography of Bertrand Russell* (London: George Allen & Unwin, 1967)

Bertrand Russell, *War Crimes in Vietnam* (London: George Allen & Unwin, 1967)

Harrison E. Salisbury, *Behind the Lines: Hanoi, December 23, 1966 – January 7, 1967* (London: Secker & Warburg, 1967)

Michael Sallah and Mitch Weiss, *Tiger Force: A True Story of Men and War* (London: Hodder & Stoughton, 2006)

Jean-Paul Sartre, *Being and Nothingness: An Essay on Phenomenological Ontology*, trans. Hazel E. Barnes (New York: Philosophical Library, 1956)

Jean-Paul Sartre, *Words*, trans. Irene Clephane (London: Hamish Hamilton, 1964)

Arthur M. Schlesinger, Jr., *A Thousand Days: John F. Kennedy in the White House* (Boston, MA: Houghton Mifflin, 1965)

John Schultz, *No One Was Killed: The Democratic National Convention, August 1968* (Chicago, IL: University of Chicago Press, 2009)

Laurent Schwartz, *A Mathematician Grappling with His Century*, trans. Leila Schneps (Basel: Birkhäuser, 2001)

Carole Seymour-Jones, *A Dangerous Liaison: Simone de Beauvoir and Jean-Paul Sartre* (London: Cornerstone, 2011)

Melvin Small, *Covering Dissent: The Media and the Anti-Vietnam War Movement* (New Brunswick, NJ: Rutgers University Press, 1994)

Lewis Sorley, *Westmoreland: The General Who Lost Vietnam* (Boston and New York: Harcourt Mifflin Harcourt, 2011)

Charles Sowerwine, *France Since 1870: Culture, Politics and Society* (London: Palgrave, 2018)

Fred L. Standley and Louis H. Pratt, eds, *Conversations with James Baldwin* (Jackson, MS: University Press of Mississippi, 1989)

Tyler Stovall, *Transnational France: The Modern History of a Universal Nation* (Harlow: Longman, 2015)

Katharine Tait, *My Father Bertrand Russell* (New York and London: Harcourt Brace Jovanovich, 1975)

Ernest Tate, *Revolutionary Activism in the 1950s & 60s, Volume 2: Britain, 1965–1970* (London: Resistance Books, 2014)

Telford Taylor, *Nuremberg and Vietnam: An American Tragedy* (New York: Bantam, 1971)

Nick Turse, *Kill Anything That Moves: The Real American War in Vietnam* (New York: Picador, 2013)

Brian VanDeMark, *Into the Quagmire: Lyndon Johnson and the Escalation of the Vietnam War* (New York: Oxford University Press, 1995)

Theodore Voorhees, Jr., *The Silent Guns of Two Octobers: Kennedy and Khrushchev Play the Double Game* (Ann Arbor, MI: University of Michigan Press, 2nd edn, 2021)

James A. Warren, *Year of the Hawk: America's Descent into Vietnam, 1965* (New York: Scribner, 2021)

William J. Weatherby, *James Baldwin: Artist on Fire* (New York: D. I. Fine, 1989)

Robert Weisbrot, *Freedom Bound: A History of America's Civil Rights Movement* (New York: W. W. Norton, 1990)

Peter Weiss, *'Limited Bombing' in Vietnam: Report on the Attacks Against the Democratic Republic of Vietnam by the US Air Force and the Seventh Fleet, After the Declaration of 'Limited Bombing' by President Lyndon B. Johnson on March 31, 1968* (London: Bertrand Russell Peace Foundation, 1969)

Peter Weiss, *Two Plays: Song of the Lusitanian Bogey and Discourse on the Progress of the Prolonged War of Liberation in Viet Nam ...* (New York: Atheneum, 1970)

Peter Weiss, *Notes on the Cultural Life of the Democratic Republic of Vietnam* (London: Calder & Boyars, 1971)

Peter Weiss, *Leavetaking* [1960], trans. Christopher Levenson (New York: Melville House, 2014)

David A. Welch, *Painful Choices: A Theory of Foreign Policy Change* (Princeton, NJ: Princeton University Press, 2005)

Robert B. Westbrook, *John Dewey and American Democracy* (Ithaca, NY: Cornell University Press, 1991)

Donald L. Westerfield, *War Powers: The President, the Congress, and the Question of War* (Westport, CT: Praeger, 1996)

Randall B. Woods, *LBJ: Architect of American Ambition* (New York: Free Press, 2006)

Cecil Woolf and John Bagguley, eds, *Authors Takes Sides on Vietnam* (New York: Simon & Schuster, 1967)

Book chapters, essays and selected articles

Vo Van Ai, 'Isle of Light: A Look Back at the Boat People and the European Left', *World Affairs*, Vol. 176, No. 6 (March/April 2014), pp. 38–46

Tariq Ali, 'Anatomy of a War', *Jacobin*, jacobin.com/2014/08/anatomy-of-a-war

Stefan Andersson, 'The Legacy of the Russell Tribunal', *Russell: The Journal of Bertrand Russell Studies*, Vol. 34, No. 2 (2014), pp. 183–90

James Baldwin, 'The War Crimes Tribunal', *Freedomways*, No. 713 (Summer 1967), pp. 242–4

David Blitz, 'Russell and the Boer War: From Imperialist to Anti-Imperialist', *Russell: The Journal of Bertrand Russell Studies*, Vol. 19, No. 2 (Winter 1999), pp. 117–42

Craig Borowiak, 'The World Tribunal on Iraq: Citizens' Tribunals and the Struggle for Accountability', *New Political Science*, Vol. 30, No. 2 (2008), pp. 161–86

Charlie Cobb and Julius Lester, 'Letters from Hanoi', *The Movement*, Vol. 3, No. 5 (May 1967), p. 5

Ben Cosgrove, 'American Atrocity: Remembering My Lai', *Life*, 13 March 2013, life.com/history/american-atrocity-remembering-my-lai/

Ayça Çubukçu, 'The Political Imaginary of the World Tribunal on Iraq', *Humanity Journal*, 13 November 2019, humanityjournal.org/blog/political-imaginary-world-tribunal-iraq/

Peter Davies, 'Sterling and Strings', *London Review of Books*, Vol. 30, No. 22 (20 November 2008)

David Dellinger, 'Report from the Tribunal', *Liberation* (April 1967), pp. 7–13

David Drake, 'Sartre, Camus and the Algerian War', *Sartre Studies International*, Vol. 5, No. 1 (1999), pp. 16–32

Donald Duncan, '"The Whole Thing Was a Lie!"', *Ramparts* (February 1966), pp. 13–24

Robert Elegant, 'How to Lose a War: The Press and Viet Nam', academics.

wellesley.edu/Polisci/wj/Vietnam/Readings/elegant.htm (originally published in *Encounter*, Vol. 57, No. 2 (August 1981), pp. 73–90)

Jordan Elgrably, 'James Baldwin, The Art of Fiction No. 78', *Paris Review*, 91 (Spring 1984)

Sylvia Ellis, 'British Public Opinion and the Vietnam War', *Journal of Transatlantic Studies*, Vol. 18, No. 3 (2020), pp. 314–32

Sylvia Ellis, 'Lyndon Johnson and Harold Wilson: Pragmatist v. Pragmatist' in Michael Patrick Cullinane and Martin Farr, eds, *The Palgrave Handbook of Presidents and Prime Ministers from Cleveland and Salisbury to Trump and Johnson* (Cham, Switzerland: Palgrave Macmillan, 2022), pp. 217–39

Lawrence Ferlinghetti, 'Moscow in the Wilderness', *Ramparts* (May 1967), p. 22–3

Max Paul Friedman, 'Of Sartre, Race, and Rabies: "Anti-Americanism" and the Transatlantic Politics of Intellectual Engagement', *Atlantic Studies*, Vol. 8, No. 3 (2011), pp. 361–77

David Horowitz, 'Bertrand Russell: The Final Passion', *Ramparts* (April 1970), pp. 36–43

Laurent Jalabert, 'Aux origines de la génération 1968: les étudiants français et la guerre du Vietnam', *Vingtième Siècle: Revue d'histoire*, Vol. 55 (July–September 1997), pp. 69–81

Perry Johansson, 'Resistance and Repetition: The Holocaust in the Art, Propaganda, and Political Discourse of Vietnam War Protests', *Cultural History*, Vol. 10, No. 1 (2021), pp. 111–32

Daniel Lang, 'Casualties of War: An Atrocity in Vietnam', *New Yorker*, 10 October 1969

Mark Atwood Lawrence, 'Mission Intolerable: Harrison Salisbury's Trip to Hanoi and the Limits of Dissent Against the Vietnam War', *Pacific Historical Review*, Vol. 75, No. 3 (2006), p. 429–60

Sara Lidman, 'The Heart of the World' in *They Have Been in North Viet Nam* (Hanoi: Foreign Languages Publishing House, 1968), pp. 9–13

Fredrik Logevall, 'The Swedish-American Conflict Over Vietnam', *Diplomatic History*, Vol. 17, No. 3 (Summer 1993), pp. 421–46

Morris Low, 'Shoichi Sakata: His Life, the Sakata Model and His Achievements', *Progress of Theoretical Physics Supplement*, Vol. 167 (February 2007), pp. 1–8

Tim Madigan, 'The Warrant Report', *Philosophy Now*, No. 66 (2008), philosophynow.org/issues/66/The_Warrant_Report

Harish C. Mehta, 'North Vietnam's Informal Diplomacy with Bertrand Russell: Peace Activism and the International War Crimes Tribunal', *Peace & Change*, Vol. 37, No. 1 (2012), pp. 64–94

Edward Miguel and Gérard Roland, 'The Long-Run Impact of Bombing Vietnam', 2005, eml.berkeley.edu/~groland/pubs/vietnam-bombs_19oct05.pdf

Julien Murphy, 'Sartre on American Racism' in Julie K. Ward and Tommy L. Lott, eds, *Philosophers on Race: Critical Essays* (Oxford: Blackwell, 2002), pp. 222–40

Carl Oglesby, 'Vietnam: This Is Guernica', *The Nation*, 5 June 1967, pp. 714–21

Taylor Owen, 'Bombs Over Cambodia', *The Walrus* (October 2006), gsp.yale.edu/sites/default/files/walrus_cambodiabombing_oct06.pdf

Normand Poirier, 'An American Atrocity', *Esquire* (August 1969), pp. 59–63, 132–41

Gail M. Presbey, 'Martin Luther King Jr. on Vietnam: King's Message Applied to the U.S. Occupation of Iraq and Afghanistan' in Robert E. Birt, ed., *The Liberatory Thought of Martin Luther King Jr.: Critical Essays on the Philosopher King* (Lanham, MD: Lexington Books, 2012), pp. 215–42

M. S. Rajan and T. Israel, 'The United Nations and the Conflict in Vietnam', *International Studies*, Vol. 12, No. 4 (December 1973), pp. 511–40

Peter Ross Range, 'Only One Man Was Found Guilty for His Role in the My Lai Massacre. This Is What It Was Like to Cover His Trial', *Time*, 16 March 2018, time.com/5202268/calley-trial-my-lai-massacre/

Bertrand Russell, 'The Atomic Bomb' in *The Collected Papers of Bertrand Russell*, russell.humanities.mcmaster.ca/our-work/collected-papers/

Jean-Paul Sartre, 'The Chances of Peace', *The Nation*, 30 December 1950, pp. 696–700

Jean-Paul Sartre, 'Preface' in Frantz Fanon, *The Wretched of the Earth* (New York: Grove Press, 1963)

Jean-Paul Sartre, 'Paris Under the Occupation', *Sartre Studies International*, Vol. 4, No. 2 (1998), pp. 1–15 (originally published in *La France libre*, November 1944)

Robert Scheer, 'Lord Russell', *Ramparts* (May 1967), pp. 15–21

Carl-Gustaf Scott, '"Sweden Might Be a Haven, But It's Not Heaven": American War Resisters in Sweden During the Vietnam War', *Immigrants & Minorities*, Vol. 33, No. 3 (2015), pp. 205–30

Tor Sellström, 'Hammarskjöld and Apartheid South Africa: Mission Unaccomplished', *African Journal on Conflict Resolution*, Vol. 11, No. 1 (2011), pp. 35–62

Brendan Smith, 'The "Tribunal Movement" Holds Court in Istanbul', *Global Policy Review*, 26 June 2005

Tony Smith, 'Idealism and People's War: Sartre on Algeria', *Political Theory*, Vol. 1, No. 4 (November 1973), pp. 426–49

Amy Davidson Sorkin, 'Madame Nhu's Match', *New Yorker*, 26 April 2011.

Luke J. Stewart, 'Too Loud to Rise Above the Silence: The United States vs. the International War Crimes Tribunal, 1966–1967', *The Sixties*, Vol. 11, No. 1 (2018), pp. 17–45

Judith Surkis, 'Ethics and Violence: Simone de Beauvoir, Djamila Boupacha, and the Algerian War', *French Politics, Culture & Society*, Vol. 28, No. 2 (2010), pp. 38–55

David Torell, 'Remember the Russell Tribunal?' in Anna Reading and Tamar Katriel, eds, *Cultural Memories of Nonviolent Struggles* (Basingstoke: Palgrave Macmillan, 2015), pp. 111–27

Setsure Tsurushima, 'What I Saw in North Vietnam', *World Outlook*, Vol. 5, No. 16 (21 April 1967), pp. 425–6

Kenneth Tynan, 'Open Letter to an American Liberal' in James K. Bell and Adrian A. Cohn, eds, *Toward the New America* (Lexington, MA: D. C. Heath, 1970)

Rhiannon Vickers, 'Harold Wilson, the British Labour Party, and the War in Vietnam', *Journal of Cold War Studies*, Vol. 10, No. 2 (Spring 2008), pp. 41–70

NOTES

Introduction

1   'The Russell Effect', *Punch*, 5 December 1962, p. 823.
2   *Private Eye*, 29 October 1965.
3   For more on the failure of the UN, see Rajan and Israel, 'The United Nations and the Conflict in Vietnam'. Amnesty International started to raise concerns about civilians only as the war reached its end. See 'Amnesty Unit Makes Appeal on 200,000 Held by Saigon', *The New York Times*, 3 December 1972, p. 5.
4   Monk, *Bertrand Russell: The Ghost of Madness*, p. xi. See also pp. 481 and 484.

1. The Coming of War

1   Peter Whitehead filmed Mitchell's performance for his documentary *Wholly Communion*. You can watch it at youtu.be/FmMCObgu_jc
2   Herring, *LBJ and Vietnam*, p. 31.
3   Halberstam, *The Best and the Brightest*.
4   Welch, *Painful Choices*, p. 119.
5   Quoted in Immerman, *John Foster Dulles and the Diplomacy of the Cold War*, p. 88.
6   Hitchcock, *The Age of Eisenhower*, p. 197.
7   Herring, *America's Longest War*, p. 62.
8   Warren, *Year of the Hawk*, p. 55.
9   Miller, *On Our Own*, p. 150.
10 'Letter from President Eisenhower to President Diem, October 26, 1960' in *Why Vietnam* (Washington, DC: US Government Printing Office, 1965), p. 3.

11 'Remarks of Senator John F. Kennedy at the Conference on Vietnam Luncheon in the Hotel Willard, Washington, D.C., June 1, 1956', John F. Kennedy Presidential Library and Museum, jfklibrary.org/archives/other-resources/john-f-kennedy-speeches/vietnam-conference-washington-dc-19560601

12 Cited in Johns, *Vietnam's Second Front*, p. 17.

13 Schlesinger, Jr., *A Thousand Days*, p. 547.

14 Nojeim and Kilroy, *Days of Decision*, p. 124.

15 Nash, *Logistics in the Vietnam Wars, 1945–1975*, p. 192.

16 Logevall, *The Origins of the Vietnam War*, p. 45.

17 Sorkin, 'Madame Nhu's Match'.

18 Roberts, *First Rough Draft*, p. 221.

19 Take a look at the US National Archives online: archives.gov/exhibits/picturing_the_century/century/century_img88.html

20 Fry, *Debating Vietnam*, p. 24.

21 Lytle, *America's Uncivil Wars*, p. 165.

22 Westerfield, *War Powers*, p. 83.

23 Langguth, *Our Vietnam*, p. 340.

24 VanDeMark, *Into the Quagmire*, p. 63.

25 Goodwin, *Lyndon Johnson and the American Dream*, p. 275.

26 Langguth, *Our Vietnam*, p. 317.

27 VanDeMark, *Into the Quagmire*, p. 19.

28 Logevall, *Choosing War*, p. 274.

29 Woods, *LBJ*, p. 603.

30 Lawrence, *The Vietnam War*, p. 99.

31 Chafe, *The Unfinished Journey*, p. 291.

32 Ibid.

33 Clotfelter, *The Military in American Politics*, p. 126.

34 The British Pathé digital archive includes an abundance of newsreel footage of these events. For a sense of the global scale of protest, see, among others, 'Japan: Tokyo Students' Demonstration Against U.S. Action in Vietnam (1965)', britishpathe.com/asset/209764/; 'USA: Holland: Vietnam Demonstration as World Confederation of Free Trade Unions Congress Opens (1965)', britishpathe.com/asset/210465/; 'Italy: Demonstrators in Rome Protest Against the War in Vietnam (1965)', britishpathe.com/asset/210020/; 'France: Demonstration

Against American Air Raids in North Vietnam at American Embassy in Paris (1965)', britishpathe.com/asset/142745/; 'Denmark: Demonstrators in Copenhagen Protest at United States Action in Vietnam (1965)', britishpathe.com/asset/142959/; 'Sweden: Teenagers Riot After Vietnam Protest (1965)', britishpathe.com/asset/107039/; 'Israel: Women Protest Against War in Vietnam (1965)', britishpathe.com/asset/154980/; 'Cyprus: Demonstration Against Vietnam Bombings (1965)', britishpathe.com/asset/209281/

35 Ellis, 'British Public Opinion and the Vietnam War', p. 321.

36 See, for instance, 'UK: Demonstration Against American Policy in Vietnam (1965)', britishpathe.com/asset/155034/; and 'UK: Second London Demonstration Protests American Policy in Vietnam (1965)', britishpathe.com/asset/143545/

37 The song, written by Mick Softley, appeared on the *Universal Soldier* EP (Pye Records, 1965).

38 Vanessa Redgrave, email to author, 18 February 2021.

2. The Passion and the Pity of Bertrand Russell

1   Cited in Kanterian, *Ludwig Wittgenstein*, p. 98.

2   Russell, *Autobiography*, p. 9.

3   Ibid., p. 17.

4   Ibid., p. 83.

5   Blitz, 'Russell and the Boer War'.

6   Monk, *Bertrand Russell: The Spirit of Solitude*, pp. 189–90.

7   Russell, *Autobiography*, p. 261.

8   Bertrand Russell, letter to the editor, 'Adsum Qui Feci', *The Times*, 17 May 1916, p. 9.

9   'A No-Conscription Pamphlet: Mr. Bertrand Russell Heavily Fined', *Manchester Guardian*, 6 June 1916, p. 7.

10 It did not stop them trying. See Walter M. Bailey, letter to the editor, 'Moral Impediments', *Manchester Guardian*, 17 July 1916, p. 10.

11 Russell, *Autobiography*, pp. 253–4.

12 'Mr. Bertrand Russell and the War Office: A Personal Statement', *Manchester Guardian*, 27 September 1916, p. 6.

13 Clark, *The Life of Bertrand Russell*, p. 299.

14 'Topics of the Times: He Is Right at Least in One Thing', *The New York Times*, 25 December 1916, p. 8.

15 '"A Very Despicable Offence": Six Months for the Hon Bertrand Russell', *Manchester Guardian*, 10 February 1918, p. 8.

16 Russell, *Autobiography*, p. 263.

17 Russell, *The Practice and Theory of Bolshevism*, p. 38.

18 'Banned Books', *Daily Mail*, 21 May 1930, p. 9; 'Ban on Lecture by Mrs. Bertrand Russell', *Dundee Evening Telegraph*, 24 February 1928, p. 7.

19 'Mrs. Bertrand Russell Sues for a Divorce; Authorities on Sex and Marriage Are Parted', *The New York Times*, 27 May 1934, p. 23; 'Dora Russell Gets a Divorce Decree', *The New York Times*, 23 November 1934, p. 22.

20 'Armament Reduction Urged', *Telegraph*, 7 September 1931, p. 4.

21 Fiala, *The Just War Myth*, p. 165.

22 Westbrook, *John Dewey and American Democracy*, p. 512.

23 Martin Armstrong, 'The Spoken Word: Good Resolutions', *Listener*, 6 January 1949, p. 34. The series is available to listen to at bbc.co.uk/sounds/play/poohgk62

24 'British Nobel Prize Winners (1950)', britishpathe.com/asset/186770/

25 Russell, *Autobiography*, p. 522.

26 Russell, 'The Atomic Bomb'.

27 'Earl Russell's Warning on Atom Bomb', *Telegraph*, 29 November 1945, p. 3.

28 'Russell–Einstein Manifesto', Atomic Heritage Foundation, atomicheritage.org/key-documents/russell-einstein-manifesto

29 The entire recording is available at bbc.co.uk/iplayer/episode/p04qgxlv/face-to-face-bertrand-russell

30 'Lord Russell on Arms Plan', *Manchester Guardian*, 21 September 1959, p. 1.

31 'Bertrand Russell', *Observer*, 19 February 1961, p. 24.

32 'Jailed – the Star Sit-Downers: Black Maria for Earl Russell', *Daily Mirror*, 13 September 1961, p. 1; 'The New Jailbirds', *Daily Mail*, 13 September 1961, p. 7; 'Now Russell Is Fined', *Daily Mail*, 14 September 1961, p. 7.

33 Mrs C. Heelas, letter to the editor, *Daily Mail*, 15 September 1961, p. 8;

Pearson Phillips, 'It's His Looking Down, Not the Sitting Down, I Resent', *Daily Mail*, 23 November 1961, p. 8.

34 Cited in Voorhees, Jr., *The Silent Guns of Two Octobers*, p. 73.

35 An audio recording of the speech is available at jfklibrary.org/learn/about-jfk/historic-speeches/address-during-the-cuban-missile-crisis

36 Feinberg and Kasrils, *Bertrand Russell's America*, p. 149.

37 'Kennedy's Reply to Russell Stern', *The New York Times*, 27 October 1962, p. 10.

38 For a sympathetic account of the following narrative, see Madigan, 'The Warrant Report'.

39 Joyce Egginton, 'Oswald's Defender Whips Up Support', *Observer*, 28 June 1964, p. 9.

40 Russell, *16 Questions on the Assassination*.

41 'Europe: J. F. K.: The Murder & the Myths', *Time*, 12 June 1964.

42 Russell, *Autobiography*, p. 662.

3. Angry Dove

1   Bertrand Russell, letter to the editor, *The New York Times*, 8 April 1963, p. 46.

2   'Lord Russell's Letter', *The New York Times*, 8 April 1963, p. 46.

3   'Russell Repeats "Atrocity" Charges', *The New York Times*, 9 April 1963, p. 12. Russell made a similar observation about the same Western media that denied atrocities in Vietnam actually being his principal source of information in a letter to the editor of *The Times*, 27 October 1964, p. 11.

4   Vernon's many publications include 'Vietnam – North and South', *Marxism Today* (April 1963), pp. 106–11; 'Vietnam: U.S. Guilt and Dilemma', *Labour Monthly* (November 1963), pp. 515–17; and *Vietnam: The War and Its Background* (London: British Vietnam Committee, 1965).

5   The correspondence is in RC0096, Series 380 – BRPF: British–Vietnam Committee, Bertrand Russell Archives.

6   'Bertrand Russell Chides U.S. on Its Vietnam Aims', *The New York Times*, 28 November 1964, p. 9; Bertrand Russell, letter to the editor, *The Times*, 25 August 1965, p. 9.

7   'UK: Earl Russell Sees World Suicide Over Vietnam (1965)', britishpathe.com/asset/209107/

8   'Russell Condemns U.S. Vietnam Action', *The New York Times*, 8 August 1964, p. 3.

9   *Private Eye*, 30 April 1965.

10 Ellis, *Britain, America, and the Vietnam War*, p. 7.

11 Cited in Davies, 'Sterling and Strings'.

12 Ellis, 'Lyndon Johnson and Harold Wilson', p. 233; Vickers, 'Harold Wilson, the British Labour Party, and the War in Vietnam', p. 42.

13 Bertrand Russell, letter to the editor, *The Times*, 25 August 1965, p. 9.

14 'Lord Russell Quits Labour Party', *The Times*, 15 October 1965, p. 12.

15 Stephen J. Spingarn, 'Letters to the *Times*: Bertrand Russell's "War Crimes Trial" Plan Is Strongly Assailed', *Los Angeles Times*, 26 August 1966, p. A4.

16 Kingsley Amis et al., 'Backing for U.S. Policies in Vietnam', *The Times*, 21 January 1967, p. 9; Kingsley Amis et al., 'American Policies in Vietnam', *The Times*, 3 February 1967, p. 11.

17 Brian G. Fish, letter to the editor, *Telegraph*, 4 October 1966, p. 14. See also, for instance, William Lewis Price, letter to the editor, *Telegraph*, 26 September 1966, p. 12.

18 'Earl Russell and Vietnam', *Observer*, 16 February 1964, p. 30.

19 Tait, *My Father Bertrand Russell*, p. 176.

20 Ibid, p. 177.

21 Muldoon, *Paul McCartney*, p. 131.

22 'Lame Start for Russell War Crime Tribunal', *The Times*, 17 November 1966, p. 12.

4. Freedom Fighters: Jean-Paul Sartre and Simone de Beauvoir

1   '$52,500 Nobel Literature Award Turned Down by Philosopher Sartre', *Washington Post*, 23 October 1964, p. A17. For further comment on his decision, see Wilfred Fleisher, 'Nobel Prize Rejected by Sartre in Advance', *Washington Post*, 21 October 1964, p. A22; Editorial, 'Anti-Laureate', *Washington Post*, 25 October 1964, p. E6.

2   Russell, *Autobiography*, p. 667.

3   Hayman, *Writing Against*, p. 31.

4   Sartre, *Words*, p. 35.

5   Hayman, *Writing Against*, p. 92.

6   Sartre, 'Paris Under the Occupation'.

7 Bakewell, *At the Existentialist Café*, p. 10.
8 Friedman, 'Of Sartre, Race, and Rabies', p. 361.
9 '7 French Writers Start Tour of U.S.', *The New York Times*, 16 January 1945, p. 8.
10 Hedda Hopper, 'Dunn Done Right By!', *Washington Post*, 22 February 1945, p. 12.
11 On the tailing of the two women, see Secret Agent in Charge (SAC), New York, memorandum to J. Edgar Hoover, 29 February 1945; R. B. Hood, SAC, Los Angeles, memorandum to Hoover, 27 February 1945; SAC, Chicago, to SAC, Washington, teletype, 23 February 1945; 'Madame Andree Viollis', memorandum, 16 February 1945, Federal Bureau of Investigation File: Jean-Paul Sartre (hereafter FBI: Sartre).
12 SAC, Albany, memorandum to Hoover, 3 March 1945; Washington Field Division, memorandum to Hoover, 7 March 1945; Kenneth L. Ladd, report, 'Madame Andree Viollis, Was; Etal', 6 March 1945; William L. Roberts, San Antonio, report, 'Mme. Andree Viollis, wa, Mme. D'Ardene De Tizac, Et Al', 15 March 1945; Eldred W. Cox, report, 'Me. Andree Viollis, with alias, et al.', 5 July 1945, FBI: Sartre.
13 'De Gaulle Foes Paid by U.S., Paris Is Told', *The New York Times*, 25 January 1945, p. 3; 'Figaro Article Disputed', *The New York Times*, 30 January 1945, p. 18; 'M. Sartre Explains Article', *The New York Times*, 1 February 1945, p. 22; 'In Reference to an Article by Mr. Sartre', 3 February 1945, FBI: Sartre.
14 Cohen-Solal, *Sartre*, p. 239.
15 Ibid., p. 269; Bakewell, *At the Existentialist Café*, p. 172.
16 Leonard Lyons, 'Manhattan Cafe Notes', *Washington Post*, 1 May 1947, p. 2.
17 Sterling North, 'Sartre's "Religion" of Human Dignity', *Washington Post*, 6 July 1947, p. B7.
18 'Sartre Now Target of Pravda's Attacks', *The New York Times*, 24 January 1947, p. 19.
19 The latter play is more commonly known in English translation as *Dirty Hands*.
20 Walter White, 'People, Politics and Places', *Chicago Defender*, 27 March 1948, p. 15; 'Aping the Beast', *Chicago Defender*, 8 January 1949, p. 6;

'Sartre Play in Moscow', *The New York Times*, 17 November 1955, p. 44; Murphy, 'Sartre on American Racism', p. 226.

21 'Boyer Opens Sartre Play at Baltimore on Nov. 15', *Washington Post*, 7 November 1948, p. L2; Richard L. Coe, '"Red Gloves" Pack an Early Punch', *Washington Post*, 29 November 1948, p. 10; 'Leonard Lyons ...', *Washington Post*, 5 February 1949, p. B12. In fairness to American critics, the Soviets also perceived the play as anti-communist and pressured for the cancellation of a Finnish production; see '2 Plays Closed by Finns After Soviet Protest', *Washington Post*, 12 December 1948, p. M1.

22 Bakewell, *At the Existentialist Café*, pp. 255–6.

23 Cohen-Solal, *Sartre*, p. 351.

24 Hayman, *Writing Against*, p. 292.

25 The image can be seen at old.delo.si/images/ slike/2018/12/17/0_416925_1024.jpg

26 'Sartre to Tour Red China', *The New York Times*, 5 September 1955, p. 3; Contat and Rybalka, *The Writings of Jean-Paul Sartre, Volume 1*, pp. 316–19.

27 Sartre condemned the 'atmosphere of hysteria' in the United States in 'The Chances of Peace'.

28 Cohen-Solal, *Sartre*, p. 285; Max Freedman, 'The "Innocence" of Sobell: M. Sartre Gives His Views', *Manchester Guardian*, 16 June 1956, p. 7.

29 George Sokolsky, 'These Days: The Sobell Case', *Washington Post*, 28 June 1956, p. 15; Freedman, 'The "Innocence" of Sobell'; 'Jean-Paul Sartre', correlation summary, 24 June 1971, FBI: Sartre. Sobell confessed all shortly before his death. See Sam Roberts, 'Figure in Rosenberg Case Admits to Soviet Spying', *The New York Times*, 11 September 2008.

30 'Upheaval on the Left Bank', *The Times*, 20 November 1956, p. 8; 'Sartre Assails Soviet for Action in Hungary', *The New York Times*, 10 November 1956, p. 4; 'Sartre Challenges Russians to Debate', *Washington Post*, 2 December 1956, p. A10. Scenes of Budapest and the Paris protests can be seen in 'Russians Crush Hungarian Revolt (1956)', britishpathe.com/ asset/206809/, and 'Anti-Communist Demonstration in Paris (1956)', britishpathe.com/asset/206787/

31 The articles appeared between 28 June and 15 July 1960.

32 My narrative of the war is based on the following sources: Jonathan Fenby, *The History of Modern France: From the Revolution to the Present*

Day (London: Simon & Schuster, 2015); Robert Gildea, *France Since 1945* (Oxford: Oxford University Press, 2nd edn, 2002); and Tyler Stovall, *Transnational France: The Modern History of a Universal Nation* (Harlow: Longman, 2015).

33 De Beauvoir, *Adieux*, p. 367.

34 Jean-Paul Sartre, 'Objections Noted', *The New York Times*, 21 March 1948, p. X3; Cohen-Solal, *Sartre*, p. 367.

35 Drake, 'Sartre, Camus and the Algerian War', pp. 16–19; Smith, 'Idealism and People's War', p. 429.

36 Jean-Paul Sartre, 'Almost as Mute as During Occupation', *Observer*, 9 March 1958, p. 1; 'Torture in Algeria: The Forbidden Sartre Article', *Observer*, 9 March 1958, p. 1; '"La Question" Sells 60,000 More', *Manchester Guardian*, 14 May 1958, p. 7.

37 'M. Sartre Defends F.L.N. Cause', *The Times*, 21 September 1960, p. 10; 'M. Sartre Demands to Be Charged', *The Times*, 2 December 1960, p. 12.

38 Daisie Gillie, 'Right Wing Out in Paris: Cries of "Death to Sartre"', *Guardian*, 4 October 1960, p. 1.

39 Sartre, 'Preface', p. 21. Sartre had been moving towards this position for some time. See his witness statement in the trial of an Algerian accused of murdering an opponent of independence in 'Algerian Murderer's Life Sentence', *The Times*, 12 December 1957, p. 8.

40 Bakewell, *At the Existentialist Café*, pp. 276–7.

41 C. L. Sulzberger, 'Foreign Affairs: Castro in the Mirror of Existentialism', *The New York Times*, 6 August 1960, p. 18. For evidence of federal officials monitoring Sartre, see Special Agent in Charge, New York, memorandum to Hoover, 30 March 1960, FBI: Sartre.

42 'Sartre talks to Tynan 2', *Observer*, 25 June 1961, p. 20.

43 Lewis D. Barton, District Director, 'Jean Paul Sartre', Department of Justice Immigration and Naturalization Service, 19 June 1964, FBI: Sartre.

44 Peter Kihss, 'Sartre Cancels Lectures in U.S. Over American Role in Vietnam', *The New York Times*, 18 March 1965, p. 4; See also 'Paris: Sartre's Choice', *The New York Times*, 21 March 1965, p. E6.

45 De Beauvoir, *All Said and Done*, p. 338.

46 De Beauvoir, *Memoirs of a Dutiful Daughter*, p. 366.

47 Kirkpatrick, *Becoming Beauvoir*, p. 107.

48 In addition to Kirkpatrick, important analyses of the relationship include Lisa Appignanesi, *Simone de Beauvoir* (London: Haus, 2005) and Carole Seymour-Jones, *A Dangerous Liaison: Simone de Beauvoir and Jean-Paul Sartre* (London: Cornerstone, 2011).

49 'Simone de Beauvoir, An American Renaissance in France', *The New York Times*, 22 June 1947, pp. 7, 29.

50 Simone de Beauvoir, 'An Existentialist Looks at Americans', *The New York Times*, 25 May 1947, p. SM13.

51 Surkis, 'Ethics and Violence'.

52 De Beauvoir, *The Long March*, p. 494.

53 Richard Hughes, 'Views from the Well-Beaten Trail of the Invited Visitor to China', *The New York Times*, 18 May 1958, p. BR7.

54 Fair Play for Cuba Committee, 'What Is Really Happening in Cuba?', *The New York Times*, 6 April 1960, p. 6.

55 Ferlinghetti, 'Moscow in the Wilderness', p. 22.

5. Appointing the Panel

1 Arthur Miller, letter to Bertrand Russell, 2 November 1966, box 10.03, Document 171059, Bertrand Russell Archives, available at dearbertie. mcmaster.ca/letter/miller

2 Other sources add the names of people who did not attend while omitting some who did. See Tate, *Revolutionary Activism in the 1950s & 60s, Volume 2*, p. 96.

3 My principal sources on Dedijer are his obituaries, especially David Binder, 'Vladimir Dedijer, Tito Biographer and Partisan Fighter, Dies at 76', *The New York Times*, 4 December 1990.

4 James Baldwin, letter to Bertrand Russell, 9 January 1967, box 10.01, Document 170335, Russell Archives, available at dearbertie.mcmaster.ca/ letter/baldwin

5 Standley and Pratt, *Conversations with James Baldwin*, p. 78.

6 Elgrably, 'James Baldwin, The Art of Fiction No. 78'.

7 James Baldwin, 'Down at the Cross: Letter from a Region of My Mind' in *The Fire Next Time*, p. 37.

8 'UK: American Negro Author James Baldwin Visits Philosopher Lord Russell in London (1965)', britishpathe.com/asset/248794/; Feinberg and Kasrils, *Bertrand Russell's America*, p. 222.

9   'End Your Silence', *The New York Times*, 18 April 1965, p. E5.

10   Woolf and Bagguley, *Authors Takes Sides on Vietnam*, p. 19.

11   'For the President's Eyes Only: Special Daily Report on North Vietnam', 1 December 1967, CIA Freedom of Information Act Electronic Reading Room, cia.gov/readingroom/docs/SPECIAL%20DAILY%20 REPORT%20ON%20N%5B15602422%5D.pdf

12   'Atlanta: Stokely's Spark', *Time*, 16 September 1966.

13   Cited in Fry, *The American South and the Vietnam War*, p. 209.

14   Feinberg and Kasrils, *Bertrand Russell's America*, p. 277.

15   On the tumultuous events in Chicago, see Schultz, *No One Was Killed*. For a fuller account of David Dellinger's life, see Hunt, *David Dellinger*.

16   Dellinger, *From Yale to Jail*, p. 80.

17   Hunt, *David Dellinger*, pp. 70–1.

18   The best source on Oglesby is his own *Ravens in the Storm: A Personal History of the 1960s Antiwar Movement* (New York: Scribner, 2008).

19   House of Representatives, *Investigation of Students for a Democratic Society, Part 1-A (Georgetown University), Hearings Before the Committee on Internal Security, Ninety-First Congress, First Session, June 3 and 4, 1969* (Washington, DC: US Government Printing Office, 1969), p. 5.

20   Oglesby, *Ravens in the Storm*, p. 97.

21   Ibid, p. 246.

22   Oliver Clausen, 'Weiss/Propagandist and Weiss/Playwright: Propagandist and Playwright', *The New York Times*, 2 October 1966, p. 255.

23   Weiss produced the best account of his earlier life, albeit in fictionalised form, in the 1960 novella *Leavetaking*.

24   'Londoners Form Lines for Long-Titled Play', *The New York Times*, 25 August 1964, p. 29.

25   Al Alvarez, 'Peter Weiss: The Truths That Are Uttered in a Madhouse', *The New York Times*, 26 December 1965, p. X3.

26   Weiss, *Notes on the Cultural Life of the Democratic Republic of Vietnam*, p. 4.

27   Interview with Sara Lidman, 6 November 1973, Studs Terkel Radio Archive, studsterkel.wfmt.com/programs/interview-sara-lidman

28   I have drawn on numerous sources to narrate Lidman's life story, the best

of which is Helena Forsås-Scott, *Swedish Women's Writing, 1850–1995*
(London and Atlantic Highlands, NJ: Athlone, 1997), pp. 197–215.

29 'South Africa Arrest of Swedish Novelist', *The Times*, 9 February 1961,
p. 12; Patrick Keatley, 'S. African Charge Against Swedish Novelist',
Guardian, 11 February 1961, p. 7; 'Authoress for Trial', *The Times*, 15
February 1961, p. 11; 'Swedish Authoress Free to Leave', *The Times*, 25
February 1961, p. 5; Sellström, 'Hammarskjöld and Apartheid South
Africa', pp. 55–6.

30 Clausen, 'Weiss/Propagandist and Weiss/Playwright'.

31 For more on Swedish opposition to the war, see Logevall, 'The Swedish-
American Conflict Over Vietnam'.

32 'Sweden Blames U.S. For Vietnam War', UPI news report, 21 March
1968.

33 CIA, Foreign Broadcast Information Service, Daily Report, No. 46 (6
March 1968), p. AA1.

34 Dembo and Pondrom, *The Contemporary Writer*, p. 124.

35 Lidman, 'The Heart of the World', pp. 11–12.

36 Cited in Johansson, 'Resistance and Repetition'.

37 On Americans who relocated to Sweden to avoid the draft, see Scott,
'"Sweden Might Be a Haven, But It's Not Heaven"'.

38 The speech is available at youtu.be/YcfHCmsMHAA

39 Low, 'Shoichi Sakata'.

40 Anders and Eatherly, *Burning Conscience*.

41 Jalabert, 'Aux origines de la génération 1968'. More broadly, see Schwartz,
A Mathematician Grappling with His Century.

42 Andrea Rodriguez, 'Melba Hernandez, a "Heroine of the Cuban
Revolution," Dies at 92', *Washington Post*, 10 March 2014; Douglas
Martin, 'Melba Hernández, a Confidante of Castro from First Volley, Is
Dead at 92', *The New York Times*, 15 March 2014.

43 Tate, *Revolutionary Activism*, p. 152.

6. Smears, Surveillance and Suppression

1 'Russell Bids Johnson to "War Crimes" Trial', *The New York Times*, 29
August 1966, p. 4; Duffett, *Against the Crime of Silence*, pp. 18–20, 25–6.

2 'Sponsors of "Trial" Withdraw', *Guardian*, 14 November 1966, p. 1; Karl

E. Meyer, "'War Trial" Backers "Unmoved" at Losses', *Washington Post*, 15 November 1966, p. A16.

3 'Tanzanian Denies Pressure Made Him Quit Peace Body', *The New York Times*, 15 November 1966, p. 2; 'Dr Nyerere Not Consulted Over LBJ Trial', *Guardian*, 15 November 1966, p. 9.

4 D. W. Ropa, 'The Bertrand Russell "Trial"', memo to Rostow, 12 December 1966, 'The Bertrand Russell "Trial"', National Security File, Country Files, Vietnam, NSF, box 191, Lyndon Baines Johnson Presidential Library, Austin, Texas (hereafter LBJ).

5 Stewart, 'Too Loud to Rise Above the Silence', p. 22.

6 Ibid., p. 23; State Department–United States Information Agency circular, 8 May 1967, FBI; Russell, *Autobiography*, p. 668.

7 Gibbons, *The U.S. Government and the Vietnam War*, p. 434.

8 Circular, Joint State Department–United States Information Agency Message, 8 May 1967, LBJ.

9 Walt Rostow, memo to William Connell, 2 December 1966; Ropa, 'The Bertrand Russell "Trial"'.

10 Memo to J. Edgar Hoover, 20 October 1966; Deputy Director of Plans, memo to J. Edgar Hoover, 5 April 1967, Central Intelligence Agency Files (hereafter CIA).

11 Information cables, 7 and 24 December 1966; information reports, 25 and 31 January 1967; Deputy Director for Plans, memo to J. Edgar Hoover, 27 March 1967, CIA.

12 'A la Mutualité, cinq mille personnes ont participé aux "Six Heures du monde pour le Vietnam"', *Le Monde*, 30 November 1966; de Beauvoir, *All Said and Done*, pp. 339–40.

13 'France: Détente Cordiale?', *Time*, 12 June 1964, p. 42.

14 'French Maintain Hard Line on War', *The New York Times*, 20 September 1966, p. 5.

15 Cited in Sowerwine, *France Since 1870*.

16 Deirdre Griswold, letter to funders, 19 April 1967, box 1, folder 6, International War Crimes Tribunal Records, Tamiment Library and Robert F. Wagner Labor Archives, New York (hereafter IWCTR); 'War "Trial" Plans Unchanged', *Guardian*, 8 October 1966, p. 21; 'Ban on War Crimes Hearing if ...', *Guardian*, 25 March 1967, p. 7.

17 'Hotel's "No" to Tribunal', *Guardian*, 12 April 1967, p. 9.

18 'Reluctance to Allow Mock Trial', *Guardian*, 6 October 1966, p. 9.

19 Cited in Duffett, *Against the Crime of Silence*, p. 31. Sartre's rebuttal of de Gaulle is available in full in box 1, folder 6, IWCTR.

20 Leslie Fielding, memo to Donald Murray, 12 April 1967, Bertrand Russell Peace Foundation War Crimes: Information Research Department correspondence with Paris, FCO 168/2771, National Archives, Kew, London.

21 'Le general de Gaulle à Jean-Paul Sartre: La justice n'appartient qu'a l'État', *Le Figaro*, 24 April 1967; 'De Gaulle Bans Tribunal', *Guardian*, 24 April 1967, p. 7; 'De Gaulle Explains Ban on "Tribunal"', *The New York Times*, 24 April 1967, p. 11.

22 Stewart, 'Too Loud to Rise Above the Silence', p. 20; N. D. Clive, Top Secret Memo, 'War Crimes Tribunal', 21 February 1967; Leslie Fielding to Donald Murray, Foreign Office, 14 April 1967, FCO 168/2771.

23 Donald Murray, memo to [ ] de la Mare, 21 March 1967; Nigel Trench, memo to Donald Murray, 27 January 1967, FCO 168/2771.

24 Stewart, 'Too Loud to Rise Above the Silence', p. 20; Duffett, *Against the Crime of Silence*, pp. 20–3.

25 'Swiss Won't Permit "War Crimes Trial"', *Los Angeles Times*, 2 March 1967, p. 24; information report, 18–20 January 1967, CIA; Canadian Committee for the International War Crimes Tribunal, press statement, 25 April 1967, box 1, folder 6, IWCTR; Duffett, *Against the Crime of Silence*, p. 36.

26 'Russell Tribunal Hits Trouble', *Guardian*, 30 April 1967, p. 3; 'Sweden's Trial Ban May Still Be Upset', *Washington Post*, 15 December 1966, p. H2; Transcript of statement by Prime Minister Erlander, 24 April 1967, box 1, folder 6, IWCTR.

27 US Embassy, Stockholm, memo to Secretary of State, 25 April 1967, LBJ.

28 Walt Rostow, memo to Lyndon B. Johnson, 27 April 1967, LBJ.

29 US Embassy, Stockholm, memo to Secretary of State, 25 April 1967, LBJ.

30 US Embassy, Stockholm, memo to Secretary of State, 7 May 1967, LBJ.

31 'U.S. Concern Expressed', *Guardian*, 9 May 1967, 15; Walt Rostow, memo to Lyndon B. Johnson, 27 April 1967, LBJ.

32 Stewart, 'Too Loud to Rise Above the Silence', p. 28.

33 Some of the more informative cables include 'Emergence of Japan Committee for Investigation of War Crimes in Vietnam as Dominant

Japanese Organization Supporting Bertrand Russell War Crimes Tribunal', 29 December 1966; 'Plans for a Session in Japan of the Russell "War Crimes" Tribunal in August 1967', 30 March 1967; and 'Japanese Differences with Russell Foundation Over Plans for Tribunal Proceedings', 14 April 1967; untitled, 20 June 1967; and untitled, 12 July 1967.

7. Hanoi

1   Gerassi, *North Vietnam*, pp. 31–6.

2   The sets of investigators were as follows:
    Team 1: Malcolm Caldwell, academic at the School of Oriental and African Studies in London; John Gerassi, US journalist; Léo Matarasso, French lawyer; Setsure Tsurushima, professor of agrarian economy at Osaka University in Japan; Jean-Pierre Vigier, former French Resistance fighter and theoretical physicist at the Sorbonne.
    Team 2: Tariq Ali, British activist; Dr Abraham Behar, French nuclear physicist; Carol Brightman, US author and activist; Lawrence Daly, Scottish trade union leader; Gustavo Tolentino, Canadian physician.
    Team 3: Lelio Basso, Italian politician; Axel Höjer, Swedish physician and public servant; Hugh Manes, US civil rights lawyer; Joe Neilands, biochemist at the University of California, Berkeley; John Takman, Swedish author and physician.
    Team 4: Dr Martin Birnstingl, consultant surgeon at St Bartholomew's Hospital, London; Marcello Cini, professor of physics at the University of Rome; Charles Cobb, US civil rights activist; Gisèle Halimi, French activist and lawyer; Marcel-Francis Kahn, French physician; Julius Lester, US civil rights activist; Conrad Lynn, US civil rights activist and lawyer. The Japanese tribunal also sent a seven-man team between December 1966 and January 1967. 'Collection of "Evidence" of Japanese Collaboration with U.S. in Vietnam by Japanese Leftists', 31 January 1967, FOIA/ESDN (CREST): 0005425057, Central Intelligence Agency, Freedom of Information Act Reading Room, cia.gov/readingroom/document/0005425057

3   'U.S. Air Attacks Are Specifically Directed Against Civilian Population', broadcast statement, 3 February 1967, Papers of Lawrence Daly, MSS. 302/4/2, Modern Records Centre, University of Warwick.

4   Horowitz, *Radical Son*, p. 131; Ferlinghetti, 'Moscow in the Wilderness', p. 22.

5   Tate, *Revolutionary Activism*, pp. 42, 45, 114–15; Horowitz, 'Bertrand Russell', p. 43; Clinton, *The Loyal Opposition*, p. 70.

6   Mehta, 'North Vietnam's Informal Diplomacy with Bertrand Russell', p. 69.

7   Ibid., pp. 63, 68; Tate, *Revolutionary Activism*, p. 98.

8   Mehta, 'North Vietnam's Informal Diplomacy with Bertrand Russell', pp. 70–1.

9   Ibid., p. 72.

10 Ibid., pp. 72, 76; Tate, *Revolutionary Activism*, pp. 98–102; 'Confidential: North Vietnam's Reservations Concerning the Planning for the Bertrand Russell "War Crimes" Tribunal and Its Intention to Coordinate with the JCP on Collection of "Evidence"', 23 February 1967, FOIA/ ESDN (CREST): 0005429136, Central Intelligence Agency, Freedom of Information Act Reading Room, cia.gov/readingroom/ document/0005429136

11 Russell, *Autobiography*, p. 603.

12 For further detail, see William McPhillips, 'Father Proud of "War Crimes" Accuser', *Los Angeles Times*, 21 May 1967, p. B1.

13 Monk, *Bertrand Russell: The Ghost of Madness*, p. 401. The word used by another American who worked alongside him was 'megalomaniac'. Horowitz, *Radical Son*, p. 131.

14 Tate, *Revolutionary Activism*, pp. 116, 121–2.

15 Ibid., pp. 112–13, 117.

16 Aptheker, *Mission to Hanoi*; Hershberger, *Traveling to Vietnam*, pp. 76–7.

17 Cameron, *Here Is Your Enemy*, p. 58.

18 Hershberger, *Traveling to Vietnam*, p. 70.

19 Dellinger, *From Yale to Jail*, pp. 230–5.

20 Gerassi, *North Vietnam*, p. 36; Ali, *Street Fighting Years*, p. 158; Clinton, *Loyal Opposition*, pp. 64, 70.

21 Ashmore and Baggs, *Mission to Hanoi*, p. 27; Gerassi, *North Vietnam*, p. 36; Ali, *Street Fighting Years*, p. 159.

22 Gerassi, *North Vietnam*, pp. 36–7.

23 Ibid., p. 39; 'Hanoi Appoints Panel to Study U.S. "War Crimes"', *The New York Times*, 24 July 1966, p. 1.

24 Clinton, *Loyal Opposition*, pp. 71–2.

25 Gerassi, *North Vietnam*, pp. 50–2.

26 Ali, *Street Fighting Years*, pp. 109–14, 130–1.

27 Ibid, pp. 164–70.

28 Ibid, p. 181.

29 Clinton, *Loyal Opposition*, p. 65; CIA, Foreign Broadcast Information Service, Daily Report: Foreign Radio Broadcasts, No. 59 (27 March 1967), pp. JJJ2–3.

30 Ali, *Street Fighting Years*, pp. 153, 155, 159.

31 Lester, *All Is Well*, pp. 136–7.

32 Gerassi, *North Vietnam*, p. 54.

33 Tsurushima, 'What I Saw in North Vietnam'.

34 Gerassi, *North Vietnam*, photo insert.

35 Cobb and Lester, 'Letters from Hanoi'; *Hearings Regarding H.R. 16742: Restraints on Travel to Hostile Areas, Committee on Internal Security, House of Representatives, 92nd Congress, 2nd Session, September 19 and 25, 1972* (Washington, DC: US Government Printing Office, 1972), pp. 7684, 7697, 7962.

36 Vietnam News Agency, 'Foreign Investigators Testify to U.S. Civilian Bombings in North Vietnam', 4 February 1967, Papers of Lawrence Daly.

37 See, for instance, the testimony of Hugh Manes in 'U.S. Bombs N. Vietnam Civilians, Lawyer Says', *Los Angeles Times*, 14 April 1967, p. A8; Clinton, *Loyal Opposition*, p. 70.

38 I have endeavoured to follow events in Stockholm as they transpired but the minutes do not include more than a provisional set of dates for the appearances of witnesses. This account is also necessarily selective, focusing on the more important evidence presented to the tribunal.

8. The Stockholm Session

1 Baldwin, 'The War Crimes Tribunal', p. 242.

2 Ibid, p. 244.

3 'Courtland Cox Attends Bertrand Russell International War Crimes Tribunal in Stockholm', SNCC Digital Gateway, snccdigital.org/events/

courtland-cox-attends-bertrand-russell-international-war-crime-tribunal-in-stockholm/; Cox interview with author.

4   Report, 31 May 1967, CIA File.

5   Baldwin, 'The War Crimes Tribunal', p. 242.

6   J. Edgar Hoover to Lyndon B. Johnson, Dean Rusk and Richard Helms, CIA Director, 13 May 1967, CIA File.

7   Weatherby, *James Baldwin*, p. 284; Charles L. Sanders, 'Paris Scratchpad', *Jet*, 13 July 1967, p. 28; 'James Arthur Baldwin', 24 March 1971, James Baldwin FBI File.

8   Mehta, 'North Vietnam's Informal Diplomacy with Bertrand Russell', p. 83; '1967, The Russell Tribunal, Stockholm, Bertrand Russell, Jean Paul Sartre, Vietnam', youtu.be/WTtlR-sS2Hw

9   'Message from Bertrand Russell to the Tribunal' in Duffett, *Against the Crime of Silence*, pp. 37–9.

10 'Jean-Paul Sartre's Inaugural Statement to the Tribunal' in Duffett, *Against the Crime of Silence*, pp. 40–5.

11 Wording adapted from 'The First, Second and Third Questions' in Duffett, *Against the Crime of Silence*, p. 48, and 'Aims of the Tribunal Agreed at the Constituting Session, London, 15 November 1966' in Coates, Limqueco and Weiss, *Prevent the Crime of Silence*, pp. 59–60.

12 Matthew McKean, 'Gabriel Kolko: A Leftist Academic Who Saw Things Differently', *Globe and Mail*, 13 June 2014; 'Summary of Historical Report by Professor Gabriel Kolko' in Duffett, *Against the Crime of Silence*, pp. 58–69, quotation p. 61.

13 'Summary of a Juridical Report by Samuel Rosenwein' in Duffett, *Against the Crime of Silence*, pp. 102–4.

14 'Juridical Report on Aggression in Vietnam, Testimony by the Japanese Legal Committee' in Duffett, *Against the Crime of Silence*, pp. 105–18, quotation p. 115.

15 The tribunal was scornful, for instance, of a statement by Cuban Raúl Valdés Vivó, which members considered 'malappropriate in tone'. IWCTR, box 1, folder 17.

16 'Extracts from the Summary Report on the Bombing of the Civil Population in the North, Testimony by Abraham Behar, M.D.' in Duffett, *Against the Crime of Silence*, p. 151.

17 Ibid, p. 153.

18 Ibid, p. 155.

19 Ibid, p. 149.

20 Ibid, p. 159.

21 Ibid, p. 160.

22 'Report on Bombing of North Vietnam, Testimony by Charles Cobb and Julius Lester' in Duffett, *Against the Crime of Silence*, pp. 206–10, quotation p. 207. For the evidence from Daly, Kugai and Schoenman, see *idem*, pp. 185–9, 196–205.

23 'Report on the Destruction of Dikes: Holland 1944–1945 and Korea 1953, Testimony by Gabriel Kolko' in Duffett, *Against the Crime of Silence*, p. 226. For the other commentary on the bombing of dykes, see *idem*, pp. 226–35.

24 'Technical Aspects of Fragmentation Bombs, Testimony by Jean-Pierre Vigier, M.D.' in Duffett, *Against the Crime of Silence*, pp. 249–58, quotation p. 252. The tribunal received further reports on fragmentation bombs from Japanese scientists. See *idem*, pp. 258–67.

25 Owen, 'Bombs Over Cambodia'.

26 'Report from Cambodia, Testimony by Bernard Couret' in Duffett, *Against the Crime of Silence*, pp. 118–29.

27 'Testimony on Cambodia by Wilfred Burchett' in Duffett, *Against the Crime of Silence*, pp. 140–4, quotation p. 142.

28 'Report from Cambodia and North Vietnam by Tariq Ali' in Duffett, *Against the Crime of Silence*, pp. 130–2, quotation p. 131.

29 'Testimony and Medical Report of Vietnamese Victims' in Duffett, *Against the Crime of Silence*, pp. 215–16, quotation p. 215.

30 Ibid., pp. 216–17.

31 Ibid., pp. 217–18, quotation p. 218. Film footage of the victims is available at Ali, 'Anatomy of a War'.

32 'Testimony and Medical Report of Vietnamese Victims', pp. 219–20; Ali, 'Anatomy of a War'.

33 'Report of Do Van Ngoc', IWCTR, box 1, folder 11.

34 'Report from North Vietnam on Civil Bombardment, Testimony by J. B. Neilands', in Duffett, *Against the Crime of Silence*, pp. 269–73.

35 'Bombardment of Civilians in North Vietnam, Testimony by John Takman, M.D. and Axel Hojer, M.D.' in Duffett, *Against the Crime of Silence*, pp. 165–74, quotation p. 172.

36 'American Bombing in North Vietnam, Testimony by Jean-Michel Krivine' in Duffett, *Against the Crime of Silence*, pp. 175–80.
37 'On the Destruction of the Leprosarium of Quinh Lap, Testimony by M. Francis Kahn, M.D.' in Duffett, *Against the Crime of Silence*, pp. 180–4, quotation p. 183.
38 'Tribunal's Verdict of "Guilty"', *Guardian*, 11 May 1967, p. 9.
39 Oglesby, *Ravens in the Storm*, pp. 133–4.
40 US Embassy, Stockholm, cable to Secretary of State, 5 May 1967, CIA.
41 Cox interview with author.
42 De Beauvoir, *All Said and Done*, pp. 343–4.
43 De Beauvoir, *All Said and Done*, p. 345.
44 Ibid.; Oglesby, *Ravens in the Storm*, p. 129.
45 Bertrand Russell to Vladimir Dedijer, 14 May 1967; Bertrand Russell to Lawrence Daly, 17 May 1967; Bertrand Russell to Jean-Paul Sartre and Laurent Schwartz, 6 June 1967; Laurent Schwartz to Bertrand Russell, 24 June 1967; Isaac Deutscher to Lawrence Daly, 24 June 1967, Papers of Lawrence Daly.
46 Isaac Deutscher to Lawrence Daly, 24 June 1967, Papers of Lawrence Daly.
47 Bertrand Russell to Members of IWCT, 4 May 1967; Laurent Schwartz to Bertrand Russell, 24 June 1967, Papers of Lawrence Daly.
48 Intelligence information cables, 5 and 9 May 1967, CIA File.

9. Second Session: Roskilde

1 De Beauvoir, *All Said and Done*, pp. 352, 360–1.
2 Ibid, p. 350.
3 'Russell Tribunal Starts 2D Session', *The New York Times*, 21 November 1967, p. 6.
4 'Russell's Tokyo "Tribunal" Rules U.S. Guilty in Vietnam', *The New York Times*, 31 August 1967, p. 2.
5 Intelligence cable, 31 August 1967, CIA File.
6 Intelligence cable, 14 July 1967; Deputy Director for Plans to Director, n.d., 'Second International War Crimes Tribunal, November 20, 1967–December 1, 1967, Copenhagen, Denmark'; Intelligence cable, 31 August 1967, 'Activities of Stokely Carmichael in Hanoi and his Plans for the Future', n.d., CIA File.

7   Intelligence cable, 29 August 1967, CIA File.

8   Intelligence cable, 8 December 1967, CIA File.

9   'Tribunal's Mind Made Up', *Guardian*, 27 November 1967, p. 9; 'Schoenman's Departure for US', *The Times*, 25 November 1967, p. 4; 'Landing Ban "Due to C.I.A."', *Telegraph*, 26 November 1967, p. 3; Intelligence cable, 13 December 1967, CIA File.

10   De Beauvoir, *All Said and Done*, p. 352.

11   'SYND 20 11 67 Famous Writers at War Crimes Tribunal in Denmark', Associated Press Archive, youtu.be/mz_Ey8_6gf4

12   'Extracts from a Report on Agricultural Chemicals Used in Vietnam, Testimony by the Japanese Scientific Committee' in Duffett, *Against the Crime of Silence*, pp. 367–73.

13   De Beauvoir, *All Said and Done*, p. 360.

14   Oglesby, *Ravens in the Storm*, p. 136.

15   De Beauvoir, *All Said and Done*, p. 361.

16   Russell had earlier liaised with the North Vietnamese government over the possible appearance before the tribunal of captured US pilots. The idea was vetoed because it would violate the rights of prisoners of war under the Geneva Convention and turn proceedings into a show trial. 'Evidence of US Pilots Ruled Out', *Guardian*, 6 May 1967, p. 7.

17   The narrative that follows including all quotations is based on 'Testimony and Questioning of David Kenneth Tuck' in Duffett, *Against the Crime of Silence*, pp. 403–25, and 'Russell "Tribunal" Hears a U.S. Negro', *The New York Times*, 26 November 1967, p. 10.

18   This information and the following narrative is adapted from 'Testimony and Questioning of Peter Martinsen' in Duffett, *Against the Crime of Silence*, pp. 425–57.

19   Sadler's performance can be seen and heard at youtu.be/ KWPwAL79vMU

20   Duncan, '"The Whole Thing Was a Lie!"'.

21   Duncan, *The New Legions*. My telling of Duncan's appearance is based on 'Testimony and Questioning of Donald Duncan' in Duffett, *Against the Crime of Silence*, pp. 457–513.

22   'Report of the Commission of Inquiry to the United States, Testimony by Gisèle Halimi' in Duffett, *Against the Crime of Silence*, pp. 514–19.

23   The following version of events is adapted from 'A Doctor Reports from

South Vietnam, testimony by Erich Wulff' in Duffett, *Against the Crime of Silence*, pp. 522–36.

24 Bertolino narrative based on 'Report on American Conduct of the War in the South, Testimony by Jean Bertolino' in Duffett, *Against the Crime of Silence*, pp. 536–50.

25 'On Treatment of Civilians' in Duffett, *Against the Crime of Silence*, pp. 551–4. The complete film is available at youtu.be/cAlp2W2a3MI

26 The following summary draws on 'On the Treatment of Women and Children in the South, Testimony by Madeleine Riffaud' in Duffett, *Against the Crime of Silence*, pp. 555–61.

27 For more information of a witness concluding that the US was committing genocide, see 'Report of the Seventh Inquiry Commission Concerning the Zones in the South Under NLF Control, Testimony by Roger Pic', in Duffett, *Against the Crime of Silence*, p. 577.

28 'Comments on the Sessions of the Copenhagen International War Crimes Tribunal (IWCT), 20 November – 2 December 1967', (FOIA)/ESDN (CREST): 0005430761, CIA Freedom of Information Act Electronic Reading Room, cia.gov/readingroom/document/0005430761; Intelligence cable, 8 December 1967, CIA File.

29 Oglesby, *Ravens in the Storm*, pp. 130–1.

30 Deputy Director for Plans to Director, 'Comments of US Student Non-Violent Coordinating Committee Leader on the International War Crimes Tribunal in Stockholm, 2–10 May 1967', 5 June 1967, CIA File.

31 Feinberg and Kasrils, *Bertrand Russell's America*, pp. 275–7.

32 'Jean-Paul Sartre, Declaration about Stokely Carmichael', 27 November 1967, box 1, folder 74, ICTWR.

33 'Comments on the Sessions of the Copenhagen International War Crimes Tribunal (IWCT), 20 November – 2 December 1967'; Intelligence cable, 8 December 1967, CIA File. For a statistical source by a later historian on Black representation within military ranks, see Weisbrot, *Freedom Bound*, p. 247.

34 'Russell "Tribunal" Finds U.S. Guilty of War Crimes', *The New York Times*, 2 December 1967, p. 3.

10. Vanquished

1 'The Games Men Play', *Newsweek*, 15 May 1967, p. 44.

2   Hedrick Smith, 'Charge at "Trial" Is Denied By U.S.', *The New York Times*, 6 May 1967, p. 3; Roland Huntford, '2d Russell "War Crimes Tribunal" Reveals It Has Entered Trying Times', *Washington Post*, 27 November 1967, p. B7.

3   Vladimir Dedijer, 'Statement on the Pentagon's Denial of the Use of CBUs' in Duffett, *Against the Crime of Silence*, pp. 267–8; Dana Adams Schmidt, 'Russell Tribunal Is "Astonished" by Denial of Attack on Civilians', *The New York Times*, 7 May 1967, p. 3. 'CBU' refers to the type of bomb – 'Cluster Bomb Unit'.

4   'That "War Crimes Tribunal"', *Washington Post*, 21 November 1966, p. 44; Henry Tanner, 'Russell Trial; Flogging a Dead Horse', *The New York Times*, 14 May 1967, p. E3.

5   Elegant, 'How to Lose a War: The Press and Viet Nam'.

6   Joel Achenbach, 'Did the News Media, Led by Walter Cronkite, Lose the War in Vietnam?', *Washington Post*, 25 May 2018. In answer to Achenbach, no.

7   My analysis draws substantially on Daniel C. Hallin's myth-busting *The 'Uncensored War': The Media and Vietnam* (Berkeley and Los Angeles: University of California Press, 1986), especially pp. 22, 42, 87–99, 105–6, 152–8.

8   'Civilized Warfare', *Washington Post*, 15 August 1965, p. E6. The CBS report can be watched at youtu.be/Mxo-8p2zdQI

9   Scheer, 'Lord Russell', p. 20.

10 William McPhillips, 'Father Proud of "War Crimes" Accuser', *Los Angeles Times*, 21 May 1967, p. B1; Flora Lewis, 'Behind the Stockholm "Tribunal" Is an American America-Hater', *Los Angeles Times*, 12 May 1967, p. A5.

11 For a fuller account of Salisbury's life and career, see Donald E. Davis and Eugene P. Trani, *The Reporter Who Knew Too Much: Harrison Salisbury and the New York Times* (Lanham, MD: Rowman & Littlefield, 2012).

12 Russell, *Autobiography*, p. 168.

13 Harrison E. Salisbury, 'A Visitor to Hanoi Inspects Damage Laid to U.S. Raids', *The New York Times*, 25 December 1966, p. 1.

14 'Statement of Harrison E. Salisbury' in *Harrison E. Salisbury's Trip to North Vietnam: Hearing Before the Committee on Foreign Relations,*

United States Senate, Ninetieth Congress, First Session (Washington, DC: US Government Printing Office, 1967), p. 7.

15 The photograph appears on the front cover of a spoken-word album based on Salisbury's book; see youtu.be/xOCMZTHmKgU

16 The Johnson and Sylvester quotes are both from Lawrence, 'Mission Intolerable', p. 444.

17 Chalmers M. Roberts, 'Ho Tries a New Propaganda Weapon', *Washington Post*, 2 January 1967, p. A10.

18 Hanson W. Baldwin, 'Bombing of the North; U.S. Officers Assert It Has Proved Effective, Restrained and Essential', *The New York Times*, 30 December 1966, p. 1. On the supposed success of bombing tactics, see Joseph Alsop, 'North Vietnam Bombing Finally Shows Results', *Los Angeles Times*, 2 February 1967, p. A5. The Pulitzer incident is recounted in Lawrence, 'Mission Intolerable', p. 452. For a rare opinion piece supporting Salisbury and encouraging the press to be less wide-eyed about what Washington officials were telling them about the war, see Walter Lippmann, 'Today and Tomorrow: Harrison Salisbury in Hanoi', *Washington Post*, 10 January 1967, p. A15.

19 Small, *Covering Dissent*, pp. 1, 23.

20 Fairclough, *Martin Luther King, Jr.*, p. 113; Presbey, 'Martin Luther King Jr. on Vietnam', p. 223.

21 Oglesby, 'Vietnam: This Is Guernica', p. 714.

22 Horowitz, *Radical Son*, p. 149.

23 The confrontation with film-maker Desmond Leslie, who sought to avenge a bad review of a show featuring his wife, can be seen at x.com/bbcarchive/status/1508403398177132545

24 Bernard Levin, 'Bertrand Russell: Prosecutor, Judge and Jury', *The New York Times*, 19 February 1967, pp. 24, 55–6, 60.

25 Nicholas Katzenbach, memo to Lyndon B. Johnson, 17 February 1967, LBJ Library.

26 C. L. Sulzberger, 'Foreign Affairs: Corpse on Horseback', *The New York Times*, 12 May 1967, p. 46. Nor did the newspaper stop at that. On the contrary, the petty insults kept coming. See 'Russell "Tribunal" Finds U.S. Guilty of War Crimes', *The New York Times*, 2 December 1967, p. 3.

27 'Sweden: Sartre's S', *Time*, 12 May 1967.

28 Among the many examples of such news stories, see 'That "War Crimes

Tribunal"', *Washington Post*, 21 November 1966, p. 44; Flora Lewis, 'Behind the Stockholm "Tribunal" Is an American America-Hater', *Los Angeles Times*, 12 May 1967, p. A5; Henry Tanner, 'Russell Trial; Flogging a Dead Horse', *The New York Times*, 14 May 1967, p. E3; 'Russell "Tribunal" Finds U.S. Guilty of War Crimes', *The New York Times*, 2 December 1967, p. 3.

29 Hallin, *The 'Uncensored War'*, pp. 152–3.

30 Cited in Tynan, 'Open Letter to an American Liberal', p. 103.

31 'Sweden: Trial's End', *Time*, 19 May 1967.

32 'Off With Their Hands', *Newsweek*, 15 May 1967, pp. 42, 44.

33 It was another unintended irony that several newspapers published stories about the supposed lack of press interest in the tribunal. See, for instance, 'Little Attention Is Being Paid to "War Tribunal"', *Washington Post*, 7 May 1967, p. A15.

34 You can listen to the still-amusing sketch at youtu.be/uKXHSfYm5wk

35 Pendennis, *Observer*, 23 April 1967, p. 40.

36 Christopher Dobson, 'The Russell Doctrine', *Daily Mail*, 5 January 1967, p. 2.

37 'Mocking Justice', *Telegraph*, 3 May 1967, p. 3; Thomas Harris, 'Vietnam, Russell and Danish Politics', *Telegraph*, 15 November 1967, p. 14.

38 'Bring Your Own Charge Sheet', *Guardian*, 2 May 1967, p. 8; 'Tribunal's Mind Made Up', *Guardian*, 27 November 1967, p. 9.

39 See, for example, Geoffrey Sinclair, 'Evidence of American War Crimes', *Tribune*, 15 December 1967, p. 13.

40 Courtland Cox oral history interview conducted by Joseph Mosnier in Washington, DC, 8 July 2011, snccdigital.org/events/ courtland-cox-attends-bertrand-russell-international-war-crime-tribunal-in-stockholm/. Cox related the same anecdote when I interviewed him.

41 Lester, *Revolutionary Notes*, p. 12; Deputy Director for Plans to Director, 'Comments of US Student Non-Violent Coordinating Committee Leader on the International War Crimes Tribunal in Stockholm, 2–10 May 1967', 5 June 1967, CIA File.

42 Lester, *All Is Well*, p. 138.

43 Lester, *Revolutionary Notes*, p. 10.

44 Ali, *Street Fighting Years*, p. 195; Oglesby, *Ravens in the Storm*, pp. 136–7; Dellinger, 'Report from the Tribunal'; Isaac Deutscher to Lawrence

Daly, 24 June 1967; Laurent Schwartz to Bertrand Russell, 24 June 1967, Papers of Lawrence Daly.

45 Russell, *Autobiography*, pp. 660–1.

46 De Beauvoir, *All Said and Done*, p. 363. Critics launched a further attack on foreign opponents of the war following the release in late 1967 of *Far from Vietnam*, a portmanteau film by some of the most esteemed film directors in Europe led by Jean-Luc Godard, which they dismissed as anti-American propaganda.

47 Walt Rostow, memo to Lyndon B. Johnson, 5 May 1967, LBJ.

48 On the support of developing countries for the tribunal, see Ali, *Street Fighting Years*, pp. 196–7; Tate, *Revolutionary Activism*, p. 99; and Tynan, 'Open Letter to an American Liberal', p. 104.

49 Mehta, 'North Vietnam's Informal Diplomacy with Bertrand Russell', p. 65; Ali, *Street Fighting Years*, p. 196.

50 *Aftonbladet*, 2 May 1967. A transcription of this and other supportive editorials in the likes of *Expressen* and *Svenska Dagbladet* are in IWCTR, box 1, folder 16. The fact that Danish radio and television 'are giving proceedings good coverage in favorable light' was one of the reasons given by diplomats for seeking to silence the tribunal. US Embassy, Stockholm, to Secretary of State, 7 May 1967, CIA File.

51 US Embassy, Stockholm, to Secretary of State, 6 May 1967, CIA File.

52 Patrick Grattan, British Embassy, Stockholm, to N. D. Clive, Joint Information Research Department, Foreign Office, confidential memo, 17 May 1967, FCO 168/2777, National Archives.

53 US Embassy, Stockholm, to Secretary of State, 7 May 1967, CIA File.

54 Grattan to Clive, 17 May 1967.

55 'Greeting to the Tribunal from American Supporters, Address by Carl Oglesby', in Duffett, *Against the Crime of Silence*, p. 322

56 Joseph Heller, letter to the editor, *The New York Times*, 12 March 1967, p. 241. This was only one of numerous letters provoked by the Bernard Levin smear piece that the *Times*, to its credit, published. The correspondence suggests that the attempt to discredit the philosopher was to some extent counterproductive.

57 Ferlinghetti, 'Moscow in the Wilderness', p. 23.

58 Tynan, 'Open Letter to an American Liberal', p. 109. Tynan's article originally appeared in the March 1968 issue of *Playboy*.

11. Vindicated

1 The story of My Lai has been recounted many times but the best place
to start is Seymour Hersh's investigative account, *My Lai 4: A Report
on the Massacre and Its Aftermath* (New York: Random House, 1970).
Other important works include Michal R. Belknap, *The Vietnam War on
Trial: The My Lai Massacre and the Court-Martial of Lieutenant Calley*
(Lawrence, KS: University Press of Kansas, 2002); Kendrick Oliver,
The My Lai Massacre in American History and Memory (Manchester:
Manchester University Press, 2006); William Thomas Allison, *My
Lai: An American Atrocity in the Vietnam War* (Baltimore, MD: Johns
Hopkins University Press, 2012); and Howard Jones, *My Lai: Vietnam,
1968, and the Descent into Darkness* (New York: Oxford University Press,
2017).

2 Goldstein, Marshall and Schwartz, *The My Lai Massacre and Its
Cover-Up*, pp. 37, 45, 50.

3 Turse, *Kill Anything That Moves*, pp. 3–4, 226–7.

4 The feature including Haeberle's photos from the 5 December 1969 issue
of *Life* are included in Cosgrove, 'American Atrocity: Remembering
My Lai'. You can hear the voices of Wallace and Meadlo at youtu.be/
ambpZnbJwdE

5 Sorley, *Westmoreland*, p. 215; Belknap, *The Vietnam War on Trial*,
pp. 122–8.

6 Marciano, *The American War in Vietnam*, p. 108.

7 Range, 'Only One Man Was Found Guilty for His Role in the My Lai
Massacre'.

8 Cody J. Foster, 'Did America Commit War Crimes in Vietnam?', *The
New York Times*, 1 December 2017.

9 Nick Turse and Deborah Nelson, 'Civilian Killings Went Unpunished',
Los Angeles Times, 6 August 2006.

10 Ibid.

11 Paul Harris, 'Vietnam Killing Spree Revelations Shock US', *Guardian*, 26
October 2003.

12 The *Toledo Blade* reporters Michael Sallah and Mitch Weiss expanded
on their original stories in the book *Tiger Force: A True Story of Men and
War* (London: Hodder & Stoughton, 2006).

13 Gregory L. Vistica, 'One Awful Night in Thanh Phong', *New York Times*

Magazine, 25 April 2001; Richard C. Paddock, 'Two Survivors Say U.S. Unit Killed Villagers "in Cold Blood"', *Los Angeles Times*, 29 April 2001.

14 Turse, *Kill Anything That Moves*, p. 12.

15 Lewy, *America in Vietnam*, p. 445.

16 Turse, *Kill Anything That Moves*, p. 81; Miguel and Roland, 'The Long-Run Impact of Bombing Vietnam'.

17 'U.S. Concedes It Hit Enemy Hospitals', *The New York Times*, 4 May 1971, p. 12.

18 Prokosch, *The Technology of Killing*, pp. 93–8, quotation p. 98.

19 Neer, *Napalm*, p. 111.

20 Greiner, *War Without Fronts*, pp. 87, 100; Lewy, *America in Vietnam*, p. 234.

21 Greiner, *War Without Fronts*, p. 35.

22 Belknap, *The Vietnam War on Trial*, p. 18; Kunen, *Standard Operating Procedure*, p. 44; Turse, *Kill Anything That Moves*, pp. 51–3.

23 'Pacification's Deadly Price', *Newsweek*, 19 June 1972, pp. 42–3; Turse, *Kill Anything That Moves*, pp. 204–21, 248–58.

24 John Pilger, email to author, 6 March 2021; Turse, *Kill Anything That Moves*, pp. 189–91.

25 Paul Johnson, 'The Stature of the Man', *The New York Times*, 21 January 1968, p. BR3. A surprising defence of Russell also appeared in an article published by the conservative *Daily Mail*, which insisted that his attacks on the Vietnam War were 'not the wanderings of a mind grown feebler with age' but the 'logical outcome' of his belief in pacifism and logical reason. Peter Lewis, 'The Cost of Being Bertrand Russell', *Daily Mail*, 25 April 1968, p. 6.

26 Leslie Fielding to J. S. Champion, 27 June 1967; J. S. Champion to Ken Coates, 27 June 1967, FCO 168/2776, National Archives.

27 'Head of Russell Tribunal Denied Visa for U.S. Trip', *The New York Times*, 9 January 1968, p. 3; '... and Retrogression Here', *The New York Times*, 13 January 1968, p. 30; 'Hanoi Visitor Firm on Passport Order', *The New York Times*, 6 February 1968, p. 54.

28 Richard A. Falk, 'Nuremberg and Vietnam', *The New York Times*, 27 December 1970, p. 165; John J. O'Connor, 'TV: Nuremberg's Relevance to the Vietnam War', *The New York Times*, 7 June 1971, p. 67.

29 'Bertrand Russell 1872–1970', *Newsweek*, 16 February 1970, pp. 62–3.

30 Ian Wright, 'The US in Asia – Mad or Bad?', *Guardian*, 20 January 1971, p. 10.

31 Neil Sheehan, 'Should We Have War Crime Trials?', *The New York Times*, 28 March 1971, p. BR1. Correspondence to the paper suggested that many readers agreed with Sheehan. See Lieutenant Roger E. Woodbury, letter to the editor, *The New York Times*, 4 April 1971, p. E12; Maurice English, letter to the editor, *The New York Times*, 25 April 1971, p. BR36.

32 Clergy and Laymen Concerned About Vietnam, *In the Name of America* (Annandale, VA: Turnpike Press, 1968). The group had submitted a report considered by the Russell tribunal in Roskilde. See Duffett, *Against the Crime of Silence*, pp. 519–21.

33 Neil Sheehan, 'Taylor Says by Yamashita Ruling Westmoreland May Be Guilty', *The New York Times*, 9 January 1971, p. 3. It is important to note though that in contrast to the Russell tribunal Taylor believed that air raids on North Vietnam did not constitute war crimes: 'Things do not look the same from a jet bomber as they do on the ground, and the possibility of error is very great.' The question of why bombing north of the 17th parallel should in that sense have been any different than south remained unanswered. See Taylor, *Nuremberg and Vietnam*, pp. 140–1.

34 'Peace Group to Set Up Panels on Atrocity Charges', *The New York Times*, 30 November 1969, p. 30. Schoenman did not calmly accept his departure from the Bertrand Russell Peace Foundation, boasting to fellow board members, 'The truth is that every major political initiative that has borne the name of Bertrand Russell since 1960 has been my work in thought and deed.' See Andersson, 'The Legacy of the Russell Tribunal', pp. 185–6. On his other personal problems, see 'Deportation Order on Schoenman', *Guardian*, 28 June 1968, p. 1; 'Schoenman "Removed"', *Guardian*, 10 December 1969, p. 4.

35 Kunen, *Standard Operating Procedure*, p. 73. My summary of the inquiry draws substantially from Kunen's account but see also Douglas Robinson, 'Ex-Pilot Alleges Civilian Slayings', *The New York Times*, 7 April 1970, p. 5.

36 The dispute focused on controversial lawyer Mark Lane and in particular his book *Conversations with Americans: Testimony from 32 Vietnam Veterans* (New York, Simon & Schuster, 1970), which included false and misleading statements by Vietnam veterans about purported war crimes.

The CCI were first to break from Lane but the VVAW also eventually decided it would no longer stand by him. Lane had earlier been an influence on Russell's decision to found the Who Killed Kennedy Committee. For more of the story, see Hunt, *The Turning*.

37 The song, 'Oh! Camil (The Winter Soldier)', appears on Nash's 1974 solo album *Wild Tales*.

38 Martin Kasindorf, 'Fonda: A Person of Many Parts', *The New York Times*, 3 February 1974, p. 19; Jane Fonda, 'Mug Shot', janefonda.com/2009/05/mug-shot/

39 Quoted in Boyle, *Flower of the Dragon*, p. 141.

40 Kunen, *Standard Operating Procedure*, pp. 62–5. 'Much of what they said had been reported or televised before,' observed one *New York Times* journalist who presumably had access to more media channels than most of his fellow Americans. Jerry M. Flint, 'Veterans Assess Atrocity Blame', *The New York Times*, 7 February 1971, p. 17. It took the *Washington Post* another three months to mention the Winter Soldier Investigation.

41 Hunt, *The Turning*, p. 73.

42 George C. Wilson, 'Viet Atrocity Probe Spurred by Veterans', *Washington Post*, 5 May 1971, p. A22.

43 The Citizens' Commission of Inquiry, *The Dellums Committee Hearings on War Crimes in Vietnam*, p. ix; Dellums and Halterman, *Lying Down with the Lions*, pp. 64–6.

44 'International Commission of Inquiry into U.S. War Crimes in Indochina', memorandum, CIA Reading Room, cia.gov/readingroom/docs/CIA-RDP80R01720R000700090029-1.pdf; *Problems of War Victims in Indochina, Part I: Vietnam, Hearing Before the Subcommittee to Investigate Problems Connected with Refugees and Escapees of the Committee on the Judiciary, United States Senate, Ninety-Second Congress, Second Session, May 8, 1972* (Washington, DC: US Government Printing Office, 1972), pp. 84–7; 'Tainted Tribunal', *Newsweek*, 5 July 1971, p. 47.

45 Douglass, *Lightning East to West*, pp. 45–6; '"U.S. War-Crimes" Hearings Are Begun in Copenhagen', *The New York Times*, 12 October 1972, p. 5.

46 Donald Macintyre, 'My Part in the Anti-War Demo That Changed Protest For Ever', *Observer*, 11 March 2018.

47 Drake, *Sartre*, pp. 123–5.

48 Tait, *My Father Bertrand Russell*, p. 177.

49 Griffin, *The Selected Letters of Bertrand Russell, Volume 2*, p. 627.

50 Margot Lyon, 'Babies Hurt in "Spray" War?', *Guardian*, 20 December
    1969, p. 2; 'A Woman Says G.I.'s Slew 300 in Village', *The New York
    Times*, 20 December 1969, p. 5; Cohen-Solal, *Sartre*, p. 454.

51 'Russell's Tribunal', *Guardian*, 19 May 1972, p. 13; Jonathan Steele, 'On a
    Wing and a Prayer', *Guardian*, 8 January 1973, p. 11; C. F. Stoneman and
    J. W. Thompson, letter to the editor, 'Mr Wilson Should Visit Hanoi',
    Guardian, 12 January 1973, p. 10.

52 Peter Weiss, *'Limited Bombing' in Vietnam: Report on the Attacks Against
    the Democratic Republic of Vietnam by the US Air Force and the Seventh
    Fleet, After the Declaration of 'Limited Bombing' by President Lyndon B.
    Johnson on March 31, 1968* (London: Bertrand Russell Peace Foundation,
    1969); *Notes on the Cultural Life of the Democratic Republic of Vietnam*
    (London: Calder & Boyars, 1970); *Two Plays: Song of the Lusitanian
    Bogey and Discourse on the Progress of the Prolonged War of Liberation in
    Viet Nam ...* (New York: Atheneum, 1970).

53 Paul Webster, '5,000 Boat People to Arrive in France', *Guardian*, 27 June
    1979, p. 7; 'UPITN 27 6 79 Jean Paul Sartre Visits Elysee Palace in Paris
    to Discuss Vietnamese Refugees', AP Archive, youtu.be/Iwjdu1_K5RI;
    Ai, 'Isle of Light'.

54 Kevin P. Phillips, 'A Case for Amnesty', *Washington Post*, 10 April 1971,
    p. A13.

55 For more on the brutalities of the North Vietnamese, see Lewy, *America
    in Vietnam*, pp. 272–9; Prokosch, *The Technology of Killing*, p. 113; and
    Taylor, *Nuremberg and Vietnam*, pp. 130–1.

56 There is more on the courage of Hugh Thompson, and the price he paid
    for it, in Jon Wiener, 'A Forgotten Hero Stopped the My Lai Massacre
    50 Years Ago Today', *Los Angeles Times*, 16 March 2018.

Epilogue

1 Mark Boal, 'The Kill Team: How U.S. Soldiers in Afghanistan Murdered
   Innocent Civilians', *Rolling Stone*, 28 March 2011.

2 Bill Frogameni, 'Revealing a 40-Year-Old Horror', *Salon*, 24 May 2006.

3 Brett Wilkins, 'No Punishment for US Troops Who Slaughtered 10
   Afghan Civilians, Says Pentagon Chief', *Common Dreams*, 13 December

2021; Charlie Savage et al., 'Newly Declassified Video Shows U.S. Killing of 10 Civilians in Drone Strike', *The New York Times*, 19 January 2022; Azmat Khan, 'Military Investigation Reveals How the U.S. Botched a Drone Strike in Kabul', *The New York Times*, 6 January 2023.

4   Glenn Greenwald, 'The Radically Changing Story of the U.S. Airstrike on Afghan Hospital: From Mistake to Justification', *The Intercept*, 5 October 2015; Gareth Porter, 'ISAF Data Show Night Raids Killed over 1,500 Afghan Civilians', Inter Press Service, 2 November 2011.

5   Emran Feroz, 'Death by Drone: America's Vicious Legacy in Afghanistan', *Foreign Policy*, 27 March 2020.

6   'Civilians Killed & Wounded', Watson Institute for International and Public Affairs, watson.brown.edu/costsofwar/costs/human/civilians

7   Toby Sterling and Stephanie Van Den Berg, 'Facing Hurdles from U.S., War Crimes Judges Reject Afghan Probe', Reuters, 12 April 2019; Lara Jakes and Michael Crowley, 'U.S. to Penalize War Crimes Investigators Looking into American Troops', *The New York Times*, 11 June 2020.

8   Jeremy Scahill, 'U.S. Hypocrisy on War Crimes Is a Gift to Putin', *The Intercept*, 10 February 2023; Alice Speri, 'Biden Administration Splits on Prosecuting Russia for War Crimes in Ukraine', *The Intercept*, 15 March 2023.

9   David Fickling, 'Pinter Demands War Crimes Trial for Blair', *Guardian*, 7 December 2005; 'Pinter Uses Nobel Talk to Accuse West of War Crimes', *The Times*, 8 December 2005; 'Pause for Thought: Harold Pinter and the Nobel Prize for ...', *The Times*, 14 October 2005, p. 23. The *Times* editorial was a model of politeness compared to some of the press reaction to Pinter.

10   The best place to learn more is at permanentpeoplestribunal.org

11   Walden Bello, 'The Perfect Storm', *Frontline*, 29 July 2005; Çubukçu, 'The Political Imaginary of the World Tribunal on Iraq'.

12   John Vidal, 'GM Seed Firm Monsanto Dismisses "Moral Trial" as a Stunt', *Guardian*, 13 October 2016.

13   Srećko Horvat, 'The Belmarsh Tribunal', openDemocracy.net, 2 October 2020. You can watch its first, Covid-affected, session at 'The Belmarsh Tribunal', youtu.be/3Zh5Nakva5Y

14   Smith, 'The "Tribunal Movement" Holds Court in Istanbul'; Borowiak,

'The World Tribunal on Iraq', pp. 182–3; Byrnes and Simm, *People's Tribunals and International Law*, pp. 20–1, 29–30.

15　Bello, 'The Perfect Storm'.

INDEX